ARABIC   ASTRONOMY   BANKING
ANISATION   CALCULUS   CANA
OMMERCIAL CORRESPONDENCE
KING   CRICKET   DRAWING   D   W9-DIJ-656
    ELECTRICITY IN THE HOUSE   ELOCUTIONIST   EMBROIDERY
ENGLISH RENASCENCE TO THE ROMANTIC REVIVAL   ROMANTIC
EVERYDAY FRENCH   TO EXPRESS YOURSELF   FISHING   TO FLY
E BOOK   GARDENING   GAS IN THE HOUSE   GEOGRAPHY OF
ONARY   GERMAN GRAMMAR   GERMAN PHRASE BOOK   GOLF
GOOD FARM ACCOUNTING   GOOD FARM CROPS   GOOD FARMING
T FARMING   GOOD GRASSLAND   GOOD AND HEALTHY ANIMALS
    GOOD POULTRY KEEPING   GOOD SHEEP FARMING   GOOD SOIL
E   HINDUSTANI   HISTORY: ABRAHAM LINCOLN   ALEXANDER THE
U   CONSTANTINE   COOK   CRANMER   ERASMUS   GLADSTONE AND
ILTON   PERICLES   PETER THE GREAT   PUSHKIN   RALEIGH   RICHELIEU
DROW   EMENT
IAN   ETTER
ENGIN   · · · · AND HE WILL BE   ANICS
DERN   ORING
HILOSO   YET WISER *Proverbs 9.9*   HYSICS
LUMBI   UBLIC
RECKO   USSIAN
: ITS   AND PURPOSE   SOCCER   SPANISH   SPE   AND
SW   SWEDISH   TEACHING   THINKING   TRIG   METRY
BRIT H RAILWAYS FOR BOYS   CAMPING FOR BOYS AND GIRLS
FOR GIRLS   MODELMAKING FOR BOYS   NEEDLEWORK FOR GIRLS
OYS AND GIRLS   SAILING AND SMALL BOATS FOR BOYS AND GIRLS
ORK FOR BOYS   ADVERTISING & PUBLICITY   ALGEBRA   AMATEUR
NG   BIOLOGY   BOOK-KEEPING   BRICKWORK   BRINGING UP
TRY   CHEMISTRY   CHESS   CHINESE   COMMERCIAL ARITHMETIC
RAVELLING   TO COMPOSE MUSIC   CONSTRUCTIONAL DETAILS
G   DUTCH   DUTTON SPEEDWORDS   ECONOMIC GEOGRAPHY
T   EMBROIDERY   ENGLISH GRAMMAR   LITERARY APPRECIATION
VAL   ROMANTIC REVIVAL   VICTORIAN AGE   CONTEMPORARY
FISHING   TO FLY   FREELANCE WRITING   FRENCH   FRENCH
USE   GEOGRAPHY OF LIVING THINGS   GEOLOGY   GEOMETRY
ASE BOOK   GOLF   GOOD CONTROL OF INSECT PESTS   GOOD
FARM CROPS   GOOD FARMING   GOOD FARMING BY MACHINE
D   GOOD AND HEALTHY ANIMALS   GOOD MARKET GARDENING
    GOOD SHEEP FARMING   GOOD SOIL   GOOD ENGLISH   GREEK
ORY   ABRAHAM LINCOLN   ALEXANDER THE GREAT   BOLIVAR   BOTHA
RANMER   ERASMUS   GLADSTONE AND LIBERALISM   HENRY V   JOAN OF
AT   PUSHKIN   RALEIGH   RICHELIEU   ROBESPIERRE   THOMAS JEFFERSON
HOME NURSING   HORSE MANAGEMENT   HOUSEHOLD DOCTOR
URNALISM   LATIN   LAWN TENNIS   LETTER WRITER   MALAY
ONENTS   WORKSHOP PRACTICE   MECHANICS   MECHANICAL
    MORE GERMAN   MOTHERCRAFT   MOTORING   MOTOR CYCLING
APHY   PHYSICAL GEOGRAPHY   PHYSICS   PHYSIOLOGY   PITMAN'S
JESE   PSYCHOLOGY   PUBLIC ADMINISTRATION   PUBLIC SPEAKING

72 K

THE TEACH YOURSELF BOOKS
EDITED BY LEONARD CUTTS

GOOD ENGLISH

TEACH YOURSELF

GOOD ENGLISH

A PRACTICAL BOOK OF SELF-INSTRUCTION IN
ENGLISH COMPOSITION BASED ON THE WORK BY
G. H. THORNTON, M.A., COMPLETELY REVISED AND
ENLARGED BY KATHLEEN BARON, B.A.

THE ENGLISH UNIVERSITIES PRESS LTD
102 NEWGATE STREET
LONDON, E.C.1

First printed in this form 1938
This impression 1958

*Printed in Great Britain for the English Universities Press, Limited,
by Richard Clay and Company, Ltd., Bungay, Suffolk*

INTRODUCTION

This book attempts to examine the principles that underlie good written English, and to suggest the best methods by which you may learn to write good English yourself.

This is a vaguer task than the grammarian's, and one more difficult to accomplish. He deals with language after it has been written down, and makes his rules to fit with current practice, not to guide it. Like the student of anatomy, his work is to probe and dissect, and he has a whole dictionary of terms by which he may label whatever he finds. To know these labels will not help you to write good English. You may be learned in all the uses of restrictive and illative and copulative clauses, and yet be unable to compose a single sentence with lucidity and ease. The study of formal grammar is useful in itself, but it will no more help you to write than a knowledge of anatomy will help a lame man to walk. This book therefore tries to avoid grammatical labels as far as possible, though in discussing sentence-structure it has sometimes been necessary to borrow them. It aims at showing the processes of prose construction, and once you understand them and have practised them for yourselves, you have no need to know the grammarian's names for them. To have talked much and read much is of more value in learning to write good English than to have parsed and analysed half a library.

Yet, you may ask, how far can good writing

be taught? It is clearly a different problem from teaching arithmetic or Latin or trigonometry. In all these subjects you may lay down definite rules, but English, written as well as spoken, is both personal and instinctive. In learning to write, you are learning to express *yourself*; if you write well, whatever you write will be plainly and unmistakably your own. It seems therefore almost as difficult to write a book on composition as it must be to write those popular and fascinating handbooks on how to cultivate your personality. The problem is fundamentally the same. Professor Raleigh is extremely severe towards all such writers: " When you go to the teachers of composition, they cannot tell you what to say. They wait until you have said something and then they carp at it. They help you to a good style about as much as detectives help a thief to a good life."

Yet, with deference to Professor Raleigh, there are many ways in which such a book as this may be useful. You learn to compose by stages, learning first to express yourself in simple sentences and to give them variety, then to link your simple sentences into longer ones, and finally to link these into a paragraph. In this way you are able to practise and perfect your writing at each stage, and so to avoid the lopsided, ungainly style of the man who writes upon instinct as the words come into his head. In considering vocabulary, and in examining examples of bad writing, you sharpen your critical sense, and in the practice of précis and paraphrase you gain accuracy and conciseness, while in the later chapters you will find advice on tackling essays, descriptions and stories. By the time you have worked through this book, you will have absorbed the principles of good writing, and you will insensibly put them into practice. Most valuable of all, your study will have taught you how to criticise your own work, and you will have no need of a teacher, since you will rarely find a severer critic than yourself.

Some of the exercises set require criticism or correction of style; others demand original writing. The first can generally be checked by the Key; for the second, it is only possible to provide specimen compositions which will serve as a standard, and illustrate a different method of approaching the same subject. You cannot be too strongly urged not to look at the Key until you have finished your own exercise, however strong the temptation. Nothing more effectively paralyses the mind than to read what someone else has written on the same subject. Never be content to answer a question in your head; to write down an answer requires clearer thinking and more precise expression, and clearness and precision are qualities indispensable to any writer.

If it is at all possible, work with another student. You will find that each stimulates the other, and in criticising another's work you become more critical of your own. But, most important of all, you must yourself continually practise writing, not only formal composition, but letters, diaries—anything that offers freedom of self-expression. Without this constant practice you will never be able to write well or fluently, but, having learnt all the graces and arts of style, will be left disconsolate with nothing at all to say.

CONTENTS

CONTENTS

CONTENTS

x

PART I

MEANING OF COMPOSITION—METHOD OF STUDY

Composition is simply the art of saying what we mean—an art which sounds easier than it really is, as we may remember from the Hatter's remarks in *Alice in Wonderland* :—

" ' Do you mean that you think you can find out the answer to it ? ' said the March Hare.

" ' Exactly so,' said Alice.

" ' Then you should say what you mean,' the March Hare went on.

" ' I do,' Alice hastily replied, ' at least—at least I mean what I say—that's the same thing, you know.'

" ' Not the same thing a bit ! ' said the Hatter. ' Why, you might just as well say that " I see what I eat " is the same thing as " I eat what I see " ! ' "

That is excellent logic, and if it is a little difficult to follow, it serves to illustrate the essential difficulty of all composition—of saying what we really mean.

For most of us, the study of composition begins at the age of two or thereabouts. A child begins to talk by saying single words, then, guided by instinct and imitation, learns to compose words into sentences, sentences into continuous speech. This process of composition is natural and unconscious, and he learns with astonishing ease.

15

Written composition carries the process a stage further, and it is less easy because less instinctive, though it is in its essentials the same. Here again he is guided by instinct, but still more by imitation, and this time he unconsciously imitates not speech, but what he has read. A Somerset child will speak with a Somerset accent because he hears it on every side. So, in the same way, in learning to write he will naturally adopt the style and vocabulary of the books and papers he reads most often.

In the past, the Authorised Version of the Bible profoundly influenced speech and writing, because it was the staple literature of the common people. The ignorant tinker who wrote *The Pilgrim's Progress* wrote great prose because his ear was attuned to the language and cadence of the English Bible. To-day, the daily newspaper has taken its place. Instead of David's lament over Jonathan, we read of " Scenes in Stepney " or " Love Tragedy in Hyde Park ". It would, of course, be foolish to condemn all newspaper-English as bad. There is much good, vigorous prose written daily in the papers. In clearness and brevity you can learn much from the journalist; in the vivid presentment of facts his is a master hand. The conditions of his work do not permit him to consider the nicety or accuracy of the words he uses, nor is a finely balanced style or intricate sentence-structure well suited to an article which will be read over a hurried breakfast or in a crowded bus or train.

If you wish to gain a good and flexible style, newspapers must not be your only reading, nor must you read them too much. Such a style can only be learnt from good and careful writers.

Read as much and as carefully as you can, and your style will insensibly be influenced by what you read. For critical reading, essays are perhaps the best study, and a book of selected essays [1] offers you great variety of style. The essays of Addison, Hazlitt, Leigh Hunt, Macaulay, R. L. Stevenson, Richard Jeffries, and W. H. Hudson are good models; so also are the essays of contemporary writers such as Robert Lynd, E. V. Lucas, H. M. Tomlinson, Aldous Huxley, Sir Arthur Quiller-Couch. [2] These names are selected from many others because they offer examples of good, direct prose, for it is best at this stage not to study authors who have a markedly individual style. Their mannerisms are easily imitated, while their essential qualities are forgotten. For this reason, essayists such as Lamb, De Quincey, Carlyle, Pater, Max Beerbohm, G. K. Chesterton, Virginia Woolf, are best reserved for later pleasure, when your own style is so far developed that it will not easily be influenced. For general reading, choose novels that are acknowledged to be well-written. You cannot read too much of that fastidious stylist, Robert Louis Stevenson; Thackeray will be good reading at this stage, while Dickens is too "mannered" a writer; but, if you prefer modern novels, you have abundant choice. The best are easily obtainable in cheap editions, and with so wide a choice, selection would be invidious. Study the book reviews in the newspaper, or consult your local librarian, if you do not know which to choose. You cannot always read slowly and critically, and your enjoyment

[1] Such as *English Essays* (World's Classics Series).
[2] Cf. *English Essay of To-day* (Oxford University Press).

of a novel would be spoiled by such a treatment. Yet nevertheless you should try every day to read a page or so of good prose slowly and with attention, noting the value of the words chosen and the rhythm and construction of the sentences. Good prose does not merely convey a clear meaning, but is written to satisfy the ear. To gain its full effect, you must read a passage aloud, so that its rhythm stays in your head like a remembered tune and your own style unconsciously takes on some of its music and balance.

The study of good prose is important in developing your critical sense and moulding your style, but study is not enough. You must constantly practise writing for yourself, and, if you wish to write well, you will not be content merely to work through the exercises in this book. This constant practice is less difficult than it sounds. Every letter you write offers you an opportunity, and the fact that someone else must read what you have written enforces a sufficiently exacting standard. Letters are especially useful in teaching you a sense of appropriateness, which is essential for success in writing. You instinctively adapt your style to your correspondent, just as in writing essays you will have to adapt your style to your subject. If you have little opportunity for letter-writing, then the next best course is to keep a diary—not the kind of diary that one used to receive at Christmas, with one half-inch of space in which to record all the pleasures, excitements and miseries of the day, but one in which you may write at ease, and may set down whatever interesting things you have done or seen or heard. The value of keeping a diary is that you may write in it without self-consciousness, with no thought that anyone else may read it. Pepys, writing carelessly for his own diversion, produced one of the pleasantest works in the world. Here is an extract from his diary for 1660 :—

" After dinner we went to the Green Dragon on Lambeth Hill, and there we sang of all sorts of things, and I ventured with good success upon things at first sight, and after that I played on my flageolet, and staid there till nine o'clock, very merry and drawn on with one song after another till it came to be so late. So parted and thence home, where I found my wife and maid a-washing. I staid up till the bellman came by with his bell just under my window as I was writing of this very line, and cried, ' Past one of the clock, and a cold, frosty, windy morning '. I then went to bed, and left my wife and the maid a-washing still."

Yet you may feel perhaps that you do not live so active or so " merry " a life as Mr. Pepys —that you have, in short, nothing to write about. There lies the root problem of all composition, and you cannot find the solution from books. A man who had lived all his life in his study, with only books for friends, would never be a great writer, even though he acquired by practice all the arts of style. Writing is the translation into words of thought and sensation and experience. If you use well your faculties of eye and ear, if you multiply and deepen your interests, then you will find the stimulus and the material for writing, and the eagerness of your thought will forge your style.

Your study should be divided between reading,

writing, and the formal lessons given in this book. It will be best at first to spend most time upon the work in this book, so that when you are writing for yourself you may put into practice the elementary rules given in the first thirteen lessons. The initial requirement in all writing is that you should say what you mean with clearness and accuracy. These are the first virtues to be cultivated; without them all elegance of style is worthless. They can be gained only by systematic practice, and for this reason the lessons of this book are arranged in systematic order, so that you will use simple sentences before you go on to more complicated constructions. When you have worked through a lesson, consider your own writing in the light of what you have learnt, and amend it where you can. Periodic revision of your work is a useful practice, but you should always allow some time to elapse before you attempt this critical survey of what you have written. When you have just finished a piece of work, especially if it has cost you a good deal of trouble, you are in no position to judge of its merits. One or two comparatively insignificant words—a *nor* or an *if*, a *this* or a *then*—have been so carefully considered that they practically dwarf their more important fellows. The whole passage is out of focus. Later—perhaps after a week or more— you will be able to judge the passage as a whole.

Although in the correction of faulty sentences given in the exercises, and in the detailed criticism of your own work, you must bear in mind the rules of grammar and style, you must try not to let them assume too much import- ance. By degrees, correct expression will come naturally without any conscious attention to rules. They must never at any time be too rigidly applied, for pedantry and good writing never go together. Even Shakespeare has sorely troubled the grammarians. The strict laws of grammar need not always be insisted on, if the meaning is clear and the expression conforms with current practice. Do not be like the Victorian lady who was so conscious of correct grammar that, when she received a letter from her husband beginning, "My dearest Maria", she replied, "My dear John, I beg that you will either mend your morals or your grammar. You call me your *dearest* Maria; am I to understand that you have other Marias?"

LESSON I

VOCABULARY—WORDS AND THEIR VALUE

Words are the raw material of the writer's craft, and in his choice of them lies very much of his skill. English offers him an immense vocabulary, enriched from many sources. French and Latin have added most to the original Saxon stock, but words have been borrowed from almost every country under the sun. French came over with the Norman conquerors; Renaissance scholars borrowed direct from Latin and Greek; fine gentlemen in Elizabeth's day garnished their speech with French, Italian and Spanish phrases; merchants and sailors and adventurers brought home new words from East and West. The process has been continuous, and continues still to-day. By these means the

English vocabulary has increased not only in size, but in richness and variety. There seems at times a bewildering number of words which might express one plain meaning. How, then, shall we select the right one?

To the writer, words have value in three different ways. Most important, of course, is the meaning. He will choose the word that seems to express most accurately what he has to say. Yet he may find that several words seem to serve his turn equally well, so that he has to consider them in two other ways—for their sound and their association.

Though the practice of reading aloud is almost dying out, you must not think of the written word as a mere collection of letters on the printed page. When we read to ourselves, we hear in imagination the sound of what we are reading. Silent reading cannot destroy the sound-value of words, and the careful writer will consider not only their individual sound, but how far that sound fits into the rhythm or musical pattern of the sentence. In the passage Pater has written on the portrait of Mona Lisa not a word could be changed without destroying the music of the whole :—

" She is older than the rocks among which she sits ; like the vampire, she has been dead many times, and learned the secrets of the grave; and has been a diver in deep seas, and keeps their fallen day about her. . . ."

Some words express sounds in themselves, and have been coined in imitation of the sounds they express. *Rustle, whisper, hush, chatter, whimper*, are examples, and you can find many

22

more, if you think (and listen) carefully. They have a special value in suggesting a sound almost directly to the imagination, and for this reason they are much used in poetry and in vivid descriptive prose.

Words are no less important for their associations than for their sounds. A word takes on colour and character according to the way it is used. From being commonly used to express a certain idea, it is always associated in the mind with that idea. You might write *The priest chuckled*, but you would feel a certain impropriety in writing *The priest giggled*, since we associate that word with the schoolgirl, and do not use it in any flattering sense. Words are constantly gathering new associations : some gain dignity, others lose it ; some are mysterious, some matter-of-fact. You must read widely and attentively if you would be aware of the subtle changes that words undergo in their journeyings.

If in writing you are to find the best words and use them well, then you must have as many words as possible at your disposal. The vocabulary of everyday speech is meagre. Comparatively few words are needed to explain material wants ; primitive people make do with very few. Civilisation increases man's vocabulary by increasing his knowledge and his needs ; but it is when man begins to think that he needs more words to express his ideas and opinions. Still more are needed when he comes to write them down. The vocabulary of speech and that of writing differ widely in scope, and words that seem forceful in speech seem vague and unconvincing when written. You may say emphatically, "This play is rotten", but if you are asked to write down your opinion, you will have to search for more precise words in which to express it. You may write instead, "This play is badly constructed, badly written and badly acted". These are common enough words, but you have had to pause a moment before finding them. Every time that you make this effort towards clearer thought and exacter expression, you will find that the right words come more easily.

If you are to have the best vocabulary for your purpose, you must constantly enlarge it by careful reading. Do not pass over any word whose meaning is not quite clear, for until you know a word in all its meanings, it is dangerous to use it. Aldous Huxley has a pleasant story of a young man who fell in love with the word "carminative", which he found on the label of a cinnamon bottle. He treasured it for its warmth and colour and sound, and used it at last in a poem to his lady, in which he expressed the carminative quality of his passion. It was a mere accident that he looked it up in the dictionary and discovered, to his grief and vexation, that it meant "good for curing flatulence".[1]

In reading use a dictionary to discover the meaning of a word; use your own critical instinct to estimate its worth. Read a piece of good prose over slowly and savour the words as you go; or, even better, read poetry, for the poet even more than the writer of prose must be aware of the sound and atmosphere of the words he uses. Poets who use a definitely poetic vocabulary will be of small use for this purpose,

[1] *Chrome Yellow*, Aldous Huxley.

but read those poets whose vocabulary is fairly close to that of modern prose.[1]

Once you are familiar with their correct use in prose use the words you have learnt, but do not in your enthusiasm use your choicest words too often. Like jewels, they are made more beautiful by their rarity. They are more effective when used with restraint. One or two rich words will lend fineness and distinction to a paragraph, where more will only weary those who read it. Shakespeare, in *Macbeth*, deliberately sets two echoing words among a crowd of plain, short ones :—

" What hands are here? ha ! they pluck out my
    eyes !
Will all great Neptune's ocean wash this blood
Clean from my hand? No; this my hand will
    rather
The *multitudinous seas incarnadine*
Making the green, one red.''

Finally, never go to the dictionary for new words, for you cannot learn from it how to use them, and will inevitably use them wrongly.

Exercise 1

(a) In the following sentences, replace the words printed in italics by more suitable words, and indicate your reasons for the change :—

1. One statesman thought the treaty *derogative* to his country's honour. 2. The Frenchman regards the *observation* of the Sabbath from a different standpoint than we do. 3. The town officials did their best to make the tram-

[1] As, for instance, Coleridge, Keats, Wordsworth, Browning, and almost any of the contemporary poets.

25

cars popular and *payable*. 4. Among the domestics she raised such *dissent* that no pair of them remained on speaking terms. 5. Your best plan is to treat her as *contemptibly* as you can. 6. Like all Scotsmen he maintained that porridge is the most *healthy* food. 7. It seemed, therefore, that Dirk ought to *decease*. 8. One of that great army of cooks sent by the devil for the *spoliation* of God's food. 9. The girl was *sick with nostalgia*. 10. By these remarks do you mean to *infer* that I know something about your miserable savings? 11. I have photographed the children of that school now for thirty years without a *breakage*. 12. The island of Ceylon is famous for its *luxurious* vegetation. 13. The *acceptation* of the sword of honour from the council does not commit the general to their policy. 14. The murderer was seen in the very *action* of firing his gun. 15. After the *invention* of chloroform, surgical operations had a much greater chance of success. 16. The body was so mangled that it could hardly be recognised as *humane*.

(*b*) Write down ten adjectives which you might use to describe a country stream.

Write down ten adjectives which you might use to describe a river flowing through a city.

(Think of the appearance, movement and sound of the water in each case.)

LESSON II

VOCABULARY—SYNONYMS

The advantage of a wide vocabulary is that you may express your thoughts with precision and grace. It is also occasionally useful in enabling you to avoid awkward repetition of the same word or sound, by substituting one word for another. It is bad to repeat the same word in two different senses, as in these examples :—

The sailors hoisted sail and sailed away.

If you do not stop crying at once you will cause your husband much needless anxiety : I promise you I have his cause at heart.

It is nevertheless even worse to make obvious efforts to avoid repetition. No sensible person would write : *The beautiful girl descended the staircase; he felt he had never seen such a lovely maiden.* But a great many people are strangely shy of repeating the same noun or proper name, and will write *our hero, the anxious husband, the handsome commander,* in the course of a single page, when all the time they merely mean *John Smith.* Your best rule is never to avoid repetition when avoidance of it is obvious.

When one word can be replaced by another, these words are said to be *synonyms,* a clumsy name for words that are similar in meaning. No word can be the exact equivalent of another, as we tried to show in the last lesson, for every word is slightly changed by its use and association. *Behaviour* and *deportment,* for instance, might seem from the dictionary to be almost interchangeable; but, if you consider them, you will find that *deportment* has a narrower meaning, and has grown rather prim through its association with Victorian standards of correctness and good manners. *Snapdragon* and *antirrhinum* are exact equivalents in meaning, but *snapdragon* is the more vivid word for general use, while *antirrhinum* is in place in a technical article on botany or gardening. *Linden* and *lime* are another pair with identical meanings, but in ordinary prose the commoner word *lime* will generally be preferable to the rarer, more poetic word *linden*.

Many so-called synonyms differ also in grammatical use. *Answer, reply, respond* are commonly called synonyms, yet they cannot be used in exactly the same way. We can say : *He answered her never a word* but not *He responded her never a word.*

English is rich in synonyms, and for this there is an historical reason. The English language is fundamentally Saxon : that is, its grammar is Saxon, and so are all the really essential words. It borrowed words from the Norman conquerors, who brought with them a higher standard of civilisation,[1] but a still larger part of our vocabulary comes from Latin, from which we still continue to borrow. Generally the Latin words are longer and more learned in sound and association than those that come to us from Saxon or direct from French. All the essential words in English are Saxon in origin—*the, with, of, out,* and all the other small necessary words on which language depends. Saxon gives us many words for concrete things—like *milk, fish, cattle, house*; many good words, too, to express simple emotions—*love, friendship, hate*—but very few indeed to express abstract things or subtle conceptions. These we have had to borrow from French and Latin.

[1] It is interesting to notice that our words for animals are plain Saxon—cow, calf, sheep, oxen—but our words for meat are French in origin—beef (*bœuf*), mutton (*mouton*), veal (*veau*), etc., the reason being that the Normans were not only more cultured, but also better cooks.

In writing prose, we inevitably use many words of Saxon origin, and they will always outnumber the rest, even in books written in what is called a Latin diction—in Dr. Johnson's essays, or Gibbon's history, or books written on scientific subjects. How far you will use words taken from Latin will depend very much on what you are writing. You will use less in a story of action than in an essay on Truth or Justice. In the following passage, taken from the eighteenth-century novel *Tristram Shandy*, Sterne uses few Latin words. A baby has just been born, and Susannah, the maid, is sent to inquire by what name it shall be christened :—

" ' Were one sure,' said my father to himself, scratching his eyebrow, ' that the child was expiring . . . it would be a pity in such a case to throw away so great a name as *Trismegistus* upon him—but he may recover.'

" ' No, no,' said my father to Susannah, ' I'll get up.'

" ' There is no time,' cried Susannah, ' the child's as black as my shoe.'

" ' *Trismegistus*,' said my father. ' But stay ! Thou art a leaky vessel, Susannah,' added my father. ' Canst thou carry *Trismegistus* in thy head the whole length of the gallery without scattering ? '

" ' Can I ? ' cried Susannah, shutting the door in a huff.

" ' If she can, I'll be shot,' said my father, bouncing out of bed in the dark, and groping for his breeches.

" Susannah ran with all speed along the gallery.

" My father made all speed to find his breeches.

" Susannah got the start and kept it. ' 'Tis

29

Tris—something,' cried Susannah. ' There is no Christian name in the world,' said the curate, ' beginning with *Tris*—but *Tristram*.'

" ' Then 'tis *Tristram-gistus*,' quoth Susannah.

" ' There is no *gistus* to it, noodle !—'tis my own name,' replied the curate, dipping his hand, as he spoke, into the basin. ' Tristram ! ' said he, etc., etc., etc., etc., so Tristram was I called, and Tristram shall I be to the day of my death. . . ."

Compare this with a characteristic passage from one of Johnson's essays, where the sentences are weighted with Latin :—

" It is asserted by Horace, that ' if matter be once got together, words will be found with very little difficulty ' ; a position which, though sufficiently plausible to be asserted in poetical precepts, is by no means strictly and philosophically true. If words were naturally and necessarily consequential to sentiments, it would always follow, that he who has most knowledge must have most eloquence, and that every man would clearly express what he fully understood."

Though you may prefer Sterne to Dr. Johnson, it is clearly impossible to say that one kind of diction is better than another. The only test is its appropriateness. Students are sometimes advised to use words of Latin derivation as little as possible. It is felt that they may be so delighted with long Latin words that they will use them in and out of season, and so develop a pompous and pedantic style. Yet it is often as stilted and pedantic to use a Saxon for a Latin word as a Latin word for a Saxon. No sensible person will speak of *lactation* when he means *milking*, but the earnest people who tried to

30

establish the Saxon coinage *folk-wain*, in place of the Latin *omnibus*, were surely equally absurd.

Do not use long Latin words where simpler words will do, but do not strain after an artificial simplicity. If you find in writing that you are using a great many Latin words, it is time to stop and consider what you have written. It is much easier to write nonsense when you are using long Latin words than when you write in plain Saxon. Their weightiness is deceptive, and may conceal the flimsiest of meanings. Examples of such a style can often be found in the leading articles of the daily papers, and it has been amusingly parodied in C. E. Montague's novel, *A Hind Let Loose*. Read it, and you will be ever after on your guard against using pompous words to conceal a pitiful lack of meaning.

Exercise 2

(*a*) In the following sentences supply a synonym for each of the words printed in italics, indicating in each case the slight change of meaning implied by the use of the new word.

1. I shall be glad if you send me the third volume of Campbell's Architecture, and with it any other *entertaining* books. 2. " Well, young gentleman," says a man that stood at the door, " you look *wishfully*." 3. The Greeks took the city of Troy by *guile*. 4. Bute and the *adjacent* island of Arran form one county. 5. Warren Hastings was a *resolute* man. 6. Some of the worst *offenders* were caught and punished. 7. A tear to grace his *obsequies*. 8. I am greatly *indebted* to you for your kindness. 9. A man

never *outlives* his conscience. 10. Some students were killed in an affray that took place at a *wedding*. 11. *Globes* of light appeared among the trees. 12. Those tyrants who have been a *reproach* to human nature. 13. Religion *intrenches* upon none of our privileges. 14. The lie that flatters I *abhor* the most. 15. Then *shrieked* the timid and stood still the brave. 16. Carlyle's manuscripts were scarcely *legible*.

(*b*) Write down ten adjectives you might use to describe a policeman, ten more to describe a speaker at an open-air meeting. (Think of their appearance, character, qualities, moods.)

LESSON III

VOCABULARY—CHOICE OF WORDS

When we speak, we suit our words to those to whom we speak; in writing, we address a wide, yet undefined audience, and must use words which will be generally understood. It follows that certain words must be excluded from our written vocabulary since their meaning will not be clear to everyone. They fall into four classes :—

(1) Slang words form the largest class, and though they are often vivid and effective in speech, there are good reasons why they should not be used in writing. Consider first what we mean by slang. *The Concise Oxford Dictionary* defines it thus :—

" Words and phrases in common colloquial use, but generally considered in some or all of their senses to be outside of standard English;

32

words and phrases either entirely peculiar to, or used in special senses by, some class or profession."

The important part of the definition lies for us in the words "outside standard English", by which we mean the English that is spoken and understood by the greatest number of educated people. Burglars, in their profession, use a very vivid and effective slang, yet, since their profession is a narrow one, it is, for the writer's purpose, useless. Slang words, if they really supply a gap in language, will one day be accepted in standard English. Till then they should be avoided in ordinary prose.

(2) Words and phrases used only in certain districts are to be avoided for the same reason. They are excellent in speech, and have often much more character than the corresponding words in standard English, yet, since they will not be generally understood, it is unwise to use them. The Scotsman may talk of his " pinkie ", but he will write " little finger "; he may use " wee " in speech, but he will use " little " or " small " in writing. Some local words, like the Scotch " caddie ", have passed into general use, but till then they must be excluded from written English.

(3) Foreign words and phrases should be used as little as possible, unless they have already been absorbed into the language. *Route, chauffeur, chef, matinée* are French words that we could hardly do without. Many other foreign words come into favour from time to time and then pass out of use. *Fuhrer, coup, putsch, duce* are modern examples which the journalist has brought to popular notice. They

are not really necessary in English, and it is unwise to use them, for their popularity may quickly fade and their meaning be forgotten. To use foreign words which will not be known by people who have not learnt a foreign language is affected and ill-mannered. Unless you are writing for a small class of people whom you know will understand you, this should at all costs be avoided.

(4) Technical words easily creep into prose if the writer is a specialist in any subject. It would be impossible, of course, to write a technical work without them, but they should be avoided in general writing.

Words of these four classes are to be avoided, lest they obscure your meaning; but there is a fifth class which must be as rigorously avoided if you wish to write good prose. To this class belong all words and phrases that have been so staled by use that they have lost their vividness and accuracy. For these the journalist is much to blame, for, writing in haste, he is tempted to use words as ciphers to fill up a line, very often using an epithet as makeweight. For him every crime becomes a *dastardly crime*, every love affair *tragic* or *romantic* ; *grave developments are awaited* in *the political arena* ; *crises* are *averted* at *the psychological moment* ; calm *ensues* ; unhappy wives make *revelations*. Hack words and phrases are created by bad writing. Examples might be endless—the misused word *transpire* ;[1] *partake* (and its falsely refined passive form—*tea was partaken of*) ; *in the sphere*

[1] *Transpire* means "emerge from secrecy into knowledge, become known by degrees". It is frequently wrongly used with the meaning "happen, turn out".

of; *under the circumstances*; *seriously inclined to*; *young hopefuls*. You may find countless others for yourself. Such words and phrases are to be avoided if you would write fresh, vigorous prose. If you find yourself using one, look it up in the dictionary, and if you are not using it in its exact sense, strike it out.

Words have a strong tendency to coalesce, to form compounds, and thus to lose their identity. This is essential if each sentence is not to be built up by the conscious effort of joining separate words. These connections should only be the commonplace ones, which are natural and fitting. If you do not know what a man means, you say, without conscious thought, "What do you mean?" which is natural and fitting. But very often words fall into set phrases, which were once witty or imaginative, but have lost their lustre through overmuch quotation. Shakespeare has contributed many : *Patience on a monument* ; *my prophetic soul !* ; *the pity of it* ; *there's the rub* ; *a snapper-up of unconsidered trifles*; *to be or not to be*; *here's metal more attractive*. These are but a few. Other phrases once witty have become merely facetious—*better half*; *conspicuous by their absence* ; *the curate's egg* ; *the inner man*, etc. Others have become current journalese—*the logic of events* ; *the irony of fate* ; *the defects of his qualities* ; *leave severely alone*, etc. Such set phrases are to be avoided; if you can invent neat phrases instead of them, well and good; if not, then stick to the plain noun and let the wearied epithet go in peace.

Exercise 3

Express the following sentences in what you feel is a better form :—

1. The Opposition must buck up if they wish to gain anything at the approaching election. 2. The judges were escorted to their hotel with all the pomp and circumstance of war. 3. In the dim, religious light of the pit he could not see to read his programme. 4. Mr. Parkins of this city last night passed over to the other side. 5. It is rumoured that the green-eyed monster was at the bottom of the tragedy that transpired at Gudburgh last night. 6. A cold collation was partaken of by the distinguished party at the witching hour. 7. The authorities were shocked when they learned how the newcomers had painted the town red. 8. The Government is rotten from gunwale to garboard streak. 9. *Al fresco* meals were for him ever the best. 10. The Countess is expecting a happy event shortly. 11. Do not burn the midnight oil over this exercise. 12. I drink cocoa every night as regularly as clockwork. 13. In the sphere of science Einstein is pre-eminent. 14. He suffers from an acute inferiority complex. 15. She declared she loved the little feathered songsters. 16. Greater development of uncorrupted conduct is a desideratum. 17. A really mondaine child now requires an engagement book in which to record her numerous social activities. 18. I am staggered by the impertinence of the honourable member who has just spoken. 19. Now is the psychological moment for the restoration of the monarchy. 20. His book will repay perusal.

LESSON IV

THE SENTENCE—MEANING

Words are the material with which composition deals, but words are not the units of composition. Some words, it is true, can express complete thoughts. Thus *Yes, Never, Listen*, may express a complete thought each. But this is exceptional. In most cases we require several words to communicate a complete thought. Even such words as *Yes* and *Never* depend upon previous words to help out their apparently independent meaning.

A group of words so arranged as to express a complete thought is called a sentence. Sometimes we have a sentence defined as a combination of words making complete sense. By "complete" we must not understand that a sentence tells us all that is to be said, but only that the sense is complete so far as that independent group of words is concerned. Examples of "incomplete sense" will be found below. The following are sentences : *All the world's a stage. I remember. Where do you buy your books ?* If you examine these, or any other sentences, you will find that they always consist of two parts : something spoken about, and something said about it. The words indicating what is spoken about form what is called the *subject* : the words indicating what is said about the subject form what is called the *predicate*. Thus *All the world* is the subject ; *is a stage* is the predicate. *I* is subject ; *remember*, predicate.

In the third sentence we seem to have two subjects ; for we are saying something about *you* and also something about *books*. Grammarians, however, are quite clear that *you* is the subject, while *do buy your books where* is the predicate. To understand why *you* is at once selected as the subject, we must consider how it is related to the verb. At first sight it appears as if the verb *buy* were as closely related to *books* as to *you*, but, as a matter of fact, *buy* is more dependent upon *you* than upon *books*. Let us take the sentence in its plain form as a statement, not as a question : *You buy your books*. Here you may change *books* into *book*, or into *clothes*, or *pencils*, or *potatoes*, without in any way changing the rest of the sentence. But if we change *you* into *he* we must change the verb. It must now read *he buys*. In other words, the verb is limited by the subject in regard to *number* and *person*.

> I have a book.
> Thou hast a book.
> She has a book.

Here *I*, *thou* and *she* are the subjects, since they cause the verb to change, while *book* is called the object. We can change the object as much as we please without changing the verb at all. *He sees*—which is the third person singular of the verb—may be followed by *me*, which is first person singular, or *thee*, which is second person singular, or *us*, which is first person plural, or *them*, which is third person plural, or by any sort of objective noun or pronoun.

All parts of the verb which can be thus affected by the number and person of the subject are called *finite* parts. The parts that are not finite are the infinitive and the participles. These do not change with their subjects, because, as a matter of fact, they do not have subjects. This is only another way of saying that infinitives and participles cannot be predicates. *I buying my books* is not a sentence, for there is not a complete thought. There is a subject, *I*, but no predicate. When we hear the words, *A gentleman walking along the street*, we wait, expecting to hear more : the gentleman must fall, or get run over, or enter a shop—he must do something before we are satisfied.

A group of words without a finite part of a verb forms not a sentence, but a phrase ; the words make sense, but not complete sense. Here, for instance, are phrases that yield a certain sense :—

Being unable to stifle his remorse . . .
To have worked well . . .
For the good of the State . . .

To turn them into sentences, we must add the finite part of some verb, thus :—

Being unable to stifle his remorse, he shot himself.

To have worked well is small satisfaction.

For the good of the State they are willing to sacrifice their happiness and their liberty.

Exercise 4

(*a*) Change the following phrases into sentences by adding some statement containing a finite part of a verb at the place where the dash occurs :—

1. Notwithstanding all he had undergone ——
2. —— after having done his utmost. 3. Proceeding up the dangerous defile ——. 4. ——

to have accosted him. 5. —— to know a little of everything. 6. After reposing some hours in the hut of a peasant —— 7. Puffed into existence by unscrupulous speculators —— 8. —— even by the appointment of a regular wit. 9. Frederick, without a guinea in his pocket, and having left not many in the pockets of his friends —— 10. —— to fall at once from the pinnacle of neglect.

(*b*) Make simple sentences introducing the three words given :—

    (i) Cuckoo—south—nest.
    (ii) Clock—hour—chime.
    (iii) Silver—light—candles.

LESSON V

THE SENTENCE—ORDER OF WORDS

The natural order of words in a sentence is : Subject—verb—object. In some cases no other order is possible. *William defeated Harold* is the only way in which we can state the fact while restricting ourselves to these three words. *Harold defeated William* is untrue. *William Harold defeated* and *Harold William defeated* are not only clumsy forms, but they leave it doubtful which of the two was defeated. *Defeated William Harold* is nonsense. Here, then, no other order is permissible than subject—verb—object.

With *William defeated him* we can take more liberties. *Him William defeated* is as clear as the regular form, though we feel that it is less natural. Even the form *Him defeated William* is intelligible, though unjustifiable.

When a sentence contains more words than the bare three necessary to give subject, verb and object still greater freedom may be allowed. The following sentence from Gray's *Elegy* keeps the normal word-order : *The ploughman homeward plods his weary way*, but it is possible to express in a great many ways without materially altering the meaning. Here are some of the more obvious :—

Homeward the ploughman plods his weary way.

His weary way the ploughman plods homeward.

Plods the ploughman his weary way homeward.

Homeward his weary way plods the ploughman.

His weary way the ploughman homeward plods.

Plods homeward the ploughman his weary way.

The ploughman plods his weary way homeward.

We might strain ingenuity still further by producing still more forms of the same sentence, but they would soon become not only unnatural, but almost unintelligible. They merely afford an example of the way in which word-order may vary. You may ask, indeed, why we should trouble to vary the order when the normal order is clear. Certainly on most occasions the normal order is to be preferred, but there are times when we must change it in order to make certain parts of the sentence more emphatic, or to gain variety.

It is found that the beginning and the end of a sentence are the important places for catching the attention of the reader. These places accordingly give greater emphasis to any words that are placed there. You have only to read over the different arrangements of Gray's sentence to see the truth of this. Every one of the variations conveys a slightly different meaning because the emphasis falls on different ideas. All the sentences convey the general meaning that a wearied ploughman is plodding his way home; but some of them make us think more of the ploughman, others more of the plodding, other again more of the home or of the weariness. The truth is that while, *for all practical purposes*, the same idea may be expressed by two or more forms of the same sentence, there is only *one* form for the *exact* expression of any given idea.

Since the beginning and the end of a sentence are the emphatic places, we easily understand why little, insignificant words should not be placed in these positions of advantage. It is sometimes said that words should be arranged in a sentence as officers used to arrange their men in the old hand-to-hand fighting days—the big ones in the front and rear, the little ones in the middle. There is this difference, however, that while in fighting the van is more important than the rear, the end of the sentence is, on the whole, more important than the beginning. It used to be given as an absolute rule that no sentence should ever begin with *And* or *But*. This rule is now not insisted on, though it is not desirable to have many sentences beginning with these. A sentence should begin and end as well as we can make it, but if one of the two must suffer, let it not be the ending. Prepositions, pronouns, small unemphatic adverbs and adjectives are endings to be avoided. A weak ending is sometimes produced by the use of a passive form, and where this happens we should turn the sentence into the active, as in the first and the last sentences given below.

Bad.	Not so Bad.
Games and other forms of amusement were indulged in.	They indulged in games and other forms of amusement.
We have no chance of learning since everything is done for us.	Since everything is done for us we have no chance of learning.
He paid all his debts to the amount of three thousand pounds then.	Then he paid . . . [if we wish to emphasise the time], or, He paid then all his debts to the amount of three thousand pounds.
Houses and lands were things he had quite lost the desire of.	He had quite lost the desire of houses and lands.

This desire to have something solid to rest on at the end of a sentence depends largely upon the ear, and may be illustrated by reference to music. Not every note of the scale can make a satisfactory ending : there are certain notes that make natural halting-places, and certain others which the ear declines to accept as final.

Exercise 5

(a) Write out the following sentence in as many different arrangements as you can without making it lose its general sense. Number your versions in order, beginning with the version that you think the most satisfactory :—

We came to our journey's end, at last, with no small difficulty, after much fatigue, through deep roads, and bad weather.

(*b*) Write a short account (about a hundred words) of a walk in the country, such as you might write in a diary. (Describe the way you went, where you had tea, how you came back, anything of interest you saw.) Use simple sentences as far as possible.

LESSON VI

THE SENTENCE—KINDS OF SIMPLE SENTENCES

The second cause which leads to variation from the natural order of subject—verb—object is the desire to avoid monotony. A page or two of direct statements of the Cows-eat-grass type would be intolerable in a book meant for general reading. In legal documents, and in business papers generally, it is often necessary to gain clearness and save time even at the expense of monotony. But in what is usually called composition a certain amount of variety is necessary.

Even the most simple sentences need not be always expressed in the standard form, so long as the change involves no loss of clearness. Those that we have hitherto dealt with have made plain, straightforward statements. Such a sentence is, *None of the soldiers was dismayed.*

But the same idea may be expressed in the

interrogative form, as Tennyson puts it : *Was there a man dismayed ?* Though this is put in the form of a question, Tennyson did not want an answer. It is what is called a rhetorical question. An orator or preacher often goes on asking questions which he would be greatly surprised if any one answered. The answer is supposed to be implied in the very nature of things. The question is, in fact, an exclamation. Sometimes, indeed, there is a difficulty in saying whether a sentence which is interrogative in form should have the question mark (?) or the exclamation mark (!) after it. In : *Who can number the stars of the firmament*, we may use either *!* or *?*

Then we have sentences which express a wish. *God speed the right. May your shadow never grow less.* Finally, we have sentences in which an order or an authoritative piece of advice is given. *Charge for the guns. Never use a big word when a little one will do as well.*

With these five kinds of simple sentences we have ample scope for variety of form. But we must not forget that the ordinary straightforward form of the sentence should always be preferred, unless there is some reason for departing from it. There is a style of writing that seeks to gain brightness by twisting the words of the sentence into unnatural positions. *Go downstairs I could not* may be passed if found as one example of inversion in a passage, particularly if the tone of the passage is somewhat elevated. But for an ordinary construction such a sentence is to be condemned.

You must note that while the following exercise gives practice in changing the form of sentences, it does not at all follow that the change is for the better. So long as wearisome monotony is avoided, the more direct you can make your sentences the better.

Exercise 6

Change the following into the interrogative form without materially altering the meaning :—

(a) 1. This is not English straightforwardness. 2. A braver man is not to be found. 3. There is no longer any doubt about the matter. 4. There is not a scrap of evidence against him. 5. I am no dog that I should do this thing.

Change the following into the exclamatory form without materially altering the meaning :—

(b) 1. He has a very ugly mouth. 2. I dislike babies very much. 3. The ways of God are wonderful. 4. There is plenty of plunder here.

(c) Write a short description of waking up on a snowy morning, using the following notes as a guide, if you are at a loss what to say :—

On waking, the lightness of the room—the stillness outside—footmarks in the snowy street—snow falling again—men sweeping the snow away—difference between snow in town and snow in the country.

LESSON VII

THE SENTENCE—COMPOUND AND COMPLEX SENTENCES

When a sentence contains only one subject and one predicate it is called a simple sentence. All the sentences we have hitherto considered are simple sentences. But sentences frequently contain several subjects and predicates. When two simple sentences are joined together we have a new sentence with two subjects and two predicates. Consider these two simple sentences :—

The Spaniard swerved aside. The dagger grazed his ear.

These can be combined in several ways, as thus :—

The Spaniard swerved aside and the dagger grazed his ear.
The Spaniard swerved aside : the dagger grazed his ear.

In both cases two simple sentences have been rolled into one : in the first they are linked by the conjunction, *and* ; in the second the conjunction has been replaced by a colon. When two sentences are thus combined, they cease to be called sentences, and, in relation to the new sentence which they form, they are called *Clauses*. In these sentences both clauses are equally important, and neither is dependent on the other. A sentence formed from such clauses is called a *Compound Sentence*. There may be any number of clauses in a Compound Sentence, provided each is independent, e.g. *The cat mewed, the dog whined, and the baby howled for its rattle.*

Sometimes the clauses are not independent. Examine the following sentences :—

1. *Here is a portrait of my grandmother, who was in her youth a very beautiful woman.* Here the clause *who was a very beautiful woman* is dependent on the first clause. Its purpose is to describe *my grandmother*, so that it really stands in place of an adjective.

47

2. *The seal was discovered where it had fallen.*
Here the clause expands what the verb tells us,
and really stands in place of an adverb.

3. *He told the cook that the house was on fire.*
Here the clause stands for what he told the cook,
and might be replaced by a noun such as *news*.
It is the object of the verb *told*, and stands in
place of a noun.

In all these cases we have a principal clause
and a subordinate one, the whole sentence being
called *Complex*. There is no limit to the number
of subordinate clauses that may be found in a
complex sentence. We may have all three
kinds present in the same sentence. *When
Edward learned the true state of affairs, he decided
that the hostages who had been sent should be at once
executed.* The relation of the clauses in this
sentence is more clearly seen if we set them out
like a family tree :—

We can also have sentences which are both complex and compound. These contain two principal clauses and one or more dependent clauses,
as : *They reached the battlements which were
deserted by the sentinels, and put the entire garrison
to the sword.*

For the purposes of composition the triple classification is sufficient—simple sentences : compound sentences (*i.e.*, those having two or more principal clauses but no subordinate clauses) : and complex sentences (*i.e.*, those having one or more principal, and one or more subordinate clauses). Compare the following example : the principal verbs are in bold type :—

John Gilpin **was** a citizen of credit and renown.
Simple.

The Queen of France, being a Spaniard, would not, he **thought,** be welcome.   Complex.

Tom **put** out his pink palm, and Bob **was** not slow to place his hard, grimy hand within it.
Compound.

You must be on your guard against the error of regarding the grammatical principal clause as really the most important clause. *He told me that my house had been burned to the ground. He told* is grammatically the principal clause, but the subordinate noun clause would be the important one for me. What does it matter who told me, compared with the fact that my house is ruined ? On the other hand, if the news were false, and the question was who had spread the disagreeable story, the grammatical principal clause would also be the really important one.

Exercise 7

(*a*) In the following sentences underline the principal (grammatical) verb or verbs, and set them out in such a way as to show the relation of the clauses (as in the example on p. 48).

1. There's a story that when the mill changes

49

hands, the river's angry. 2. Nevertheless we have reason to be thankful that the thing, well or ill, is over. 3. Love heaven; let your heart be on it. 4. I could easily give you more definite, but very disagreeable proofs of the evil of knowing the anatomy of the human face too intimately.

(b) Combine the simple sentences of your account of a country walk into longer sentences.

(c) Do the same in the passage given on p. 189.

LESSON VIII

THE SENTENCE—KINDS OF COMPOUND SENTENCES

When simple sentences are joined together to make compound sentences, the combination may be effected in different ways. First, the two parts may be of equal importance and of the same character. They may be joined by a conjunction : *The mate opened his mouth, and the pipe fell from it* ; or they may have only a colon between them : *Fox went into Parliament at twenty : Pitt when just of age.* Or one part of the sentence may be opposed to or contrasted with the other. *Acids turn litmus red, but alkalies turn it blue.* Speaking generally, the conjunction *and* is the mark of the first kind of sentence, the conjunction *but* of the second. But the meaning alone can determine the relation between the clauses. *Lord Bruce was made an earl for a blunder in prosody : and Nelson was made a baron for the victory of the Nile.* Here the clauses are clearly contrasted, though joined by *and*. If Pitt had been old when he entered Parliament, the clauses of the sentence above would become contrasted, though the form remained unchanged.

The two clauses may be separated from one another as alternatives, or plainly disjoined from each other : *She must weep or she will die. You will neither use the material yourself nor allow others to do so.*

Again, the two clauses may be so related that one of them gives the cause of what is stated in the other : *The King had abdicated : therefore Henry's course was clear.*

In the examples given above both subjects and both predicates are expressed, but it frequently happens that one verb has to do duty for several subjects, and as frequently one subject has several verbs. *The populace, the patricians, the Emperor himself yielded to the impulse of the moment. The interloper fawned, flattered, yet failed.* Each of these two compound sentences is made up of three simple sentences.

In the first case we have three sentences with the same predicate :—

The populace yielded to the impulse of the moment.

The patricians yielded to the impulse of the moment.

The Emperor himself yielded to the impulse of the moment.

In the second case we have three sentences with the same subject :—

The interloper fawned.

The interloper flattered.

The interloper failed.

51

Exercise 8

(a) Complete the following sentences :—

1. Such treatment I did not expect, for ——
2. Sir, you are either ignorant or —— 3. Cain as well as Abel —— 4. The table was literally loaded with good cheer, and —— 5. Man proposes —— 6. —— in consequence the work had to be re-written. 7. —— but his pleadings were in vain. 8. —— and ready to forgive. 9. This made Christian give a little back; Apollyon therefore —— 10. He shuddered; he grew pale; he —— 11. —— accordingly Wellington gave it an emphatic denial. 12. Forster counterfeits a passion too, but ——

(b) Turn the simple sentences in your description of a snowy morning into longer sentences by turning them into complex or compound sentences.

(c) Do the same for the passage given on p. 190.

LESSON IX

THE SENTENCE—RELATIVE CLAUSES

Simple sentences are often rolled into one with the help of a relative clause.

He supports his mother.   She has bad health.

These sentences in combination become :—

He supports his mother who has bad health.

This is the just and proper use of the relative. It should not, however, be used where it is possible to use an adjective or participle instead.

If we wish to roll the following sentences into one, we should do so by transferring the adjective :—

He supports his mother. She is an invalid.
He supports his invalid mother.

The next can be linked by a participle in the same way :—

Sir William has a favourite dog. Its name is Diamond.
Sir William has a favourite dog named Diamond.

These copulative relative clauses, as they are called, should always be used in moderation; they are clumsy and unwieldy when used in excess. They are most abused when they are hitched one behind another, like a train of carriages behind a railway engine. The classic example of this chain construction is the nursery rhyme, " The House that Jack Built," but it is found also in serious prose, as, for example :—

" Sir William used to show with pride a silver casket which he had received from an Indian prince whom he had been able to accommodate in a small matter which had arisen out of the diplomatic entanglements which necessarily arise in countries which are broken up into petty states, whose rulers are kept at peace only by fear of the force which the Government can bring to bear upon those princes who transgress the limits which it marks out."

In this monstrous sentence, nine simple sentences have been tacked together, and the connection between the first and the last is remote in the extreme.

There is another use of the relative clause that must be distinguished from that we have illustrated. *The soul that sinneth shall die*. In this case we cannot split the sentence up into two independent sentences. *The soul shall die* is complete so far as it goes. But it is not true as it stands. We are not told that the soul in general shall die, but only a particular kind of soul, the kind that sins. In other words, the relative clause *that sinneth* really limits the meaning of the whole sentence. This is called the restrictive use of the relative; the other kind illustrates what may be called the copulative or co-ordinative use. Generally speaking, the restrictive use prefers *that*, while the copulative use prefers *who* or *which*. But this cannot be depended on in discriminating the two. It is carrying criticism too far to ask a Scotsman to change his patriotic song from *Scots wha hae* to *Scots that hae*. The rule, in fact, is not rigid, as is seen in Ruskin's : " The man who does not know when to die, does not know how to live ". We should in most cases use *that* in restrictive clauses, but we need not bind ourselves to the one form. Sometimes the flow of the sentence is improved by a *who* or *which*.

The best way of discriminating between the two uses is to note whether the relative clause is in any way parenthetic. Try if the main sentence can stand quite alone, and mean exactly the same thing, *so far as it goes*, after we have taken away the relative clause. *The man who writes for fools is always sure of a large audience*. Here, if we cut out *who writes for fools* we take away the whole point of the sentence. The real subject is not *man* but man-who-writes-for-fools.

In the sentence, *That man, who is talking to the porter, is her brother,* we find that the relative clause tells us more about *that man* than is found in the main clause, but does not materially affect the main clause.

In the copulative or co-ordinative use of the relative it is found that *who* and *which* are practically equal to *and he* (or *she*) *and it.* *My father, whom I left at home, will be here presently* really equals *My father (and I left him at home) will be here presently.* But *The friend that I left at home will be here presently* cannot be separated in this way.

Students who are studying, or intend to study, French or Latin should attend specially to this distinction between restrictive and copulative relative clauses.

Exercise 9

(*a*) Combine the following sets of simple sentences into complex sentences; first with a restrictive relative clause, and secondly with a copulative relative clause, in each case :—

1. The man was exempted from military service. His mother was a widow. 2. The ship was built by Jackson & Co. It was wrecked. 3. Mary had a little lamb. It went with her to school. 4. The novelist has few friends. He is despised. He is conceited.

(*b*) Break up the sentence about Sir William (on p. 53) into simple sentences, and then combine them into sentences of suitable length.

LESSON X

THE SENTENCE—LOOSE AND PERIODIC SENTENCES

There are said to be two great classes of sentences according to the general principles on which they are constructed. There is first the **loose** sentence. Its characteristic is that it puts the main idea of the sentence in the front, and adds piecemeal whatever is thought necessary. In this form of sentence the author is tempted to add fact after fact as they occur to him, and as they all have some sort of connection with the main idea, they may fairly be included in the same sentence, though the looseness of the connection is often apparent enough to justify the name. The first sentence of *Robinson Crusoe* supplies an excellent example.

"I was born in the year 1632, in the city of York, of a good family, though not of that country, my father being a foreigner of Bremen, who settled first at Hull : he got a good estate by merchandise, and leaving off his trade, lived afterward at York, from whence he had married my mother, whose relations were named Robinson, a very good family in that country, and from whom I was called Robinson Kreutznaer; but, by the usual corruption of words in England, we are now called, nay, we call ourselves, and write our name Crusoe, and so my companions always called me."

Defoe is here writing in a conversational manner. He seems to lengthen his sentence as the facts occur to him, and there seems no reason why it should ever come to end. This kind of sentence is very appropriate to informal writing, especially where the first person is used.

The other kind of sentence, known as the **periodic,** arranges for a termination by keeping the principal statement to the end. In Dr. Johnson we find :—

" If, therefore, he whose crimes have deprived him of the favour of God can reflect upon his conduct without disturbance, or can at will banish the reflection ; if he who considers himself as suspended over the abyss of eternal perdition only by the thread of life, which must soon part by its own weakness, and which the wing of every minute may divide, can cast his eyes round him without shuddering with horror or panting with security, what can he judge of himself but that he is not yet awakened to sufficient conviction ? "

The name *periodic* is apt to convey the impression that this sort of sentence must be long, and generally speaking the impression is correct. But the real test is not the length of the whole sentence, but the place of the principal idea at the end rather than at the beginning.

After the most straitest sect of our religion I lived a Pharisee is periodic ; *I lived a Pharisee after the most straitest sect of our religion* is loose.

A very common kind of periodic sentence begins with clauses preceded by *that*.

" That the life and progress on which he built such hopes, should be endangered in the outset by so mean a want : that Dombey and Son should be tottering for a nurse, was a sore humiliation."

It is not to be supposed that all sentences obligingly fall into the two classes : those that begin with the main idea, and those that end with it. In many cases the main idea comes about the middle, as in the following sentences quoted from Charles Lamb :—

" With great deference to the old lady's judgment in these matters, I think I have experienced some moments in my life, when playing at cards for nothing has even been agreeable. When I am in sickness, or not in the best of spirits, I sometimes call for the cards, and play a game at piquet for love with my cousin Bridget—Bridget Elia."

These seem to be neither loose nor periodic, but those who lay great store upon exact definitions will be glad to learn that all sentences that do not begin with the main statement are called periodic, so that the sentences just quoted are technically known as periodic sentences. The original sentence given in Exercise 5 is loose. All the variations on it are periodic.

The very name " loose " is sufficient to prejudice the unwary against the first kind of sentence. Almost invariably a student when asked which is the better form of sentence answers, " The periodic ". The answer should be, " It depends upon the connection in which it is used ". In speaking, as opposed to writing, the loose construction is frequently to be preferred. If the hearer knows what the sentence is about in general terms, he can examine each new statement as it is presented : but if all the subordinate clauses come first, he cannot understand their bearing, and is very apt to get tired and give up attending before the explanatory ending is reached. " That St. Paul was struck blind at Damascus, that he had to gaze steadfastly in order to distinguish the High Priest, that he wrote to the Galatians in large characters, that these same Galatians were at one time willing to give even their own eyes for him, all lead us to believe that St. Paul's ' thorn in the flesh ' consisted in a weakness of the eyes."

Such a sentence demands a second reading; for the first four clauses cannot be estimated as arguments till it is known what position they are used to establish. In a speech the sentence is bad; in a written argument it is quite permissible. It cannot be too strongly impressed upon writers and speakers that it is not enough that they should so express themselves that any one who cares to take pains can understand what they write or speak : the ideal is to express oneself so that hearers or readers cannot help understanding.

The true view is that both loose and periodic sentences ought to be used in all kinds of composition, but that in speaking the loose should predominate, and in writing the periodic. It has been made clear already that a periodic sentence is not necessarily either long or heavy. *Reduced to his last cartridge he fired it and fell* is regarded by some authorities as a more finished sentence than *He fell after he had fired his last cartridge*. But there is not difference enough to quarrel over. The important thing is to use both forms in a composition, so that monotony of structure may be avoided.

Exercise 10

(a) State in the case of each of the following eight sentences whether it is loose or periodic : if it is loose turn it into the periodic form, if it is periodic then change it to the loose form.

1. When Edward the Black Prince made your king his prisoner, he reverenced his age, his station, his misfortunes; attending him, serving him, consoling him, like a son. 2. He would, as became him, have kept behind his master, if the knight had not called him to his side, complaining that the length and roughness of the roads had shaken his saddle so as to make it uneven and uneasy. 3. Among the beautiful and simple-hearted customs of rural life which still linger in some parts of England, are those of strewing flowers before the funerals, and planting them at the graves of departed friends. 4. There is something genuine and affectionate in the gaiety of the young, when it is excited by the bounty and familiarity of their elders. 5. The simple truth is that the Aristotelians erected their castles upon a basis far less reliable than air. 6. In attempting to appreciate this interval by the aid of any considerations of velocity, as we did in endeavouring to estimate the distance of the moon, we must leave out of sight altogether such nothings as the speed of a cannon ball or of sound. 7. If any pretend that they have the Spirit, and so turn away from the straight rule of the Holy Scriptures, they have a spirit indeed, but it is a fanatical spirit, the spirit of delusion and giddiness. 8. From the circumstance of the dinner being composed of pig's head mock-turtle soup, of pig's fry and roast

ribs of pork, I am led to imagine that one of Ponto's black Hampshires had been sacrificed a short time before my visit.

(b) Make up a loose sentence on the pleasures of living in a city, and a periodic sentence on the pleasures of living in the country.

LESSON XI

THE SENTENCE—LENGTH AND BALANCE OF SENTENCES

The claims of long and short sentences must be treated in exactly the same way as we have treated those of loose and periodic sentences. There is room in composition for both : each in its own place is best. They ought to be used together; the one kind acts as a foil to the other. A passage written entirely in very short sentences lacks dignity and weight : it conveys the impression of being very brittle and ready to fall to pieces : it is jerky, and gives no resting-places for the mind. On the other hand, long sentences, such as Johnson sometimes uses, are exceedingly cumbrous, and make an unnecessarily heavy demand on our attention. It is true that many of those long sentences are not sentences at all, since they are merely several sentences joined together by semicolons, instead of being separated by periods. They are really paragraphs.

The short sentence must, on the whole, have the preference. Wherever there is any doubt, always decide for the shorter sentence. But it is well to recognise that the long sentence has its place and use. Short sentences are very useful to introduce a general principle which is to be elaborated. Somewhat longer sentences are useful in working out the principle. Shorter sentences are again useful in gathering up conclusions drawn from the treatment of a subject.

Different kinds of writing demand different lengths of sentence. Description usually permits of pretty equal proportions of long and short; argument often requires a preponderance of long sentences; narrative generally prefers the short sentence. Especially in the case of rapid action the short sentence is useful. Thus, in telling how Crusoe prepared to meet the savages, Defoe says :—

" I turned to Friday. ' Now, Friday,' said I, ' do as I bid thee.' Friday said he would. ' Then, Friday,' says I, ' do exactly as you see me do—fail in nothing.' "

This is followed by longer sentences describing how things were done : the dramatic short sentence is no longer needed. Apart from this need for variety in length, the short sentence justifies its existence because it tends, on the whole, to greater clearness.[1]

We have seen that neither the loose nor the periodic form is necessarily long : but the loose sentence has a natural tendency to swell beyond its legitimate size. When once the main idea has been expressed, the way seems so clear for less important matter that we are tempted to go

[1] Of modern writers, Ernest Hemingway shows marked preference for short sentences, and uses them with great effect.

on adding clause after clause till the sentence becomes monstrous. To a certain extent the subordinate matters are kept in their place, since they follow the main statement. But there are degrees of subordination, and the less important clauses should be so arranged as to indicate the greater or less importance of each. The loose sentence tempts us to put them down in the mere order in which they occur to us.

Try to complete every sentence in your mind before setting it down on paper. This does not mean that you are to sit mouthing over every word in a sentence before you write it down : but it does mean that you must know the exact kind of sentence you are dealing with, and its exact scope. Afterthoughts in the middle of a sentence often cause what is called a broken construction (see p. 121), and almost always cause an unpleasant lopsidedness in sentences. Clearly the loose sentence is more liable to abuse in this way than is the periodic. From the very beginning the important point of the periodic sentence must be kept in view : we are working up to that main point, and are therefore not likely to let too many smaller ideas come between us and our goal. In the loose sentence we can make a beginning and go on without having well considered the end. In the periodic, the end must be clearly conceived from the very beginning.

In sentence-building the matter of balance is too often neglected. Wherever possible the parts should be so arranged that each supports the others, and that similar parts are grouped together, and dissimilar parts contrasted with each other. A sentence, for example, may contain three principal clauses, the first with one subordinate clause, the second with three, the last with none. Here we have a clear case of lack of balance. The sentence is lopsided. We must not, however, go to the opposite extreme, and arrange that each of the clauses shall have three subordinate clauses, whether the meaning demands it or not. Nothing can justify the padding out of sentences when the meaning is clear enough already.

" The tower was captured in spite of all the villagers could do, the baron was killed in the very room in which he had caused Gerald to be put to death because of his refusal to sign the declaration when the first troop of insurgents had arrived in defiance of the orders the cardinal had issued, and Fenton had to seek a new master."

The sentence is so lopsided as to be unpleasant, but the remedy is not to be sought in adding balancing clauses at the beginning and the end. The whole requires to be recast. Take the following sentence from Gibbon, and you cannot fail to find satisfaction in the balance of the two final clauses.

" The unsuccessful expedition of Hannibal served only to display the character of the senate and people; of a senate degraded, rather than ennobled, by the comparison of an assembly of kings; and of a people to whom the ambassador of Pyrrhus ascribed the inexhaustible resources of the Hydra."

It is generally supposed that the periodic sentence lends itself more readily than the loose to this just balancing; but the sentence quoted is loose and yet perfectly balanced.

Johnson is noted for his balanced sentences. Indeed, he cannot be regarded as quite guiltless of sacrificing matter to style in the rounding of his periods. The following is an excellent example of a Johnsonian sentence :—

"The power of invention has been conferred by nature upon few, and the labour of learning those sciences which may by mere labour be obtained, is too great to be willingly endured; but every man can exert such judgment as he has upon the works of others; and he whom nature has made weak, and idleness keeps ignorant, may yet support his vanity by the name of a critic."

There is first the general balance of the part that precedes and the part that follows the first semicolon. Then there is the balance of the two main clauses that make up the second part. Finally, there is the balance of the two subordinate clauses contained in the final main clause.

This may be called the double or two-pulse balance, but Johnson is very fond of the three-pulse or triple balance. It has been sarcastically said that each of Johnson's essays could be made into three essays by simply selecting, one after the other, the first, the second and the third of his balanced nouns, adjectives and verbs. Most people would be content with saying that at certain periods the world is filled with bloodshed. Johnson makes it filled with "ravage, bloodshed and devastation".

"Men then grow weary of debate and altercation, and apply themselves to the arts of profit; trading companies are formed, manufactures improved, and navigation extended; and nothing is any longer thought on but the increase and preservation of property, the artifices of getting money, and the pleasures of spending it."

Here the whole sentence, as separated by the semicolons, represents the triple balance, each of the three parts having a subordinate balance of its own; the first subordinate balance is double, the next two triple.

This poised style, though it can be applied to both the loose and the periodic sentence, is generally known as the periodic style. It is no longer popular, which is not altogether to be regretted, as it formed a strong temptation to subordinate thought to expression. Nature has not arranged that things shall fall into well-ordered groups of pairs and elegant series of trilogies to suit the convenience of the writer of periods. But the reaction goes too far. Our ordinary style pays too little heed to the flow of words. Our sentences are often so short that we feel as if our minds were jolted from one idea to the other. More frequently our longer sentences are mere huddles of clauses, badly joined together or not joined at all.

" It ought to be presumed that a publisher who conducts a respectable and honourable business will, when he retires from it, probably do so, however suddenly, respectably and honourably; and he ought not to be deprived of the right, which he himself allows the author, of assigning his interest in the work if necessary."

Here we have neither balance nor flow. Ask any one to read the sentence aloud, and you will find how essentially bad it is. *This test of reading aloud ought to be applied to all the sentences that you write by way of practice.* It is not meant that prose should flow as smoothly as verse, but it should flow; it should not be a series of gasps or pistol shots. The sentence quoted gasps along in puffs, till it comes to *suddenly* : there, where it ought to halt, it begins to flow. *Suddenly, respectably and honourably* run into one another with an ease that is as vicious as is the preceding stiffness.

Exercise 11

(*a*) Re-cast the first half of the sentence about the publisher.

(*b*) Throw the whole of the Crusoe sentences into one.

(*c*) The following passage is taken from *Pickwick Papers*. Bob Sawyer is giving a party, and his friend Jack Hopkins is telling Mr. Pickwick a very tall story about his experiences as a medical student. Re-write the story as it might appear in a daily paper, leaving out all unnecessary details (the conversation, the shoulder of mutton, etc.). Make the account as dramatic as possible, using longer sentences for the plainer parts of the narrative, short sentences for the exciting parts.

" By the bye," said Hopkins, ". . . we had a curious accident last night. A child was brought in, who had swallowed a necklace."

" Swallowed what, sir ? " interrupted Mr. Pickwick.

" A necklace," replied Jack Hopkins. " Not all at once, you know, that would be too much. . . . No, the way was this. Child's parents

67

were poor people who lived in a court. Child's eldest sister bought a necklace; common necklace, made of large wooden beads. Child, being fond of toys, cribbed the necklace, hid it, played with it, cut the string, swallowed a bead. Child thought it capital fun, went back next day, swallowed another bead."

" Bless my heart," said Mr. Pickwick, " what a dreadful thing ! I beg your pardon, sir. Go on."

" Next day, child swallowed two beads; the day after that, he treated himself to three, and so on, till in a week's time he had got through the necklace—five and twenty beads in all. The sister . . . cried her eyes out at the loss of the necklace; looked high and low for it; but, I needn't say, didn't find it. A few days afterwards, the family were at dinner—baked shoulder of mutton, and potatoes under it—the child, who wasn't hungry, was playing about the room, when suddenly there was heard a devil of a noise, like a small hailstorm. ' Don't do that, my boy,' said the father. ' I ain't doin' nothing,' said the child. ' Well, don't do it again,' said the father. There was a short silence, and then the noise began again, worse than ever. ' If you don't mind what I say, my boy,' said the father, ' you'll find yourself in bed in something less than a pig's whisper.' He gave the child a shake to make him obedient, and such a rattling ensued as nobody ever heard before. ' Why, damme, it's *in* the child ! ' said the father, ' he's got croup in the wrong place ! ' ' No, I haven't, father,' said the child, beginning to cry, ' it's the necklace; I swallowed it, father.'—The father caught the child up and ran with him to the hospital, the beads in the boy's stomach rattling all the way with the jolting, and the people looking up in the air, and down in the cellars to see where the unusual noise came from. He's in the hospital now," said Jack Hopkins, " and he makes such a devil of a noise when he walks about, that they're obliged to muffle him in a watchman's coat, for fear he should wake the patients ! "

(*Note*.—Your own version should be about two-thirds the length of the original.)

LESSON XII

THE PARAGRAPH

The paragraph bears the same relation to an essay, an article or a chapter that the sentence does to the paragraph. The sentence is often said to be "complete in itself", but in many cases this is true only in a grammatical sense. Take the isolated sentences given in the exercises of this book, and you cannot fail to see how incomplete they are as they stand. There is the proper number of verbs and subjects : all the grammatical rules have been attended to : yet we feel that in many cases we cannot be quite sure about the real meaning. When several sentences have been so grouped as to explain each other, and together make up a more or less independent part of a longer composition, they form a paragraph.

A great many of the points dealt with regarding sentences have to be considered in connection with paragraphs. To begin with, a paragraph has only a modified independence. It must depend upon the other paragraphs for its full meaning. If this is not so, it is not a paragraph, but a little essay by itself.

Next comes the question whether paragraphs should be long or short. Here we must be guided by the same principles that we applied to sentences. If we are dealing with events rapidly taking place we must have short paragraphs. In ordinary descriptive or argumentative work they ought to be longer. The modern tendency is to shorten the paragraph unduly. A page of solid printing is almost as distasteful to the public as to the compositor. The very same matter that repels when presented in a block, seems attractive when broken up into four or five portions. Within limits the tendency to shorten paragraphs is to be encouraged. To feel that you must say all that you have to say on each aspect of your subject in the fewest possible sentences has a wholesome effect. One danger is that the thought expressed in paragraphs may become unduly compressed. The more serious danger is that short paragraphs are made by the simple process of cutting up a long paragraph into bits of the required length. The resulting groups of sentences are no longer paragraphs in any respect but appearance. In consequence of this mechanical shortening of paragraphs many modern books have a very spasmodic, jerky style that interferes with the flow of thought. The following illustrates the jerky effect of too short paragraphs :—

" Let me face it quietly. To-day I am actually beset with a fresh disaster and a worse one.

" ' You are a pauper, Archibald Seaton.'

" This is what the city roared to me an hour or two ago.

" The simple story of a stupid investor once again.

" When I married I wanted my income stretched to its utmost extent, and against the advice of the family solicitor invested all *The Demon* does not claim in the Del Norte Gold Mines, then paying 10 per cent.

" An old Oxford acquaintance of Hebrew extraction, who had adopted the name of an ancient Scotch family, tempted me, and I fell.

" For two years the dividends were paid. Yesterday the company went into liquidation, and my few poor thousands have vanished into thin air like a ghost in Virgil.

" In the City, where I ran like a frightened rabbit, I met fellow-shareholders in a similar plight—a white-faced, panic-stricken crew.

" To me there is a certain grim humour in the situation.

" I distinctly hear two voices.

" My Uncle Linton is saying, ' That unlucky ass, Archibald ! ' My father-in-law is rubbing the back of his left hand with the palm of his right, exclaiming to Christabel, ' What a calamity ! What a calamity ! How is it he never consulted me ? Was ever any one so unbusinesslike ? ' And what is my wife saying ? She, I know, will say nothing—only wonder silently how we are to live.

" And how do I feel ? Much like a sentient cork drifting with the blind black tide of disaster.''

Even in verse, where the stanza forms the

71

natural paragraph, we find that poets are frequently compelled to carry on the thought of one stanza into the next, and to do this have sometimes to split a sentence between the stanzas. The truth is that paragraphs must vary in length according to the requirements of each case, exactly as do sentences. The tendency should always be towards shortness.

As to the arrangement of sentences in a paragraph, no hard and fast rules can be laid down. It is generally more effective to begin and end with shorter sentences, while the middle is occupied with those of more complicated construction. In an essay the shorter sentences introduce clearly and boldly the argument of the paragraph, the longer sentences unfold it, and the short closing sentences gather up and clinch what has gone before. In a descriptive paragraph the same process is very often followed. Here is a simple, yet effective, paragraph from Cowper's letters :—

" I have a kitten, my dearest Cousin, the drollest of all creatures that ever wore a cat's skin. Her gambols are not to be described, and would be incredible, if they could. In point of size she is likely to be a kitten always, being extremely small of her age, but time, I suppose, that spoils everything, will make her also a cat. You will see her, I hope, before that melancholy period shall arrive, for no wisdom that she may gain by experience and reflection hereafter, will compensate the loss of her present hilarity. She is dressed in a tortoise-shell suit, and I know that you will delight in her."

Exercise 12

(*a*) The following passage from Lamb's essay, " Mrs. Battle's Opinions on Whist ", is divided in the original into four paragraphs. Read it over carefully and try to discover where each new paragraph begins.

" ' A clear fire, a clean hearth, and the rigour of the game.' This was the celebrated *wish* of old Sarah Battle (now with God) who, next to her devotions, loved a good game at whist. She was none of your lukewarm gamesters, your half and half players, who have no objection to take a hand, if you want one to make up a rubber ; who affirm they have no pleasure in winning ; that they like to win one game and lose another ; that they can while away an hour very agreeably at a card table, but are indifferent whether they play or no ; and will desire an adversary, who has slipt a wrong card, to take it up and play another. These insufferable triflers are the curse of a table. One of these flies will spoil a whole pot. Of such may it be said, that they do not play at cards, but only play at playing at them. Sarah Battle was none of that breed. She detested them, as I do, from her heart and soul ; and would not, save upon a striking emergency, willingly seat herself at the same table with them. She loved a thorough-paced partner, a determined enemy. She took, and gave, no concessions. She hated favours. She fought a good fight : cut and thrust. She held not her good sword (her cards) ' like a dancer '. She sat bolt upright ; and neither showed you her cards, nor desired to see yours.

All people have their blind side—their superstitions; and I have heard her declare, under the rose, that Hearts was her favourite suit. I never in my life—and I knew Sarah Battle many of the best years of it—saw her take out her snuff-box when it was her turn to play; or snuff a candle in the middle of a game; or ring for a servant, till it was fairly over. She never introduced, or connived at, miscellaneous conversation during its process. As she emphatically observed, cards were cards: and if ever I saw unmingled distaste in her fine last-century countenance, it was at the airs of a young gentleman of a literary turn, who had been with difficulty persuaded to take a hand; and who, in his excess of candour, declared, that he thought there was no harm in unbending the mind now and then, after serious studies, in recreations of that kind! She could not bear to have her noble occupation, to which she wound up her faculties, considered in that light. It was her business, her duty, the thing she came into the world to do,—and she did it. She unbent her mind afterwards—over a book. Pope was her favourite author: his Rape of the Lock her favourite work. She once did me the favour to play over with me (with the cards) his celebrated game of Ombre in that poem; and to explain to me how far it agreed with, and in what points it would be found to differ from, tradrille. Her illustrations were apposite and poignant; and I had the pleasure of sending the substance of them to Mr. Bowles: but I suppose they came too late to be inserted among his ingenious notes upon that author."

(b) Write a descriptive paragraph about a

fruiterer's shop, using the following notes as a guide if necessary :—

The gaiety and colour of the window—the various fruit—where it comes from—the English fruit.

LESSON XIII

PUNCTUATION

Certain marks have been agreed upon by writers and printers so as to help readers to understand exactly what is meant by the written or printed page. The importance of these marks may be well shown in the two different meanings that may be attached to the following couplet found above a barber's door :—

What do you think
I'll shave you for nothing and give you a drink

There were no points at all, but the passer-by naturally took the view that here was an unusually generous offer. He read *What do you think ?* as an exclamation calling attention to the promise that follows. After the shave the barber punctuated it for himself—*What ! do you think I'll shave you for nothing and give you a drink ?*

The meaning of this sentence depends entirely upon its punctuation. This is regarded as a bad quality. The best sentence is that which stands least in need of punctuation. It is impossible to do without it altogether, but the aim of the good writer is to depend upon it as little as possible. Some books give very elaborate rules for the use of each of the punctuation marks, but these rules have the evil effect of giving them an undue importance in the mind of the writer. They must be servants, not masters.

The **full stop** or **period** need give no trouble, since it is only used to mark the end of a complete sentence that is neither a question nor an exclamation. Its use to indicate a contraction hardly enters into composition, though it is highly desirable that you should know the exact meaning of certain contractions—if only to avoid them in ordinary prose.

I.e. means that is (*id est*); *e.g.* means for example (*exempli gratiâ*); *viz.* means namely (*videlicet*); *&c.* or *etc.* means and so forth (*etcetera*).

These contractions are excellent things to omit, unless you happen to be an auctioneer or a catalogue-maker. In general, one should always take the trouble to write out *for example* if one wishes to use these words. In writing lists or purely explanatory matter where no pretence of style is made, all manner of intelligible contractions may be used. But in continuous prose it is an excellent rule to write out everything in full, even numbers.

The **comma** is unfortunate enough to labour under a great number of rules. Its duty is to show the slightest amount of separation that demands punctuation at all. It should be omitted wherever possible.

1. Simple sentences joined but not opposed to each other are separated by a comma. *A faint wind moaned through the trees, and Tom*

feared it might be the spirits of the dead com-
plaining at being disturbed. " It's awful solemn
like, ain't it ? "

2. Generally speaking, a series of words or
phrases has its parts separated by commas :—

Conjuration, sleight of hand, magic, witchcraft, were the subjects of the evening.

The enemy waver, break, flee.

The brave, honest, dull Lefèvre died fighting
against the captain he thought he was saving.

3. When the subject of a sentence is itself a
clause or a longish phrase a comma is frequently
placed after the subject :—

That the accused had been under the influence
of drink when the man was killed, did not
appear to the judge as an extenuating circumstance.

Speechless, abject reverence, with a blue coat
and brass buttons, fails to express the porter's
state of mind towards the six-hundred-pounders
of the first landing.

4. An adjectival clause is marked off by
commas when the qualifying clause does not
indicate something essential in the thing quali-
fied. *Du Maurier's house, which I saw lately,
is now turned into some sort of Home.* But in
the sentence, *How we like men who can be amused
where most people would get into a passion,* we
have no commas ; for all that comes after *men*
is really a part of the essential idea. We do
not say that we like men in general, but only
men-who-can-be-amused and the rest.

This rule may be shortly expressed : the
copulative relative clause is marked off by
commas, but not the restrictive (see Lesson IX).

Here the essentially parenthetical nature of clauses marked off by commas becomes evident. This is equally conspicuous in the next rule.

5. After an introductory phrase or word, before and after a term of address, and, indeed, generally before and after anything that may be omitted without altering the main sense of the sentence we may use the comma. Thus we have :—

Moreover, it does not pay.

Fetch me *Rasselas*, my dear, out of the book room.

The goddess Nicotine has a fund of good sense, which prompts her, as a general thing, to put a smile, either broad or latent, into the carving of her pipes and cigar-holders.

Here " *as a general thing* " and " *either broad or latent* " are both parenthetical. It must be admitted that the sentence, though by a good author, is over-punctuated. There are too many commas, which gives a jerkiness to the whole. The comma after *smile* and *latent* could go.

A real **parenthesis,** that is, one which is more markedly independent of its surroundings, is usually indicated by being enclosed within brackets ( ). Thus :—

He believed in her so much (often to his annoyance) that she was a religion to him.

The parenthesis should be used sparingly. It is a confession that something is being brought into the sentence that has no right to be there. It is less abused in the form of brackets than in that of the dash, which is becoming so common as to threaten to take the place of all the other punctuation.

The **dash** (—) may be legitimately used to indicate a parenthesis, but it should be confined to those cases in which there is a more sudden break from the general run of the passage :—

In the unknown land called Markland, which may or may not have been Rhode Island, the Skrælings—and the Lord He knows who these may or may not have been—came to trade with the Vikings.

Another use of the dash is to indicate a conclusion without expressing it. This conclusion is quite clear to the hearer, though the speaker is unwilling to state it baldly :—

Business is business, and you may be sure I shouldn't give that price unless——

This use of the dash always implies a pause, though Scott thought it necessary to state this in the following passage :—

" 'I would rather work these ten bones to the knuckles, and live by my labour; but '—(and here he paused)."

A very common use of the dash is to indicate that what follows it is of special significance, or is not the natural or expected outcome of what goes before :—

Removing envelope after envelope with ever-increasing eagerness he finally disclosed—his own letter.

The **semicolon** (;) marks a slighter connection

between the parts of a sentence than does the comma : it is particularly useful in indicating contrasts :—

Permission was readily granted; and he set out for Italy.

The zeal of Burke was still fiercer; but it was far purer.

A very common use of the semicolon is to mark off parts of a long sentence that might quite naturally be separated by commas were it not that commas are already used largely in the sentence for subordinate divisions :—

Twice, while residing in the Writers' Buildings, he attempted to destroy himself; and twice the pistol which he snapped at his own head failed to go off.

Old-fashioned teachers of reading used to give their pupils the mechanical rule : at a comma stop as long as to count *one*, at a semicolon to count *two*, at a colon *three*, and at a full-stop *four*. This somewhat wooden plan was not very satisfactory in teaching reading, but it is at least useful in fixing in the pupils' minds the comparative degrees of separation indicated by the various marks.

The **colon** (:) does for a long sentence, containing semicolons and commas, what the semicolon does for one containing commas : it marks off broader distinctions than either of the other two. Thus :—

No person shall be permitted to visit more than one picture in one day : at which rate it would take at least three years to see a gallery of any extent; and true picture-lovers would probably confine their attentions to two or three favourites; spending day after day at their houses, not always gazing on the very canvas, but musing upon the fine symbolism of the surroundings, and leisurely accumulating fresh power to see and understand.

A very common use of the colon is to introduce the details of a group of things already referred to in the mass :—

The captain's excuses for not firing a royal salute were : first, he did not know that the king was on board; secondly, he was afraid lest the firing should cause a panic in the port; thirdly, his gunpowder had given out.

The **exclamation mark** (!) should be very sparingly used, particularly in prose. In no case should it be doubled (!!), however great the occasion.

The **question mark** (?) is to be used after every direct question, but never after an indirect.

Six men are to be hanged on the morrow : comes no hammering on the Rabenstein ? But in the indirect form,—*Carlyle asked why there came no hammering on the Rabenstein,*—there is no question mark.

The use of **quotation marks** (" ") is easily stated. They always enclose the very words that came out of the speaker's mouth, or are quoted direct from any author :—

" I can't get out," said the starling. But : The starling said that he could not get out.

Clearly the bird did not open its mouth and utter the words—*that he could not get out.* Accordingly these are not enclosed in quotation marks.

When a quotation occurs within a quotation the inner quotation is marked by single points

(' '), as in this passage from Meredith : " Beauchamp continued in the street : ' Tyrannies like this fellow's have made the English the dullest and wretchedest people in Europe ' ".

Capital letters are necessary at the beginning of every sentence, at the first word of every line of verse, at the beginning of every direct quotation. All proper nouns are written with capitals, the pronoun I, the vocative O, and all names applied to the Deity. In the titles of books or chapters all the important words have capitals—only articles, demonstratives, prepositions and little adverbs beginning with small letters. The days of the week, the months of the year, the great festivals, and generally any outstanding thing or event—the House of Commons, the Reformation—are dignified with capitals. Note particularly that adjectives formed from proper nouns retain the capital—Chinese, Lenten. A personified word (see Lesson XIV) is written with a capital.

Exercise 13

Punctuate the following, insert capitals where necessary, and arrange any verse into its proper lines :—

(a) 1. A man going to sea his wife desires the prayers of the congregation. 2. The woman that deliberates is lost. 3. Ask wheres the north at york tis on the tweed in scotland at the orcades and there at greenland zembla or the lord knows where. 4. At length mary died elizabeth succeeded and cecil rose at once to greatness. 5. And what did your uncle say to that asked the judge he said you must never breathe a word of this to a living soul was the reply. 6. I go to a convention of philanthropists do what I can I cannot keep my eyes off the clock but if there should appear in the company some gentle soul who knows little of persons or parties of carolina or cuba but who announces a law that disposes these particulars and so certifies me of the equity which checkmates every false player bankrupts every self seeker and apprises me of my independence on any conditions of country or time or human body that man liberates me I forget the clock I pass out of the sore relation to persons I am healed of my hurts I am made immortal by apprehending my possession of incorruptible goods. 7. If he was an inhumane old gentleman and I am afraid it is a fact that he was inhumane he was also perfectly intrepid. 8. He promised to go down first and boldly he did so for william give him his due had the heart of a lion. 9. Im no leech said adam let me go no not yet I will convict thee of ignorance thou dost not even know where the liver is placed I do answered adam shortly but what then thou dost I deny it here is a pin stick it into this wax man where thou sayest the liver lies in the human frame adam unsuspiciously obeyed. 10. You and I master worthy have worked hard many years and think it very well to have scraped a trifle of money together you a few hundreds I suppose and I a few thousands.

(*b*) Punctuate the following conversation between Alice in Wonderland, the Hatter and the March Hare, insert capitals and apostrophes, and break it up into paragraphs :—

there was a table set out under a tree in front of the house and the march hare and the hatter were having tea at it a dormouse was sitting between them fast asleep and the other two were using it as a cushion resting their elbows on it and talking over its head very uncomfortable for the dormouse thought alice only as its asleep i suppose it doesnt mind the table was a large one but the three were all crowded together at one corner of it no room no room they cried out when they saw alice coming theres plenty of room said alice indignantly and she sat down in a large armchair at one end of the table have some wine the march hare said in an encouraging tone alice looked all round the table but there was nothing on it but tea i dont see any wine she remarked there isn't any said the march hare then it wasn't very civil of you to offer it said alice angrily it wasn't very civil of you to sit down without being invited said the march hare i didn't know it was your table said alice its laid for a great many more than three your hair wants cutting said the hatter he had been looking at alice for some time with great curiosity and this was his first speech you should learn not to make personal remarks alice said with some severity its very rude the hatter opened his eyes very wide on hearing this but all he said was why is a raven like a writing desk come we shall have some fun now thought alice im glad theyve begun asking riddles i believe i can guess that she added aloud do you mean that you think you can find out the answer to it said the march hare exactly so said alice then you should say what you mean the march hare went on i do

alice hastily replied at least at least i mean what
i say thats the same thing you know

LESSON XIV

ORNAMENT—FIGURATIVE SPEECH

We have been considering so far the structure
of prose, and we have now to consider its
external graces, which, for want of a better
name, we may call ornament. The writer, like
the architect and the designer, has now a
problem to face. What part shall ornament
play in the whole? How far can use and
elegance be combined? How he answers these
questions will depend on his own taste and the
taste of his age. To writers in the sixteenth
and seventeenth centuries, ornament seemed
all-important. They did not study composition,
but rhetoric—which is the art of ornament :
their books of rhetoric were categories of the
various figures of speech. Taste has changed,
and most modern writers prefer a simpler style.
This is certainly better for the student, and he
will do well to imitate a plain prose style. He
may admire the richly decorated style of G. K.
Chesterton, but it is not one to be imitated—if
indeed imitation were possible. The writer, like
the designer, must use ornament sparingly if he
is to use it with effect. He must take care also
to use it in the right place and for the right
subject, or it will appear as ridiculous as a fine
lady tripping down a country lane in gold-
brocaded shoes.

Ornament commonly takes the form of figurative speech. We are not satisfied with a plain term, and choose a more imaginative way to express our meaning. We say—*His reproaches cut her to the quick*, which is of course literally impossible, but is more emphatic than saying simply—" His reproaches hurt her ". Here a comparison is implied between the mental pain she feels at his reproaches, and the physical pain she would feel if she were stabbed with a knife. Such implied comparisons are called *metaphors*. When a comparison is actually made, we call it a *simile*. In the sentence, *The ungodly flourish like a green bay tree* we use a simile; but if we say, *The ungodly flourish and bear goodly fruit*, then we use a metaphor. Similes are often worked out at some length, and include several points of comparison, while a metaphor is often expressed in a single word.

Our language is full of metaphors. We frequently use them quite unconsciously. When we talk about the *bed* of a river, the *shoulder* of a mountain, the *hands* of a watch, the *key* of a position, we are apt to think that we are using literal language, and so, for practical purposes, we are. A considerable proportion of our vocabulary was originally metaphorical, but by long use the comparison has become so unobtrusive that we do not observe it unless our attention is specially called to it. Such dead metaphors do not serve to quicken the imagination. If you wish to make a vivid comparison, then you must make up a metaphor or simile for yourself.

Milton is content to say *When the dappled dawn doth rise*. This is literal. Homer is fond

86

of talking of *Rosy-fingered Morn*. Here we have a kind of metaphor. Kipling gives us : *And the dawn comes up like thunder*, which is a simile. In the Homeric metaphor we have the dawn compared to a person, and this kind of metaphor usually gets the name of **personification.** When we make the sea greedy or justice lame or love tyrannical we are using personification just as much as when we let the trees clap their hands. It is customary to write the personified word with a capital.

When we turn aside from our main subject to address some person or thing that is not present, we use the figure called **apostrophe,** as in the familiar " O woman, in our hours of ease," etc.

Some other forms of figurative speech resemble metaphor. If two things are so closely associated that the mention of one recalls the other, then the most vivid word is sometimes used, as in this sentence, *The armoured train vomited khaki*. Here the verb implies a metaphor, but the word khaki stands for soldiers, not from any likeness between the stuff and the men, but because the two are firmly connected in our minds. In the same way, *The Crescent fell before the Cross* means that the followers of Mahomet were defeated by the Christians. Again, a part may stand for the whole in such a sentence as, *All the blue bonnets are over the Border*, or *Eighteen lances could hold that pass against an army*. Sometimes an individual is made to stand for a class, or the abstract for the concrete, as thus :—

Her salon attracted the learning of a dozen provinces.

87

Mr. Lloyd George is the Peter Pan of politics.

or, to take a more modern example :—

The deliberations of the parish council seem to be directly guided by Colonel Blimp.

A comparison sustained through a long passage, and worked into a story, becomes an *allegory*. We are given a plain story with a clear surface meaning, and a less apparent under-meaning. The parables of the New Testament are little allegories, told by way of illustrating general truths. In our own literature, *The Pilgrim's Progress* and *Gulliver's Travels* are well-known allegories, which are read and enjoyed by children for the sake of the story, yet have a profound underlying seriousness. Interesting modern examples of allegory are *The Happy Hypocrite* by Max Beerbohm, and Rebecca West's novel, *Harriet Hume*.

Many writers have a natural tendency towards figurative speech, but such a tendency must be held in check. Over-use of metaphor and simile destroys their value, and often produces the absurdities of mixed metaphor. This most often occurs when one writes or speaks in " the grand manner " :—

Let us build our house upon a sure foundation, that its life-blood be not sapped, and the waves of enmity and malice wash not over us.

Here the metaphors from house-building, trees, blood and stormy seas are wildly mixed. It is not enough to apologise for a mixed metaphor by such a phrase as, " if we may change the metaphor ". If you feel the necessity for apology, then it is time you considered how your sentence may be amended. In general, use metaphor sparingly, unless you have especial need to make some detail emphatic, or have to express an abstract meaning in concrete form, or are describing something that cannot easily be expressed in plain terms. Milton, when he describes Hell in *Paradise Lost*, cannot make it real to his readers except by constant comparison and simile, since no one can imagine what Hell is like except by comparing it to the familiar things of earth. If you wish to describe a fire, or a great storm, or a wild sea, or anything else which is not part of normal everyday experience, then you will naturally fall back on comparisons to make your meaning clear. Stevenson uses metaphor and simile sparingly and always with justification, as in this description of a storm in the Hebrides :—

" All round the isle of Aros the surf, with an incessant, hammering thunder, beat upon the reefs and beaches. Now louder in one place, now lower in another, like the combinations of orchestral music, the constant mass of sound was hardly varied for a moment. And loud above all this hurly-burly I could hear the changeful voices of the Roost, and the intermittent roaring of the Merry Men. The noise of them seemed almost mirthful, as it out-topped the other noises of the night; or if not mirthful, yet instinct with a portentous joviality. Nay, and it seemed even human. As when savage men have drunk away their reason, and discarding speech, bawl together in their madness by the hour; so, to my ears, these deadly breakers shouted by Aros in the night."

Exercise 14

(*a*) Write out the meaning of each sentence in plain literal language, and say which forms you think most suitable.

1. Babies rolled about like tumbled fruit in grass. 2. Shut your 'ead. 3. Lovers' watches stand still. 4. The ashes of Mr. Foster's note seemed to crinkle into a sour grin. 5. Literature had jilted him; henceforth Law was to be his mistress. 6. That shop, which was dark and smelt of Bibles, was a loadstone rock for all that bore the name of boy. 7. Habit is habit, and not to be flung out of the window by any man, but coaxed downstairs a step at a time. 8. Do you hear the wood crying for us? It's sorry for our little troubles. 9. There are always plenty of men ready to lick the blacking off one's boots provided always that that doubtful fare be varied by champagne and truffles at appropriate intervals. 10. Mrs. Agar toyed with a biscuit. 11. The lid of the kettle clattered like a deaf and dumb young cymbal that had never known the use of its twin-brother. 12. An Ogilvie's sword never ploughed so deep a furrow. 13. His evil soul went down to its place squeaking, like a bat into the darkness of a cave. 14. " No," said his daughter, taking a weapon of fine cambric out of her pocket. 15. With these words he retired, leaving a seething volcano to pace the deck.

(*b*) Find a metaphor and a simile for each of the following:—a rocket, a sailing ship, flood water.

LESSON XV

SOME OTHER FORMS OF ORNAMENT

Several recognised ornaments of style owe their effect to the force of contrast. In what is called antitheses the contrast is expressly stated.

Coleridge tells us that his teacher flogged him on a certain occasion, "wisely, I think, soundly, I know". Here we have a double contrast plainly stated—*wisely, soundly ; think, know.* Sometimes the contrast gains point by one part being left out. In that most familiar figure known as **irony** the contrast is between the surface statement which is pleasant, and the underlying truth which is bitter. It is ironical to dismiss a candidate for an assistant-clerkship in the Foreign Office with the words, "I'm very sorry we have no vacancy worthy of your talents. You see, the Prime Minister *will* not retire." In the still more popular figure of **hyperbole** the contrast is between the plain truth and the deliberately exaggerated statement of it. When we say that the trees of California are very tall, we use the words of truth and soberness ; when we declare that they are so high that it takes two men and a boy to look at the top of them, we drop into hyperbole.

To the class of figures of contrast belong those witty sayings called **epigrams.** An epigram must be short, pointed, with enough falsehood to make it piquant and with enough truth to make it worth saying :—*A science is nothing but a well-made language. A man who has stolen sixty thousand pounds ought to be able to live* *honestly*. Another contrast figure, known as **euphemism,** consists in putting things in an unduly favourable way. It may be kindly meant, as when we call a shoemaker a leather merchant, or it may only intensify the disagreeable fact it seems to palliate, as in *the independent candidate nowhere showed his independence so markedly as in relation to the truth.*

Another class of figures of speech depend largely upon the order in which ideas are expressed. If we arrange ideas in the order of increasing intensity or importance we have what is known as **climax.** *Swiftly Napoleon mounted— lieutenant, general, First Consul, Emperor.* It is not always easy to have a climax so accurately graded as this. Often some of the terms will be understood in a different way by various readers. In the following example from Sir Walter Scott's *Woodstock* we have a double climax in which Sir Henry Lee relieves his mind about two of his political opponents. " What ! John Milton, the blasphemous and bloody-minded author of the *Defensio Populi Anglicani* ! —the advocate of the infernal High Court of Fiends !—the creature and parasite of that grand impostor, that loathsome hypocrite, that detestable monster, that prodigy of the universe, that disgrace of mankind, that landscape of iniquity, that sink of sin, and that compendium of baseness, Oliver Cromwell ! " Here the old cavalier is so eager to vent his anger that he does not take time to arrange his abuse in exact order of merit. But while we may quarrel about which of the old gentleman's epithets is the most stinging, we cannot but agree that the effect of the whole goes on increasing, and that, therefore, the figure is a genuine climax.

When the climax breaks down, whether by accident or by the deliberate design of the writer, we have anti-climax. *Our hills and dales, our hearths and homes, our wives and daughters, our flocks and herds, lie at the mercy of the invaders.* Here everything goes well till the end. The *flocks and herds* should come in after the *hills and dales*. Note that anti-climax does not mean a descending order, but a sudden drop from a height. " A month to consider it ! Not a week, not a day, an hour, a minute ! I demand instant submission." Here we have really an ascending order of imperious demand, though the time periods are in descending order.

Inversion is a figure that is very commonly used to give emphasis and variety. It consists in reversing the usual order of words, particularly of subject and predicate. It is very common in verse, so common as to be almost the normal construction there. *As bends the bark's mast in the gale.* In prose it may be very effectively used as in, *Pitiful is the case of the blind who cannot read the face ; pitiful that of the deaf who cannot follow the changes of the voice.* But this figure seems peculiarly liable to abuse by those who seek to be effective in common speech. It is barbarous to write *Understood him she has not.*

Alliteration is more often used in poetry than in prose. It consists in using words beginning with the same letter or sound, and when used with restraint it can be very effective,—as in *Macbeth*,

> " Duncan is in his grave,
> After life's fitful fever he sleeps well."

In prose it is often used in hack phrases, which

should be earnestly avoided; *fair, fat and forty*; *happy Hampstead*; *ministerial mendacity*. Yet it can be used in prose with exquisite effect, as in this passage from Kingsley's *Water Babies*, where the same sounds are not too often repeated :—

" And what sort of river was it? Was it like an Irish stream, winding through the brown bogs, where the wild ducks squatter up from among the white water-lilies, and the curlews flit to and fro, crying ' Tullie-wheep, mind your sheep '; and Dennis tells you strange stories of the Peishtamore, the great bogy-snake which lies in the black peat pools, among the old pine-stems, and puts his head out at night to snap at the cattle as they come down to drink? "

Exercise 15

State which figure of speech each of the following exemplifies, and write out the meaning of each sentence in plain literal language :—

1. As a dog doesn't comprehend good English we naturally talk bad to him. 2. Let us endeavour so to live that when we come to die even the undertaker will be sorry. 3. The Duke of Wellington's English despatches were written in fine idiomatic English—and so were his French ones. 4. Some German words are so long that they have a perspective. 5. Women hate a debt as men a gift. 6. In order to love mankind we must expect little from them. 7. The bareness of the hills in the south of Scotland is such that a bluebottle can be seen against the sky when it walks along their profile. 8. We are near awakening when we dream

that we were dreaming.   9. The love-light was
in her eyes, but Andrew did not open the door
for her, for he was a Scotch graduate.   Besides,
she might one day be his wife.   10. Paris is not
a city, but a Bedlam.   11. It is better to be a
young June-bug than an old bird of paradise.
12. And the verse halts like the best of Luther's
psalms.   13. If we still love those we lose can
we altogether lose those we love?   14. Absence
destroys small passions and increases great ones,
as the wind extinguishes tapers and kindles
fires.   15. The prime minister was set free from
the cares of office.

LESSON XVI

DIRECT AND REPORTED SPEECH

When we give the very words used by a speaker
we are said to use the direct form.   " I can't get
out," cried the starling, is an example of this
direct form.   The starling opened his mouth
and out came these actual words : " I can't
get out ".   In reported speech this would have
to read something like this : *The starling said
that it* (or *he*, if you prefer that form) *could not
get out.*   Thus the tense is always changed to
the past in reported speech, and the person of
verbs and pronouns is changed.

There are other changes too.   " Here stand
I," said Luther, is the direct form, and becomes
Luther said that he stood there.   Thus *here* is
changed to *there*.   Similarly *this* becomes *that*.

The best way to get a real knowledge of the

difference between the two forms is to practise turning passages from the one to the other.

It is more difficult turning from the direct to the indirect, for there are often a great number of *he's* and *him's* that are apt to get confounded. This confusion is usually avoided by inserting a proper name in brackets after the doubtful pronoun.

Ellicock said to Wilberforce that his father had bought him the gold watch that he was then wearing. Here we are not sure whose father bought the watch, for whom the watch was bought, who was then wearing it. The probable meaning is, *Ellicock said to Wilberforce that his* (Ellicock's) *father had bought him* (Ellicock) *the gold watch that he* (Ellicock) *was then wearing.* This labelling of pronouns is better than confusion—*any-thing* is better than lack of clearness. But the expedient is very clumsy and should be avoided. It may be pardoned in a reported speech; but in a piece of original composition it is a public confession of faulty construction.

" There is nothing at all unusual in this, and I have no doubt Burke would have stuck to his bargain, had not Hamilton conceived the fatal idea that Burke's brains were *exclusively* his (Hamilton's)."

Here the clumsiness could be averted, and the author's point equally well made, by saying, ". . . had not Hamilton conceived the fatal idea that he had bought the *exclusive* use of Burke's brains ".

In the following exercises, in turning from the direct to the reported form you will find it necessary to make occasional use of the noun in parenthesis. You must try to avoid the construction so far as is possible by repeating the noun in the text as often as that can be done without unseemly repetition.

Exercise 16

Change the passages (*a*) and (*b*) into the direct form, and passages (*c*) and (*d*) into the reported form.

(*a*) Mr. Wetherell said that he had half guessed there might be some hanky-panky of this sort, and he had therefore taken such steps as would prevent him from being left out in the cold. He proposed to deal with this affair as he dealt with matters of politics or of organisation, in that he should use plain language, and speak out his mind like a man. If a man or a woman behaved straight to him, he behaved straight to them; if *they* behaved crooked, *he* behaved crooked. That was him all the world over. Mr. Wetherell added that if he were then and there to undertake to write his own epitaph, he would simply take a pen, dip it in the ink, seat himself at the table, and write these words : " He was as open as the day ".

(*b*) Mr. PICKWICK observed (says the secretary) that fame was dear to the heart of every man. Poetic fame was dear to the heart of his friend Snodgrass; the fame of conquest was equally dear to his friend Tupman ; and the desire of earning fame in the sports of the field, the air, and the water, was uppermost in the breast of his friend Winkle. He (Mr. Pickwick) would not deny that he was influenced by human passions, and human feelings—(cheers)—possibly

by human weaknesses—(loud cries of " No ");
but this he would say, that if ever the fire of
self-importance broke out in his bosom, the
desire to benefit the human race in preference
effectually quenched it. The praise of mankind
was his Swing; philanthropy was his insurance
office. (Vehement cheering.) He had felt some
pride—he acknowledged it freely, and let his
enemies make the most of it—he had felt some
pride when he presented his Tittlebatian Theory
to the world; it might be celebrated or it might
not. (A cry of " It is ", and great cheering.)
He would take the assertion of that honourable
Pickwickian whose voice he had just heard—it
was celebrated; but if the fame of that treatise
were to extend to the farthest confines of the
known world, the pride with which he should
reflect on the authorship of that production
would be as nothing compared with the pride
with which he looked around him on this, the
proudest moment of his existence. (Cheers.)
He was a humble individual. (" No, no.")
Still he could not but feel that they had selected
him for a service of great honour, and of some
danger. Travelling was in a troubled state, and
the minds of coachmen were unsettled. Let
them look abroad and contemplate the scenes
which are enacting around them. Stage coaches
were upsetting in all directions, horses were
bolting, boats were overturning, and boilers were
bursting. (Cheers—a voice, " No".) No !
(Cheers.) Let that honourable Pickwickian who
cried " No " so loudly come forward and deny
it, if he could. (Cheers.) Who was it that
cried " No "? (Enthusiastic cheering.) Was it
some vain and disappointed man—he would not

say haberdasher—(loud cheers)—who, jealous of
the praise which had been—perhaps undeservedly
—bestowed on his (Mr. Pickwick's) researches,
and smarting under the censure which had been
heaped upon his own feeble attempts at rivalry,
now took this vile and calumnious mode of—

Mr. BLOTTON (of Aldgate) rose to order. Did
the honourable Pickwickian allude to him?
(Cries of "Order", "Chair", "Yes", "No",
"Go on", "Leave off", etc.)

Mr. PICKWICK would not put up to be put
down by clamour. He *had* alluded to the
honourable gentleman. (Great excitement.)

Mr. BLOTTON would only say then, that he
repelled the hon. gent.'s false and scurrilous
accusation with profound contempt. (Great
cheering.) The hon. gent. was a humbug.

(*c*) Sir,—The atrocious crime of being a young
man, which the honourable gentleman has, with
such spirit and decency, charged upon me, I
shall neither attempt to palliate nor deny; but
content myself with wishing, that I may be one
of those whose follies may cease with their
youth, and not of those who continue ignorant
in spite of age and experience.

Whether youth can be attributed to any man
as a reproach, I will not, Sir, assume the province
of determining; but surely, age may justly
become contemptible, if the opportunities which
it brings have passed away without improvement, and vice appear to prevail when the
passions have subsided. The wretch who, after
having seen the consequences of a thousand
errors, continues still to blunder, and in whom
age has only added obstinacy to stupidity, is
surely the object either of abhorrence or con-

tempt; and deserves not that his grey head should secure him from insults. Much more, Sir, is he to be abhorred, who, as he has advanced in age, has receded from virtue, and become more wicked with less temptation; who prostitutes himself for money which he cannot enjoy, and spends the remains of his life in the ruin of his country.

(d) I cannot, my Lords, I will not, join in congratulation on misfortune and disgrace. This, my Lords, is a perilous and tremendous moment. It is not a time for adulation; the smoothness of flattery cannot save us in this rugged and awful crisis. It is now necessary to instruct the throne in the language of truth. We must, if possible, dispel the delusion and darkness which envelop it; and display, in its full danger and genuine colours, the ruin which is brought to our doors. Can ministers still presume to expect support in their infatuation? Can Parliament be so dead to its dignity and duty, as to give its support to measures thus obtruded and forced upon it? Measures, my Lords, which have reduced this late flourishing empire to scorn and contempt! " But yesterday, and Britain might have stood against the world : now, none so poor as do her reverence ! " —The people, whom we at first despised as rebels, but whom we now acknowledge as enemies, are abetted against us, supplied with every military store, have their interests consulted, and their ambassadors entertained, by our inveterate enemy; and ministers do not— and dare not—interpose with dignity or effect. The desperate state of our army abroad is in part known. No man more highly esteems and

honours the British troops than I do; I know
their virtues and their valour; I know they
can achieve anything but impossibilities; and
I know that the conquest of British America is
an impossibility. You cannot, my Lords, you
can not conquer America. What is your present
situation there? We do not know the worst;
but we know that in three campaigns we have
done nothing, and suffered much. You may
swell every expense, accumulate every assistance, and extend your traffic to the shambles
of every German despot : your attempts will
be for ever vain and impotent.

LESSON XVII

WRITING IN THIRD PERSON

There is a formal kind of composition that
sometimes takes the place of a letter. It is
marked by the exclusive use of the third person
where one would naturally expect the first and
the second. It is the recognised language of
invitations, particularly when these are of a
public or formal character. " The Mayor and
Corporation of Blanktown request the pleasure
of Mr. Dash's presence at dinner in the Town
Hall, on Thursday, the 24th March, 1938, at
7.30 P.M." The regulation reply is : " Mr. Dash
has much pleasure in accepting the invitation
of the Mayor and Corporation of Blanktown to
dinner in the Town Hall, on Thursday, the 24th
March, 1938, at 7.30 P.M."

Those who claim to be authorities on these

matters maintain that the reply should repeat all the details, as in Mr. Dash's specimen, and perhaps it is as well to gratify form-lovers by giving them plenty of form. The argument in favour of this fullness is that all chance of misunderstanding is thus removed. Invitations in the third person are used in private life wherever a certain formality is kept up. An invitation in the third person from an intimate friend ought to imply a specially good dinner.

A very common error in replying to invitations is to use the future instead of the present. " Mr. Dash-Blank will have much pleasure in accepting the kind invitation of . . ." This should read " has much pleasure ". Mr. Dash-Blank does not intend to accept the invitation, he is accepting it as he writes. The confusion is caused by thinking of the dinner rather than of the invitation.

Another and less pleasant use of the third person is in communicating with people with whom we wish to have nothing to do, beyond the business of the moment. A lady writes to learn from another, who is not of her circle, the character of a servant. This is the sort of reply that comes. " Mrs. Dash-Blank has always found Susan Liskens careful, honest, and willing. She has been in her service only nine months, but she came to her with a four years' character, and has done nothing to forfeit it. She leaves her of her own accord."

The *she's* and *her's* are a little mixed, but no serious misunderstanding can arise. The following presents more difficulty :—

" Mr. Brown presents his compliments to

Mr. Johnson, and will be much obliged if he will keep his dog on his own side of the wall during the day, and on the other side of the house during the night, as neither he nor Mrs. Brown get a wink of sleep while he occupies his present position."

Bad as this is, it does not fall into the worst error of all—that of mixing up different persons. The writer gets tired of the formal third person, and drops into a more natural form.

" If advertiser RS 4309 will call at 47 Arlington Villas he will find a suite of rooms that fulfil all the conditions he specifies. Mrs. Spross can assure him that nothing will be wanting on her part to make him comfortable. I do my own washing so you can rely upon your linen being well attended to."

The whole style of writing is cumbersome and stilted. It is to be avoided as far as possible, but when it has to be used there must be no lapses into first or second person. Ambiguity may to a great extent be avoided by the frequent repetition of the proper names. This is perhaps not very elegant, but the style is already so clumsy that nothing can make it much worse.

Exercise 17

Rewrite the three examples of third personal composition in the preceding lesson, improving them wherever you see a chance.

LESSON XVIII

OBSCURITY AND AMBIGUITY

A sentence or a passage is obscure when it is difficult to gather the meaning. It may be that there *is* no meaning, as in the irritating conundrum, *Why is a mouse when it spins?* and its aggravating answer, *Because the fewer the higher.* In this case the lack of meaning is concealed only for a moment, but sometimes a long passage of apparently reasonable words conveys no real meaning to the mind. The following is quoted by an eminent psychologist, who confesses that he fails to make any sort of sense out of it.

" The flow of the efferent fluids of all these vessels from their outlets at the terminal loop of each culminate link on the surface of the nuclear organism is continuous as their respective atmospheric fruitage up to the altitudinal limit of their expansibility, whence, when atmosphered by like but coalescing essences from higher altitudes—those sensibly expressed as the essential qualities of external forms—they descend, and become assimilated by the afferents of the nuclear organism."

These are extreme cases. A writer usually has a meaning behind his words.

" We mean only a man having some sort of arms—a club, or a dart, or a matchlock, or a poker—anything which would give him the idea that he had to fight, and which would perhaps delay his death a moment while myriads of others swept over those who had killed him."

The man who wrote this meant to say that

an undisciplined and ill-armed horde, if only numerous enough, could overcome the best drilled and equipped army by the mere process of keeping the soldiers so busy killing some of the rabble that the rest of the rabble would have time to swarm over the soldiers and overcome them by sheer avoirdupois weight.

To convey this meaning the whole sentence after the words " his death a moment " would require to be re-cast, and might run thus, . . . " while myriads of his comrades swarmed over those who were in the act of killing him ". In this case the sentence has had to be expanded; for the obscurity arises from the brevity of the explanation.

Speaking generally, it may be said that writers who are thoroughly at home in their subject are liable to become obscure because they take too much for granted. They themselves see so clearly the connection between cause and effect that they think it unnecessary to state many things which are plain to them, but are quite unknown to ordinary readers. Learned men who seek to popularise their subjects almost always become obscure by omitting certain steps in their reasoning.

In Lord Bacon's essays we find excellent examples of the advantages and defects of a condensed style. No words are wasted, and wherever the sense does not suffer there is a clear gain. But very frequently Bacon's economy of words leads to unnecessary labour on the part of his readers. In the very first essay we find this sentence : " Doth any man doubt, that if there were taken out of men's minds, vain opinions, flattering hopes, false valuations, imaginations as one would, and the like; but it would leave the minds of a number of men, poor shrunken things ". The phrase *imaginations as one would* is an unduly condensed way of saying the habit of trying to persuade ourselves that things are what our desires would have them to be. Sometimes this condensation is justifiable, since it takes the form of an epigram in which the charm lies in getting at the true meaning through an apparently inadequate expression. " It is good that a man's face give his tongue leave to speak ", is a more striking way of conveying the meaning—*A man should not betray his thoughts by the expression of his face, but should make disclosures only by his tongue.* In the following examples, however, the gain in force is more than counter-balanced by the loss in clearness :—

The master of superstition is the people.	The real origin of superstition is not with the people, but there is in them a predisposition to be deceived.
And they would be thought wits of direction.	They desire to be considered able men who are capable of directing others.
Finally he waxeth wiser than himself.	He becomes wiser than he could become without the advice of some friend.
But ignorance severally disguised.	But ignorance concealing itself under various forms.
A wound or solution of continuity.	A severance of parts of the body that ought to be joined.

Alchemy pretendeth to make separation of all the unlike parts of bodies, which in mixtures of nature are incorporate.	. . . which are incorporated in substances as these substances are found in nature.

It is easy to understand how a passage may become obscure through lack of sufficient words. At first sight it may seem impossible to become obscure by using too many words. It would appear that the only evil result would be a weariness rising from the repetition of explanations of matters already clearly understood. But in two ways excess of words darkens knowledge. In the first way the meaning is lost in its expression : there is such a small idea hidden away among such a heap of words that it becomes difficult to dig it out. In the second place every word that is used in composition is understood to mean something that is necessary to the sense of the passage in which it occurs. The orator who maintained that it was " cowardly to shoot bad landlords in Ireland " obscured his meaning, unless, indeed, he really meant that it was not cowardly to shoot good landlords so long as they did not happen to be in Ireland.

A very common form of obscurity in writing is known as ambiguity. When a sentence may convey either of two meanings it is said to be ambiguous. " The duke yet lives that Henry shall depose," is a case of deliberate ambiguity. If you think over the sentence for a moment, you will see that it does not tell which of the two—Henry or the duke—is to depose the other. So in ancient history we read of a king who was assured by an oracle that if he invaded a certain country he would " destroy a great kingdom ". When this king was defeated and complained of the falsehood of the oracle, he was reminded that the oracle had not stated whose great kingdom was to be destroyed. The king had jumped to the conclusion that the prophecy had only one meaning : the oracle knew it had two.

There is no snare more difficult to avoid than this same ambiguity. The preceding paragraph was meant to illustrate the vice, but not quite in the way it is illustrated in the concluding clause, " the oracle knew it had two ". Here *it* may mean either the prophecy or the oracle. It was meant to mean the prophecy, but since the oracle may be treated as neuter, there is no escape. The clause is ambiguous. This word *it* is, indeed, a particularly troublesome one. *She held the tea-cup to her cheek to keep it warm.* You might bring forward many arguments for believing that it was the cheek that was being kept warm, and as many in favour of the tea-cup. The relative pronoun sometimes causes ambiguity. *The castle was taken from him by William Rufus, son of the Conqueror, who had made the original grant.* Since the relative should always be allocated to the nearest legitimate antecedent, this sentence should mean that William, the son of the Conqueror, had taken away the castle, but that the original grant had been made by the Conqueror himself. If Rufus both made the grant and withdrew it, the sentence should run : *The castle was taken from him by the Conqueror's son, William Rufus, who had made the original grant.*

In the following exercise write out clearly each of the two possible meanings, after this fashion. 1. (a) The duke yet lives who shall depose Henry. 1. (b) The duke yet lives whom Henry shall depose. 2. (a) If you invade that country you will destroy the great nation which inhabits it. 2. (b) If you invade that country you will destroy your own great nation. 3. (a) To keep her cheek warm she held the tea-cup to it. 3. (b) To keep the tea-cup warm she held it to her cheek.

Exercise 18

In each case mark with the letter (a) the meaning that you think the writer intended to convey.

1. For do I now persuade God or men?
2. We know little individually of his hearers.
3. I shall lose no time in reading your verses.
4. Drink to me only with thine eyes. 5. From that place where fixed you be by His decree you cannot pass. 6. The only work we have seen in the exhibition by James Collinson is a small portrait of Christina G. Rossetti, sister of Rossetti, and a poor thing. 7. They forget that character makes the man and not the profession. 8. That is either a man or a woman's voice. 9. For sale a fine bull dog. Eats anything. Very fond of children. 10. The fearful creatures stealthily approached the edge of the precipice.

LESSON XIX

VERBOSITY, PLEONASM, TAUTOLOGY

Tautology and pleonasm are forms of the vice of using more words than are necessary to express our meaning. By many writers the two terms are treated as synonymous, but others try to establish a distinction. Tautology is said to mean the repetition of the same idea in different words, while pleonasm is the use of words of which the meaning is implied in words already employed. Thus it is tautological to say, *The earth under the trees was wet, damp and moist*, or, *You may enter this show free, gratis and for nothing*. Examples of pleonasm are, *I have seen it with my own eyes. The two friends went for a walking tour through France on foot.*

Still other writers are inclined to call all the above examples tautologies, and prefer to limit pleonasm to the vice of adding words which convey nothing really new, though their meaning is not actually implied in any previous expression. *This club treats all other clubs with an eye of contempt.* Here *an eye of* is obviously pleonastic.

Verbosity is the general name for the vice of wordiness. Tautology and pleonasm are forms of verbosity, but there are many other forms. Talkative persons and diffuse writers may never actually repeat their ideas, but they frequently use a very large number of words to express a very small number of ideas.

We shall now proceed to begin to illustrate this objectionable vice of verbosity by referring

to a passage that may be found in the pages of
a well-known author, or rather authoress, who,
however, must not be held responsible for the
high-sounding but somewhat empty and frivolous
maunderings which she puts into the mouth of
a rather austere and very precise old maiden
lady who is delightfully portrayed in the charming chapters of that gem of Mrs. Gaskell's art—
Cranford.

That paragraph is a verbose way of making
the simple statement : Miss Jenkyns, in *Cranford*, is responsible for the following example of
verbosity.

" The Honourable Mrs. Jamieson has only just
quitted me ; and, in the course of conversation,
she communicated to me the intelligence that
she had yesterday received a call from her
revered husband's quondam friend, Lord Mauleverer. You will not easily conjecture what
brought his lordship within the precincts of our
little town. It was to see Captain Brown, with
whom, it appears, his lordship was acquainted
in the ' plumed wars ', and who had the privi-
lege of averting destruction from his lordship's
head when some great peril was impending over
it, off the misnomered Cape of Good Hope. You
know our friend the Honourable Mrs. Jamieson's
deficiency in the spirit of innocent curiosity;
and you will therefore not be so much surprised
when I tell you she was quite unable to disclose
to me the exact nature of the peril in question.
I was anxious, I confess, to ascertain in what
manner Captain Brown, with his limited estab-
lishment, could receive so distinguished a guest;
and I discovered that his lordship retired to rest,

and, let us hope, to refreshing slumbers, at the Angel Hotel; but shared the Brunonian meals during the two days that he honoured Cranford with his august presence. Mrs. Johnston, our civil butcher's wife, informs me that Miss Jessie purchased a leg of lamb; but, besides this, I can hear of no preparation whatever to give a suitable reception to so distinguished a visitor. Perhaps they entertained him with ' the feast of reason and the flow of soul '; and to us, who are acquainted with Captain Brown's sad want of relish for ' the pure wells of English undefiled ', it may be matter for congratulation that he has had the opportunity of improving his taste by holding converse with an elegant and refined member of the British aristocracy. But from some mundane failings who is altogether free ? "

Another form of verbosity arises from feebleness of thought. A person who cannot select the essential parts of his subject becomes verbose by introducing a wearisome series of unimportant details. One thing recalls another and the speaker instead of directing his speech is directed by it. This is well illustrated in the following extract from Miss Austen's *Emma* :—

" ' But where could *you* hear it ? ' cried Miss Bates. ' Where could you possibly hear it, Mr. Knightley ? For it is not five minutes since I received Mrs. Cole's note—no, it cannot be more than five—or at least ten—for I had got my bonnet and spencer on, just ready to come out—I was only gone down to speak to Patty again about the pork—Jane was standing in the passage—were not you, Jane ?—for my mother was so afraid that we had not any salt-ing-pan large enough. So I said I would go down and see, and Jane said, " Shall I go down instead? for I think you have a little cold, and Patty has been washing the kitchen ". " Oh, my dear," said I—well, and just then came the note. A Miss Hawkins—that's all I know—a Miss Hawkins, of Bath. But, Mr. Knightley, how could you possibly have heard it? for the very moment Mr. Cole told Mrs. Cole of it, she sat down and wrote to me. A Miss Haw-kins——' "

Exercise 19

(a) Re-write the passage from *Cranford* making it as brief as possible without any loss of meaning.

(b) Reduce Miss Bates' speech to one sentence containing all that is really to the point.

(c) Correct the pleonasm, tautology or general verbosity of each of the following sentences :—

1. An annual grant is voted every year by Parliament. 2. The reluctant boy proceeded unwillingly to school because it was necessary that he should go thither. 3. *There's* a type of man that can't allow for a single moment that anybody should possess certain, what I may call, principles, and be prepared to argue in favour of these principles from early morn till dewy eve. Such is the base, the cowardly, the unmanly condition of that person there standing amongst your midst, that he can't recognise a honest 'eart when he meets one walking about. 4. He locked the door after he had previously seen that his prisoner was all right. 5. The guides rapidly made their way

downward along a narrow descending foot-path. 6. You can enter this show free, gratis and for nothing. 7. I put my hat upon my head and walked into the Strand. 8. She is of the same age as her twin brother. 9. He was mounted on the top of a horse. 10. The de-faulter was caused to enter a compartment in the London train and so was conveyed to the metropolis. 11. The birds filled the tree tops with their morning song, making the air moist, cool, and pleasant. 12. His elder brother was his senior. 13. This incomparable picture can-not be compared with the others in that gallery. 14. If the picture is incomparable there is no need to make the remark that it cannot be compared.

LESSON XX

COMMON ERRORS

The number of ways in which writers go wrong is legion, and no complete classification of them can be made. But there are some typical kinds of errors that occur so frequently in composition that it is worth while giving them special attention.

1. **Attraction.**—It frequently happens that the nominative is separated from its verb by several words. In this case we have a tendency to make the verb agree with whichever subject happens to be nearest it. "The misleading power of the verse divisions—which seem to be guides and are not—constantly betray him into a difficulty."

Here the nominative is *power*, so the verb

should be *betrays*. This is a very natural yielding to the force of attraction of the nearer nouns *guides* and *divisions*. But it shows a clearer grip of the thought implied in a sentence when the writer proves by his very words that he keeps the grammatical subject in view. There is no ambiguity in saying that *A suite of rooms were engaged*, but it is better to make the verb agree with its singular nominative.

2. **Ellipses or Omissions.**—It is desirable to save words by proper ellipses. *He gave five books to his sister and three to his brother.* Here there is a gain rather than a loss from the omission of *books* after *three*. But it often happens that the omission covers an error. If the omitted word is inserted it is seen to be wrong, but when it is elided the implied blunder passes unnoticed. This occurs chiefly with prepositions.

" His objection and condoning of faults marked an ill-balanced judgment." Here we must insert *to* after *objection*. The same blunder is said to be made in the following :—

" Many sentences are miserably mangled, and the force of the emphasis totally lost."

It is maintained that the verb omitted after *emphasis* is *are* which is clearly ungrammatical. Many writers maintain that we are entitled to assume the right verb *is*, but it is better to err on the safe side and express the verb.

3. **The Loose Participle.**—A participle or participial phrase is naturally referred to the nearest nominative. If only one nominative is expressed, it claims all the participles that are not by the construction of the sentence

otherwise fixed. "Entering the house the door closed with a bang."

Here the nominative *door* claims the participle *entering*, which is clearly lying about loose. The meaning expressed is, *When the door entered the house the door closed with a bang*. The meaning intended is, *When I* (or he, or she, or it, or they, or John Smith) *entered the house, the door closed with a bang*.

Broken by distress and ill-health, I could do nothing to help the unfortunate fellow. As this sentence stands it is *I* who am broken, but the context in which it was found shows that it is "the unfortunate fellow" who is ill and distressed. Even in the improved form, *I could do nothing to help the unfortunate fellow, broken by distress and ill-health*, the participle is not quite securely fastened to the fellow. The words *who was* interpolated between *fellow* and *broken* prevent all possibility of mistake.

Sometimes the participle is said to be used absolutely. *A gun having gone off, the picket turned out. Our stores giving out, we thought it prudent to withdraw*. This use of the participle is permissible, as it is quite clear to which word the participle refers.

4. **The Split Infinitive.**—There is a growing tendency to place modifying words between the *to* and the remaining part of the infinitive, thus splitting the infinitive. *He was hardly able to even crawl*, should be . . . *even to crawl*. *To clumsily handle a musket* should be *to handle a musket clumsily*. So frequently is the infinitive now split in everyday writing that in a few years it may become permissible in good writing. It is better indeed to leave a split infinitive than

make a very obvious attempt to avoid it, as in this sentence—*The nations should combine to forbid flatly hostilities.* To flatly forbid is preferable to this distortion, but it would be best to re-model the sentence : *The nations should combine and should flatly forbid. . . .*[1]

5. *And* **with the Relative.**—*And* must never be used with the relative unless there be a parallel relative in the preceding clause. *There is a house on the hill, and which I have bought,* is so clearly wrong that one is ashamed to speak of the error : but experience shows that this error is quite common, particularly when sentences become long. *On the hill there is a house which I bought, and which I hope to occupy,* is correct. So is *I am a man who speaks the truth and fears no overlord.*

Certain Dangerous Words.—*Other* and *another.* These are what may be called boomerang words. They recoil upon us, and often make us say what we had no intention of saying. *We have no connection with the other quacks across the street* is not exactly what the shopkeeper meant. *Meanwhile my friend and another shady character proceeded to the pier* is clearly a bad sentence, though in the context in which it was used " my friend " did not really suffer; for certain other shady characters had been spoken of in the previous sentence, and the *another* obviously referred to them. It is well, however, to make each sentence independent of contextual aid.

One.—The sort of impersonal use of this word in epigrammatic or proverbial saying (its gnomic use, as it is called) frequently leads to confusion.

[1] H. W. Fowler discusses the question very thoroughly, and very amusingly, in *Modern English Usage.*

If you begin with *one* you must keep on with *one* : you must not drop into *his*. *One must mind one's business if one wishes to succeed*. It is wrong to write, *One must mind his business if he wishes to succeed*. It is still worse to write, *One must mind their business if they wish to succeed*. *Any one*, on the other hand, does admit of *he, his* and *him*. *If any one guesses the truth he must not betray it*, or *let him not betray it*.

Only is perhaps the most ill-used word in the dictionary. Its grievance is that it is very often put in the wrong place.

> *I only cuffed him that time.*

As this sentence stands it means : The only thing I did to him that time was to cuff him— that is, I did not kick him, or knock him down. But we may wish it to mean : I cuffed him on that one occasion only. This meaning is conveyed by putting the *only* just before *that time*. The rule is that *only* should always come immediately before the word or phrase it limits. As a matter of fact, in speaking we are able, by emphasis, to make it quite clear what we mean without changing the position of the *only* : but in writing we cannot depend on anything but the arrangement of the words.

Meaning indicated by emphasis.	Meaning indicated by arrangement.
1. I only *cuffed* him that time.	I only cuffed him that time.
2. I only cuffed him *that time*.	I cuffed him only that time.
3. I only cuffed *him* that time.	I cuffed only him that time.
4. *I* only cuffed him that time.	Only I cuffed him that time.

The word *alone* is often of service in easing

the work of *only*. Thus the meaning of the fourth sentence above could be most exactly expressed by *I alone cuffed him that time*. If we make a pause after *only*, it conveys a totally different meaning, as in the sentence : *I would follow your plan of pretending I did not object to his tricks, only, I cuffed him that time*. With *alone* this meaning is impossible.

This rule about placing adverbs immediately before the words they modify applies to other words besides *only*.

" Born in England, trained as a weaver, he had really wandered to America and the South Seas at the dictation of a restless and inquiring spirit."

Here *really* ought to come immediately before *at the dictation*. There is no question about the reality of his wandering.

Exercise 20

Correct the following sentences. The defects are not confined to those dealt with in the preceding lesson.

1. In every occurrence there are always some elements which are generally known or recognised by only a few. 2. It would be quite unfair if we read party newspapers and formed our opinions in unison with the opinions stated there. 3. Judged from this point of view, the picture may seem entirely different from a person who had been without the same knowledge. 4. We have no universal law to include under its sway everything. 5. They fall naturally into grooves which are smooth though well-worn. 6. The arguments may be perfectly logical of

each, and yet each arrives at a different result. 7. Progress would be impossible and our brains would be mere mechanism without reason. 8. We assume certain data known to be correct and consider the question in the light of this data. 9. He who has a complete and exhaustive knowledge of a subject is most likely to be correct. 10. The jury must be allowed to decide which is right and which is wrong. 11. Poor Paddy will alter his opinions, and see without shame that it was all for the best that Home Rule was denied them. 12. This will often prevent us from becoming too much prejudiced for or against any one particular conclusion. 13. This is the point at which we begin to enlighten any one to our views. 14. In discussion of any sort or thinking, the truth must be the goal towards which we strive. 15. Yet although two different opinions may be formed and may seem opposed to one another—yet on closer examination it sometimes happens that both are absolutely correct. 16. The newspaper man puts in a great many unnecessary details in order to add to his number of pennies per line. 17. The essentials of the story in each case is the same. 18. Conservative and Liberal Clubs, debating societies, and such institutions, have many good uses, social and otherwise, but none is more useful than the use which, in the second I have named, is the chief object of the society, namely debate. 19. There is no more difficult thing than to look at a subject from both sides of the question. 20. Seldom do we get many persons who think absolutely alike on a subject and never do we get any one who thinks exactly like his neighbour.

LESSON XXI

COMMON ERRORS—*continued*

He or she.—One of the most irritating inelegancies in English is the wooden insistence upon the alternatives *he or she* when dealing with a noun of common gender.

" The teacher must give his or her whole time to his or her professional duties; and if he or she undertakes extra professional duties a corresponding reduction will be made in his or her salary."

This is clumsy pedantry. A stocking may be made by a man, a woman or a machine; but we do not say, " If the maker of stockings is thorough in his, her or its work there will be no need for him, her or it to make provision for the immediate darning of weak places".

An Act of Parliament now permits us to understand *he, his* and *him* in statutes as including *she, her* (or *hers*) and *her* respectively. We may therefore with a fair show of justice claim that the barbarous repetition of these alternatives shall from this date cease and determine. Talking of a class that is made up of women mainly, *she* may be made the standard. It is interesting to note, for example, that in America the pronoun corresponding to *teacher* is commonly *she*. But in all ordinary cases the authorised *he* should be preferred.

Broken Construction.—A very common vice in writing arises from carelessness. The end of the sentence forgets its beginning. It begins with one grammatical construction, and ends with another.

"Good principles, good temper and good manners will carry a man through the world much better than with the absence of either."

This is a hopeless sentence, take it how you will. The only thing that is clear about it is that *either* is wrong, whatever the sentence-maker meant. Did she mean the absence of any one of the three, or any two of them, or of the whole three? There is nothing to show. But for our present purpose the point is that the construction is broken at *than*: it should go on "he could be carried without them". Or we may reconstruct the sentence from the latter part and make it read *The presence of good principles . . . will carry . . . than their absence.*

The Double Negative.—In the mathematical formula of the grammars, two negatives make an affirmative. *He was not allowed not to stay* is held to mean he was allowed to stay, whatever the man who made the sentence intended it to mean. Mistakes of this crude kind are seldom made, but some confusion arises by the occasional use of the double negative to convey a mild affirmative. *It is not impossible that I may be in town next week.* This is not liable to misconception, but the construction is not to be recommended. It frequently leads to confusion. Charles Lamb, speaking of Defoe's secondary novels, says : " It is impossible to believe while you are reading them, that a real person is not narrating to you everywhere nothing but what really happened to himself ". We have here three negatives, and nothing short of an algebraic equation can bring the meaning out straight. No writer is entitled to irritate his readers in this way, even though the meaning can be ultimately dug out of the clumsy construction.

A good deal of trouble arises from confusion in what is called the **sequence of tenses.** When two verbs depend on each other, their tenses must have a definite relation to each other. *I shall have much pleasure in accepting your kind invitation* is wrong, unless you really mean that just now you decline, though by-and-by you intend to accept; or unless you mean that you do accept now, though you have no pleasure in doing so, but look forward to be more pleased by-and-by.

I should have liked to have gone to see that play. Ask yourself the plain question : What is it that I " should have liked " to do? The plain, straightforward answer is—to go to see that play. To answer : to have gone to see that play would mean that at a certain moment you would have liked to be in the position of having gone to see that play. This is clearly not what you mean. You mean that at the moment *at* which you are speaking, you wish that at the moment *of* which you are speaking you had gone to see that play. *I should have liked* carries you back to the time at which you had the chance : once you are back at that time, the going to the play is a thing of the present.

If you are in doubt about any tenses of this kind your best plan is to carry yourself in thought back to the time in question, and use the tense you would *then* naturally use.

The difficulty that many experience in using

shall and **will** correctly arises from a confusion between two different kinds of futurity. In the first place there is what may be called the future of fate. Things that are going to happen will happen without our stir, or in spite of it. The person who describes things that must take place because of the nature of things, has clearly nothing to do with their happening beyond stating that they are going to happen. The following is the form in which this sort of futurity is expressed.

1. I shall.   We shall.
2. Thou wilt.   You will.
3. He (she or it) will. They will.

But sometimes the future does depend on the will of somebody, and then we have the future of will or the volitional future as it is called. The form for the volitional future is :—

1. I will.   We will.
2. Thou shalt.   You shall.
3. He (she or it) shall. They shall.

Notice particularly that the will upon which this future depends is not the will of *thou*, or *he*, or *she*, or *it*, or *you*, or *they*, but of the person who is writing or speaking. *You shall write two hundred lines*—here the will of the teacher prevails, not the will of the pupil whom he addresses. *Thou shalt not kill*—here God's will dominates the future, not ours to whom the command is addressed.

If we say to one who has ill-treated us *You will repent of this*, we mean that things are so arranged in this world that sooner or later those who do ill have cause to repent. But if we say *You shall repent it*, we mean that we intend to take active measures to secure the repentance.

Take the case of a wet day and examine the following correct statements of the future : You will get wet if you do not put up your umbrella. I shall get wet if I do not put up my umbrella. I will get wet rather than put up my umbrella. He will get wet if he does not put up his umbrella. He shall get wet if my service demands it. You shall put up your umbrella, for I cannot afford to buy you a new hat.

The **first personal pronoun** should not too often be used in general writing. Its proper place is in passages where you are stating a view that is not generally held, and that is likely to meet with opposition, and in familiar forms of composition it is permissible. Never introduce it by way of apology. *In my opinion, so far as I can see, it appears to me*, are all unnecessary, since they are implied in the fact that you are writing at all.

Exercise 21

State what is wrong with each of the following sentences, and show how to improve them :—

1. The lion made a gracious bow to his hostess and said that there had not been at a better gathering since the time of Noah's Ark. 2. After thinking for a long time a bright idea struck her. 3. " Five score guests ! " she said to herself, " where will I get food for them all ? " 4. I called upon the editor and wished to have

submitted my manuscript to him. 5. Regard is to be had to every one's circumstances, healths and abilities. 6. Five score were no joke to feed. 7. Unlike all the other beasts of the forest the fish could not accept the ant's invitation. 8. The accused neither admitted the charge nor did he not deny it. 9. After enjoying the day in dancing and frolicking all thoughts turned towards supper. 10. The admiration of this poem was unanimous. 11. For want of debt he died in poverty. 12. We admit the gift's generosity, but the Town Council in accepting it will, we believe, be found to have saddled themselves with a white elephant. 13. Paris is larger than any city in France. 14. I am one of those who cannot describe what I do not see. 15. Put one of the pills in a little water and swallow it three times daily before meals. 16. She has a bad habit of procrastinating everything till to-morrow. 17. The sparring with words between Beatrice, who says " nobody marks you " and yet she herself does, and Benedick made us wonder how all that will end. 18. Little Hop-o'-my-thumb was the cleverest of all his brothers. 19. The old woman who received the coin was mother of the girl whose marriage all these years she had come between. 20. There was nothing for it but to let her have her wish, and, if possible, to aid her towards the consummation of it.

LESSON XXII

PARAPHRASING

When we take a passage, examine it carefully so as to grasp its meaning, and then try to express that meaning in another form, we are said to paraphrase the passage. It is plain that several of the exercises we have already worked are really examples of paraphrasing. When, for example, we express in literal terms what was before expressed in a figure of speech, we are paraphrasing.

There is a great difference of opinion about the value of paraphrasing as an exercise in composition. As used in schools there is certainly a great deal to be said against it. An especially good passage is chosen from an especially good author, and the pupil is invited to express its meaning in other words. Now, in a selected passage from a selected author we may assume that the best words and the most suitable constructions have been employed. Accordingly, we find the pupil forced to content himself with words and constructions that are not the best. The most that intelligent and assiduous students can hope for, is to succeed in selecting the second-best modes of expression.

That there is a great deal of truth in this objection no one who has had experience in marking paraphrasing exercises will deny. But it must not be forgotten that there are compensating advantages. The exercise demands a careful examination of the passage to be paraphrased. This has the same value for the student of letters that dissection has for the student of medicine. In both cases, no doubt, the subject is spoiled, but much has been learned in the spoiling. Further, the very badness of the version produced by the student increases his appreciation of the model. It may be said that a student can learn nothing by writing poor English. To this it is enough to reply that he may at least learn that it is poor English. An exercise in composition is not to be tested by the quality of the work produced at the time, but by the effect upon the student. After all, the written exercise itself finds its way into the waste-paper basket : the effect of having written it remains with him.

All the same, we naturally want the English used to be as good as possible in the circumstances. We must therefore guard against some common errors in paraphrasing. The first of these is the belief that every word of the original must be changed. This produces such abortions as *the bovine race* for *cattle*, and *lacteal fluid* for *milk*. In paraphrasing, the dictionary must be very cautiously used. The exercise should consist in reading and understanding the passage set, taking it all in, assimilating it, making it our own, and then expressing it in our own way with the least possible change in meaning or tone. Those who seek to dig the meaning out of a dictionary will produce something like the following which was handed in by a dull boy of sixteen. The passage is from Scott. Speaking of James IV. allowing Surrey to cross the Till unopposed, the poet asks :—

> But why stands Scotland idly now,
> Dark Flodden, on thy airy brow ?

The paraphrase ran, *But why does Scotland hold herself upright at the present moment on the atmospherical forehead of black Flodden?* The proper rendering in good second-rate English would be : *But why do the Scottish forces still remain inactive on the breezy heights of gloomy Flodden?* The original contains two figures of speech. *Scotland* is metonymy, *dark Flodden* is apostrophe : both are omitted in the paraphrase, for it is a recognised rule that we must not seek to carry our figures over from the original. Not infrequently we meet phrases that defy paraphrasing as they stand. We must not take the phrase, or even the sentence, as the unit of paraphrasing, but the whole passage. This enables us so to change the whole structure as to preserve the complete meaning, while avoiding literal renderings of individual phrases. *Motherly dove* is a phrase of this kind. We may insinuate the idea somewhere in a passage, but we cannot carry the phrase over bodily without disaster. No sentence, however skilful, could redeem *maternal pigeon*.

It is to be remembered that paraphrasing does not necessarily mean changing from first-class to second-class English. The custom of the school has rather favoured the assumption that paraphrasing can act in only one direction—from good to bad. Take the following example from a book whose purpose is not primarily educational. The magistrate asks the accused :—

" ' Is it a fact, my girl, that you absconded from your situation?'

" Mord Em'ly requested the sergeant to translate the question, and the sergeant complied.

Did she do a bunk from the shop her mother got for her?

" ' You may take it at that,' replied Mord Em'ly gruffly. ' Please yourself.'

" ' It seems to me that we must look on you as incorrigible.'

" The sergeant obliged again. ' His worship says that you're a bad nut.' "

As a matter of fact Mord Em'ly had not been in a shop, but in a house as domestic servant, yet *shop* is none the less an excellent paraphrase, for in Em'ly's language it is inexactly equivalent to *situation*. The *bad nut* paraphrase, again, is quite accurate. It is to be noted that the author makes the sergeant *translate*, but from our point of view *paraphrase* would be a better word, as the meaning has not to be transferred from one language to another, but only from one form of English to another. From the point of view of the author of the passage quoted, however, *translate* is the better word, as he wishes to impress the fact that Em'ly and the magistrate really speak two different languages. In fact *translate* is here a figure of speech—hyperbole.

Real translation is indeed one of the best ways of practising composition. The ideas are supplied in a clear and intelligible form, and yet neither the words nor the constructions of the English version are anticipated. If you know a little of any other language than English you should *write out* every week an English version of a page or so from that other language. The passage need not be a difficult one, as it is not a test of knowledge of French or Latin or

German, but an exercise in the use of English to express given ideas.

Turning passages written in dialect into standard English is another useful exercise in paraphrasing, for you have to find equivalents for dialect words and very often to use different constructions.

In translating, students are frequently at a loss whether they should adopt a literal or a free rendering of the passage set. A literal rendering is useful as indicating a clear grasp of the grammatical structure of the language from which the translation is made. Teachers of foreign languages are naturally inclined to favour a literal rendering, particularly at the early stages of studying a language. At later stages the free translation is to be preferred. The real test of a good translation is the degree in which it conveys to the reader the same impression as the original conveys to one who is master of the original language. *To do a bunk* is not a literal translation of *to abscond*, but it meant for Em'ly exactly what the big verb meant for the magistrate.

The paraphrasing of fine passages of poetry is seldom well done. The logical meaning may be accurately conveyed, but the tone of the passage is so different that the real meaning is lost. In dealing with poetry the *literal* rendering is nearly always wrong. This is particularly the case where numbers are concerned—*Half a league, half a league, half a league onward*, does not mean quite the same thing as *a league and a half*, while *four and a half miles* is still farther from the original.

Besides conveying exactly the same impression as the original, a translation should not read like a translation : it should not suggest the language from which it has come, but should read exactly as if the ideas had come straight from the mind of the writer, without the intervention of another language. So with paraphrasing—when finished it should read like a bit of original composition. It must express the meaning of the original, but it must do this without sacrificing its claim to be good ordinary idiomatic English. This is a case where the method of testing by time is specially useful. A paraphrase should always be judged by the effect it produces as English, when read after time has been allowed for the original to pass from the memory.

There is one great advantage connected with the practice of paraphrasing. It enforces the widening of the student's vocabulary. We all fall into ruts in our use of words. If we write a letter or an essay we are at liberty to choose our own words, and we naturally fall back upon those we are familiar with. In this way our stock of available words tends to remain fixed. In paraphrasing, the very fact that a certain number of words and phrases are already used, sets us seeking farther afield for others. Further, since the ideas expressed are not our own, it is probable that our familiar words do not fit them so well as they do our own familiar thoughts, so that again we are forced to call in words from our reading vocabulary, and in many cases these are added to our permanent writing vocabulary.

In dealing with the following passages set

for paraphrase it will be worth your while to attend to the following rules :—

1. Read over the passage carefully two or three times to get a clear grasp of the meaning of the whole and the inter-relations of the parts. If need be, turn up any doubtful words in your dictionary, not so much to find equivalents as to make sure of the meaning of the passage.

2. Having made the matter your own, consider carefully in what form it can be most suitably expressed. If it is poetry it will be necessary to give your paraphrase an elevated tone. Do not try to write what is sometimes called prose poetry : let your prose be plain prose, but in this case certain familiar words and constructions cannot be admitted.

3. The tone is the only thing that *must* be preserved. The general form may be completely changed. The original may be highly figurative, the paraphrase severely literal.

4. Paraphrasing is not so exacting as the police court which demands the truth, the whole truth and nothing but the truth. It does not rigidly insist on the middle demand. Details, if they have not an important bearing on the main subject, need not be reproduced, or may have different but parallel details introduced in their place. The writer is left free here, so long as the details in the paraphrase give the same background effect as the details in the original. The " nothing but the truth " is rigidly exacted. No important idea must appear in the paraphrase unless it appears in the original.

5. When the paraphrase has been written out, leave it for a day or two, and then take it up and read it through apart from any consideration of the original, merely to see if it reads like English.

Exercise 22

Paraphrase the following passages :—

(a) I'll get this juggler, if he quits him well,
An audience here as choice as can be lured.
For me, when a poor devil does his best,
'Tis my delight to soothe his soul with praise.
What though the best be bad? remains the good
Of throwing food to a lean hungry dog.
I'd give up the best jugglery in life
To see a miserable juggler pleased.
But that's my humour. Crowds are malcontent
And cruel as the Holy —— Shall we go?
All of us now together?

(b) In this case give two paraphrases, a close one and a free.

It is a notable tale, that old Syr Roger Chamloe, sometime chiefe Justice, wold tell of himselfe. When he was Auncient [Senior Barrister] in Inne of Courte, certaine yong Ientlemen were brought before him, to be corrected for certain misorders : And one of the lustiest saide : Syr, we be yong ientlemen, and wise men before vs, haue proued all facion and yet those haue done full well : this they said, because it was well knowen, that Syr Roger had bene a good feloe in his yougth. But he aunswered them verie wiselie. In deede saith he, I was, as you are now : and I had twelue feloes like vnto my self, but not one of them came to a good ende. And therfore, folow not my example in yougth, but folow my councell in aige, if ever ye thinke to cum to his place, or to thies yeares, that I am cum vnto, lesse ye meete either with pouertie or Tiburn in the way.

(c) Our amusements for the fortnit we stopt here were boath numerous and daliteful; nothink, in fact, could be more *pickong*, as they say. In the morning before breakfast, we boath walked on the Peer; master in a blue mareen jackit, and me in a slap-up new livry; both provided with long sliding opra-glasses, called as I said (I don't know Y, but I spose it's a scientafick term) tallowscoops. With these we igsamined, very attentively the otion, the sea-weed, the pebbils, the dead cats, the fishwimmin, and the waives (like little children playing at leap-frog), which came tumbling over I another on to the shoar. It seemed to me as if they were scrambling to get there, as well they might, being sick of the sea, and anxious for the blessid, peaceable *terry firmy*.

After brexfast, down we went again (that is, master on his beat, and me on mine—for my place in this foring town was a complete *shiny-cure*), and putting our tallyscoops again in our eyes, we egsamined a little more the otion, pebbils, dead cats, and so on; and this lasted till dinner, and dinner lasted till bed-time, and bed-time lasted till nex day, when came brexfast, and dinner, and tally-scooping, as befoar.

This is the way with all people of this town, of which, as I've heard say, there is ten thousand happy English, who lead this plesnt life from year's end to year's end.

(d) "Weel, the presbytery be't," says I, for I saw that my wife's patience, never verra lang at the best, was comin' near an end. I ken the length o't to a hair as by this time I hae a good richt to do. "Weel, the coort met an' was constitutit."

"What's that?" asked Bob Adair.

"Fegs, I do not ken, ye'll hae to ask the clerk, it was him that said it," says I, "an' then there was reports, an' strings o' feegures like laddies' coonts [sums]; but naebody payed muckle attention, but talkit to their neebours till the clerk caaed ' Order ! ' Then they were quaite for half a meenit, an' syne at it again. Deed the clerk talkit too when he didna mind."

"Deer sirce, 'an that's a presbytery. I thocht it was like a week o' sacraments!" said my wife.

"Verra far frae that," says I, "for o' a' the craiturs to fecht, doos an' ministers are the maist quarrelsome."

"Did oor minister fecht?" asked the mistress, verra pointed.

"Na, he was raither a peacemaker, so to speak," says I cautious like; "of coorse a man haes whiles to speak his mind."

"Ow ! he's the wee white hen that never lays away, oor minister, I ken," says she, dried like.

"Ye never war the bird to fyle yer ain kirk riggin," said Rob. Whiles I'm feared that auld Rob is gettin' a wee doited.

LESSON XXIII

PRÉCIS-WRITING

In paraphrasing you have to re-cast a given passage in your own words. In writing a précis, or summary, you go further, for you have to re-cast a given passage in the smallest number of words possible. Précis-writing is frequently used for official purposes, when a summary of letters or documents must be prepared for an official who has no time to read the originals; but there are many other occasions when it is useful to be able to express a number of ideas in the smallest possible space, and practice in précis-writing will help you to form a clear concise style.

In condensing ten pages of print into two or three, it is clear that much must be omitted. The art of précis-writing lies in making the right omissions, and in skilfully combining what is left. We may take certain general rules as a guide :—

(1) Omit all matters that have no bearing on the general topic—and all details that are merely picturesque, e.g. *Princess —— was bareheaded and wore a sealskin coat, when she visited the hospital. . . .*

(2) When two or more subjects, more or less distinct, are discussed, keep them in separate paragraphs.

(3) Use indirect speech.

(4) Be simple, concise and direct. Avoid repetition. E.g. *He wrote a letter in which he*

gave the Prime Minister the information that . . . would become : *The Prime Minister was informed that.* . . . Omit all metaphorical expressions, or, if they are necessary in the summary, replace them by plainer terms.

(5) Use your own words as a rule. A précis which is made up of words and phrases borrowed from the original will in most cases not be clear to anyone who has not read the original. (You must of course keep the most important words of the original.)

It is an excellent exercise to condense a longish essay by stages. Take an essay of some dozen pages, and try to express its substance in eight pages, then in six, then in four, in two, in one, and finally in half a page. You will find that you do not omit equally throughout the essay. More goes at one point than at another. Three pages may be reduced to a dozen lines, while some pages can hardly be reduced by a third. The essential thing is to retain the really important points, and to arrange them according to their value in the essay. The great advantage of thus making abstracts of long compositions is the training it gives in the discrimination of the various parts in their relation to the whole, and in this way you will cultivate a feeling for proportion.

The following is a specially useful exercise for two students working together. Let each choose an essay of about a dozen pages, and reduce it to a précis of about one page. Let them exchange their précis. Then let each elaborate the other's précis into an essay of about six pages, and condense his own twelve-page essay into a six-page précis. The interest lies in comparing the six-page essays on the same subject. For in each pair one is a précis of a twelve-page essay, and the other an elaboration of a single-page précis. For example, A condenses a twelve-page essay on Capital Punishment into one page : B does the same for an essay of the same length on Fox-hunting into six, and B expands A's one page of Capital Punishment into six. Next A condenses his twelve pages of Capital Punishment into six, and B does the like with his Fox-hunting. If A's six-page abstract on Capital Punishment agrees in essentials with B's six-page elaboration on the same subject, it may be fairly assumed that both A and B have appreciated and maintained the relative importance of the different elements of the essays. If the two versions differ materially, they offer a capital field for discussion, which cannot fail to train both students in the perception of proportion in literary style.

Excellent examples of this process of précis-writing are to be found in our daily newspapers. The little paragraphs over the leading articles usually express very clearly the substance of several columns in the middle of the paper. You cannot do better than turn from the three-column report of some political meeting to the quarter-column paragraph over the leader. In most cases you will be sorry you read the three columns.

Exercise 23

As an exercise in abstract-making, give the substance of the following passage in as few words as you can, without omitting anything essential.

" It is asserted by Horace, that ' if matter be once got together, words will be found with very little difficulty '; a position which though sufficiently plausible to be inserted in poetical precepts, is by no means strictly and philosophically true. If words were naturally and necessarily consequential to sentiments it would always follow, that he who has most knowledge must have most eloquence, and that every man would clearly express what he fully understood : yet we find, that to think, and discourse, are often the qualities of different persons: and many books might surely be produced where just and noble sentiments are degraded and obscured by unsuitable diction. Words, therefore, as well as things, claim the care of an author. Indeed of many authors, and those not useless or contemptible, words are almost the only care : many make it their study, not so much to strike out new sentiments, as to recommend those which are already known to more favourable notice by fairer decorations : but every man, whether he copies or invents, whether he delivers his own thoughts or those of another, has often found himself deficient in the power of expression, big with ideas which he could not utter, obliged to ransack his memory for terms adequate to his conceptions, and at last unable to impress upon his reader the image existing in his own mind. It is one of the common distresses of a writer, to be within a word of a happy period, to want only a single epithet to give amplification its full force, to require only a correspondent term in order to finish a paragraph with elegance, and make one of its members answer to the other : but these deficiencies cannot always be supplied : and after a long study and vexation, the passage is turned anew, and the web unwoven that was so nearly finished. But when thoughts and words are collected and adjusted, and the whole composition at last concluded, it seldom gratifies the author when he comes coolly and deliberately to review it, with the hopes which had been excited in the fury of the performance : novelty always captivates the mind; as our thoughts rise fresh upon us, we readily believe them just and original, which, when the pleasure of production is over, we find to be mean and common, or borrowed from the works of others, and supplied by memory rather than invention."

LESSON XXIV

COMPOSITION—FINDING MATERIAL

In earlier exercises you have been asked to write short compositions, but the matter has in most cases been suggested for your use. In this lesson we shall consider the problem of collecting material and expressing it in a suitable form.

Your attitude to this problem will depend on yourself. You may find that, when you are faced with a subject on which to write, your ideas come tumbling out in such profusion that when you come to set them down you hardly know where to begin. In despair, you take the first that comes, and let the others follow in what order they will. The result is a rich disorder, in which significant and insignificant facts jostle together, and no clear argument can be discerned. If you have to write an essay or description, your best plan is to write down all your ideas, as they come, on a piece of rough paper. When you have finished, go through them carefully, striking out whatever is irrelevant to the main theme. (How you are to decide which facts are irrelevant, we shall discuss later.) Then go through your list once more, this time grouping the facts which are connected with each other, and arranging the groups so that one group naturally leads on to the next. Your material is thus sorted and you are now almost ready to begin your essay.

You may, on the other hand, find that when you are faced with a subject for an essay or description, your ideas will not come. The virgin blankness of your paper paralyses your mind; you write down the title and can write no more. Your case is worse at first sight than that of the student with too much to say. You could write a brilliant essay, wittily expressed, elegantly arranged—if only you had something to say in it. Your difficulty is more than half psychological. You are like the nervous guest at a party who can say nothing until he has been drawn out by skilful questioning. For such a one, the question and answer method will prove the most stimulating, in essay-writing as in conversation. But you yourself must ask the questions, and how are you to find them?

Let us take a concrete example. Suppose you are asked to write an essay on your favourite season of the year, then your first instinctive question will be—" How to decide? " To this there is the obvious answer : your choice will depend (1) on the weather ; (2) on the way you spend your leisure (for this will clearly be more affected by the weather than your regular work). The first point suggests the obvious question : what kind of weather do you like best? When you have decided this, you will be able to expand your answer into a more detailed description. The second point suggests two more questions : (1) what are your favourite leisure occupations? (2) to what season are they suited? The answers to these questions may also be developed at length. If, for example, your favourite pastime is bathing, then you can describe the pleasures of bathing on a hot day (in sea or river or pool), the delicious coolness that follows your bathe, or the pleasures of sun-bathing afterwards. Thus one question has led on to another, until you end with ample material for your essay, and you have the advantage over the quicker student in that your ideas are then arranged in a logical order. Whether the subject of your essay is simple, like this one, or demands more thought, the important part is to find a leading question, and the rest will follow of their own accord.

If you are asked for plain description, your questions will be different. If you have to describe a concrete object, you may begin by asking : What does it look like, in colour, shape, size? What is its use? What associations has it for me? Or, if you are describing a person : What does he look like? What do I know of his character, way of living? What is his use and importance? These are general questions, but they can be modified to suit the needs of the subject. When you have practised this method several times, it will be easy to find questions, and you will ask and answer them almost unconsciously.

But your work is not yet over. As you gain practice in collecting ideas, you will find that you have too many ideas to fit into a single essay, and that they differ too widely to fit into an orderly scheme. You cannot express every view on the subject given, and you have doubtless unconsciously adopted a single point of view. Yet you will be wise nevertheless to look through your material, and consider whether all your ideas are consistent. If, for instance, you are writing an essay condemning capital punishment, you must not say at one point that the death penalty is a survival of barbarism, and later aver that it is still necessary in a civilised community. If you are unable to make up your mind, then you must make it clear from the beginning that you are going to examine both sides of the question. Even if you can find no inconsistencies in your material, pruning may still be necessary, and all irrelevancies must be cut away. You may class as irrelevant all that does not enlighten or explain or expand your main argument. We all recognise irrelevancy in conversation, and Jane Austen has caricatured it in the person of Miss Bates.[1] It is almost as easy to be garrulous and irrelevant in writing as in conversation, especially if you have a gift for writing fluently. To decide what is irrelevant, you must put your-

---

[1] In *Emma*, see p. 112.

self in the position of your reader, and think what he expects to find in your work. He may come to you for exact and useful knowledge. In that case your description or your argument must be clear in outline and exact in detail, and all that is fanciful or in any way personal must be left out. He may, on the other hand, come to you for entertainment, wishing to receive your impressions or reflections in a pleasant form. In that case, you must strike out all that is obvious and uninteresting. You must not begin an essay on a railway terminus with the definition : "A railway terminus is a place from which trains begin and at which they end their journeys". Your task is to please, and such bald facts are as out of place in such an essay as they would be in polite conversation. In short, your final tests in selecting material, as in all other problems of writing, must be the question : Is this appropriate?

Exercise 24

Prepare the material for a short general essay on a big railway station.

LESSON XXV

DESCRIPTION

Description, as was shown in the last lesson, may be of two kinds. You may write a plain, exact description, designed to give practical information, or you may write a general description with no other purpose than to entertain. Persons with any gift for writing will usually find the second kind of description easier than the first; for them exercises in plain description are very useful, since they demand clear accurate writing, and clearness and accuracy are virtues which imaginative people often forget to cultivate.

It is to be remembered that the value of a description depends upon the combined work of two persons. The writer really analyses mentally the thing to be described, and places the parts in what he considers the most suitable order before the reader, who must in turn try to reconstruct these parts into the whole with which the writer started. In describing scenery, for example, the writer mentions that there was a mountain here, a stream there, a certain tree or group of trees elsewhere, and so on. He probably uses an adjective or two about each object, and certain prepositions and adverbs of direction. From these indications the reader dips into his own storehouse of ideas, selects mountains, streams, and trees that seem to fit the case, and combines them in such a way as not to contradict any of the prepositions or adverbs. The result is a mental picture which coincides sufficiently with the author's mental picture to allow of author and reader each using his own picture as a background for what follows.

It is good practice to try to describe some practical process to a friend to whom it is unfamiliar, and to see how far he can understand it from your description. When you can accurately describe a process such as touch-typing or hand-

weaving, or can give clear directions for reaching
a certain meeting-place, then you will know
that your style has gained accuracy and precision.
Mrs. Beeton's cookery book might serve as a
model for this kind of writing. Clearness and
conciseness are essential in a recipe, and Mrs.
Beeton had both these virtues. Her secret is
that like all good cooks, she thought clearly and
methodically. In practising this style you will
do well to follow her example.

In describing a scene or a background, you
will need a different technique, but your practice
in exact description will have done you good
service. Detailed description is now somewhat
out of fashion : few modern novels begin with a
lengthy description of the house in which the
hero was born. It is recognised that such exact
detail does not necessarily make the scene more
vivid, and that a few clear touches are more
effective and put less strain on the reader.

Yet the writer must not thereby save himself
trouble. He may be content to say that his hero
was born in " a low white house with a cedar
tree leaning over it ", but he must himself know
much more about it. He must have peeped into
all the rooms, he must know the position of the
pantry, and whether the drawing-room has a
french window. It is only when he sees the house
clearly in his imagination that he can select the
points that are important to his reader. He
must not make up the details as he goes along :
such a feckless method betrays itself, and will
render the background of the story unconvincing
and unsubstantial. Jane Austen, it is said,
worked with a map before her showing the
imaginary village in which her novel was set,

with the houses in which the characters lived, clearly marked upon it. Her imaginary world was thus made real; everything that happened in it was credible, because correct in detail. Even if you do not draw a map, you should imitate Jane Austen in getting the background clear in your head before you begin to write.

Let us assume, then, that you have followed this method. Your imaginary country is mapped; you know precisely the number of bedrooms in your imaginary house, and have decided the colour of the drawing-room curtains. Now, all this detail must be pushed back into a corner of your mind. Imagine the scene now in its entirety and pick out the details which will be most vivid to your reader. " A low white house with a cedar tree leaning over it. . . ." Perhaps that is enough for the present, yet, if the house is to play an important part in your story, you may perhaps say a little more, something like this perhaps : " It was a low white house, standing back from the road; its green front door opened on to a small neat garden, and its windows were darkened by a great cedar tree."

You will ask, perhaps, how you are to decide which details are to be selected, which forgotten. It is impossible to make general rules, but three suggestions may be given. You must, of course, give some general features that the readers' imagination may have something to work on. These will be obvious—trees, river, houses and the rest—you can describe nothing without giving some definite features such as these. Next in importance is colour, for this is very easy to carry in the mind; given one or two colours, the imagination can create a picture in bold outline. Lastly, you may add whatever details are unusual or arresting (like the cedar tree in the example given). If you are interested in this kind of description, you should notice very carefully the descriptions given in any good novels, noting what is included and what left out. Then try yourself to describe some well-known place or scene—your own house—for example—choosing the details which would make it vivid to a stranger.

Exercise 25

(*a*) For practice do as many of the following descriptions as your knowledge permits. The two fundamental rules to be attended to are: (1) Assume nothing on the part of your reader but a fair knowledge of English and a moderate amount of common sense. (2) Pay special attention to the order in which you present matters. In describing a process it is well to take the different parts in the order in which they actually occur. For example, in describing how to fumigate a green-house it is too late to remark when the description is half finished: " Close all the ventilators ".

The Process of	Instruments.
Cyclostyling.	A pair of opera-glasses.
Folding table-napkins.	A roll-top desk.
Fumigating a green-house.	A trouser-stretcher.
Propelling a boat with one oar.	A fountain-pen.
Mounting a bicycle.	A cyclometer.
Preparing a salad-dressing.	An automobile.
Driving at golf.	A pianola.
Focusing in photography.	An hour-glass.

(*b*) " For Sale : Country cottage, one reception, 3 bedrooms, kitchen, bath, h. and c., all modern conveniences, old-world garden with lily pond. Apply Dodger & Dodger, House-agents, Dumbleditch."

Using this house-agents' description as a guide, imagine what the country cottage might really look like, and then describe it, pretending that your description is part of a story.

LESSON XXVI

NARRATIVE

In Lesson XXIV no mention was made of collecting material for narrative. It must be assumed that you have the material for your story in your head, or you would not be sitting down to write it. Your problem is to decide what is to be omitted, what briefly told, and how you are to arrange the material that is left.

The arrangement of matter is to a large extent imposed from without. Things happen in a certain order, and in most cases the narrator should follow that order. It is true that in dealing with a long series of events, as in history or in an epic poem, it may be necessary to present various incidents rather in the order of importance than in the exact order in which they occurred. Epics almost never begin at the beginning : they start off in the middle of an interesting situation and go on, gradually picking up preceding events as the story develops. The same is true of many novels.

On the other hand, many narratives, such as *Robinson Crusoe* and *The Pilgrim's Progress*, follow the time order : they begin at the beginning and go right on.

Even in those cases where series of events are grouped according to their importance in the whole narrative, the events within each series must be given in their time order. It would appear, therefore, that once the general arrangement of series is made, the rest is a mere matter of memory. You start at the beginning of each series, and let the mind recall each event as it happened. But the matter is not quite so easy as it looks. Two opposite lines of error present themselves : we may omit essential points, or we may include points that have no value in the narrative.

Listen to children telling stories. One of the commonest remarks you will hear is " Oh, but I forgot to tell you that . . .". This is said when the child finds that the development of the story demands a knowledge of some preceding incident, that at an earlier part of the narrative was not of sufficient consequence to command his attention. On the other hand, when we listen to the stories of certain garrulous persons we are not spared a single detail, however unimportant.

The true view is that here as elsewhere we must make a selection among the facts that present themselves, we must choose only those that are of consequence in respect of the purpose we have at the time. The reader of a narrative is entitled to assume that every fact set forth does something towards aiding the development of the story. For example, if we are told that a man walked to town " by the nearest way ", we have a right to assume that he was in a hurry to get there. If the context shows that there was no need for haste, then we are justified in assuming that later on in the story we shall find that something depended on his taking this particular way to town. Sometimes, it is true, a remark is introduced not for its own sake, or for future use, but merely to convey a present impression. *I heard the click of Aunt Maria's knitting needles* need not lead us to expect those needles to play a prominent part in the story. The context shows that the reference is made in order to strengthen the impression of the silence that reigned at a critical moment in the story.

While in narrative there is thus the usual need for a point of view and for a corresponding selection of material, there is always the great help of the time order. You must choose the proper incidents, but the incidents all pass through your mind in the order in which they originally occurred. In description, on the other hand, the facts may present themselves to the mind in any order. We must adopt our point of view, and then determine the relative importance of the facts at our disposal. It is true that, speaking generally, we have in description all the facts arranged according to space, as in a narrative they are arranged according to time. We may describe emotions, theories and other immaterial things, but the beginner in description will do well to confine himself to things seen, and there he has the aid of space arrangement. Even with this limitation he has to determine which facts are, for his present purpose, the most suitable to begin with.

Your treatment of the facts will be decided in part by your method of telling the story. The most usual method is to pretend that the author knows everything and is everywhere. In telling the story he can enter the minds of the characters and proclaim their secret thoughts; he can describe what happened in one place, and afterwards what was happening at the same time in another; he can traverse infinite distance, and leap across the years. This method is clearly most convenient since it imposes no restraint upon the writer, but there are times when other methods are appropriate.

When a story deals very particularly with the experience of a single character, it is common to make that character the narrator, and to write in the first person. *David Copperfield* and *Robinson Crusoe* are examples of this method. It has certain limitations in that you can only present what the narrator himself heard or saw or experienced, but it is often a more convincing method, since the reader easily imagines himself in the place of the character who is telling the story.

A third method is to make an imaginary character tell the story for you—a difficult method, which should not be attempted by the inexperienced. It is often used when the story would be incredible if told in a more direct form. Reading it, you feel that the author is not vouching for the truth himself, but heard it from another, who possibly heard it from a third. Henry James uses it very brilliantly in his ghost story *The Turn of the Screw*, where the events would seem utterly beyond belief if the story were told more directly. Many ghosts stories employ this method. It is used with different effect when the narrator is a " character " like W. W. Jacobs' night watchman,[1] for then much of the fun of the story lies in the way it is told. " Q " uses all three methods in a very skilful way in a short story, *The Roll-call of the Reef*.[2] It opens in the first person, with a conversation between the author and his host, but this merely serves as introduction. His host tells a ghost story, which he himself heard from his father, and because he is telling a story well-known to him he uses the freer direct method as if he himself were the author. He thus reaps the advantages of all three methods. You will be well advised not to try any such intricate methods of story-telling yourself, but you will learn very much from studying how they are handled by accomplished writers.

Exercise 26

For practice in narrative give an account of the Adventures of a Shilling, as told by itself. Make up your mind before you start, (*a*) when your shilling began its life, (*b*) which incidents in its life you consider worth narrating, (*c*) what is its present state. You may include a long or a short period, but you should try to account for the whole period you have chosen, even though great parts of it were spent in uninteresting ways. The dull parts should be indicated, the interesting parts told fully.

[1] *Captains All* and other volumes.
[2] From *Wandering Heath*.

LESSON XXVII

LETTER-WRITING

Letter-writing is the freest of all forms of composition and probably the pleasantest. You may feel self-conscious in writing an essay or an exercise, but a letter is an extension of conversation, a substitute for speech. Those who find essay-writing too formal will find it the best medium, for a letter is the converse of an essay in that the less you think about it the better it will be. Naturalness and ease are its chief essentials, and these must come unconsciously, if they come at all. The best letters are written for an immediate purpose, and destined for the waste-paper basket as soon as that purpose is fulfilled. Once you begin to think of a letter as a piece of literary work its charm vanishes—a warning that is less necessary to-day than it has been in the past when a young man could send his friend the earnest injunction—" Remember to put my letters in a book, *neatly* ".[1]

Since letters are really conversations by post, the nearer they approach the freedom of conversation the better. That is the charm of Charles Lamb's letters—that they give this illusion of talk, so that reading them you can hear in fancy all the changes in his voice. This intimacy is the essence of good letter-writing. Its secret is beyond analysis, yet two ingredients are clear—simplicity and appropriateness. Your aim must be to produce the simplicity of con-

[1] Boswell, Dr. Johnson's chronicler, writing to his friend, Temple.

versation without its flatness. You are free in a letter to use the colloquialisms and the looser constructions of speech (provided you respect the rules of grammar), but you must avoid the pitfalls of excessive simplicity. You must use the arts of style, but use them unobtrusively. The banalities which pass unnoticed in conversation are glaring when written down. If you write of an experience, you must make it as vivid to your correspondent as it is to yourself. If you write of a book or a play, your opinion must be sensible and persuasive.

The interest of your letter will depend very much on its appropriateness. Since your reader is chiefly to be considered, you must write on matters which interest him. A letter which differs from an essay only in beginning "Dear—" and ending "Yours affectionately" does not deserve the name. Your business in a letter is not only to express yourself, but to express your relationship to the person to whom you are writing. Let not your friends say of you, as Queen Victoria said of Mr. Gladstone : " He addresses me as if I were a public meeting ! "

Clearly the manner is more important than the matter, and some of the best letters in the world have been written on the lightest of subjects. If you write naturally, simply, and appropriately, then your letters are sure to be pleasant. The following extract from a young lady's letter is a happy example of this kind of writing, though she[1] has no claim whatever to literary pretensions. She has been sea-bathing— a bold adventure in 1792 :

" We had a nice dip : the machines are very

[1] Louisa Holroyd.

convenient with a curtain all round so that nobody can see you. You are not put in as at Brighton, only one woman gives you her hand and in you jump. Aunt and I went in two machines, but close together, so she had the satisfaction of hearing me flounce in, and I of hearing how she behaved as the same woman executed us both."

A very ordinary passage, you may say—loosely constructed, badly punctuated, yet it remains, after nearly a century and a half—still gay, still charming.

Letters written for a practical purpose or to people whom you hardly know will naturally demand a different style from personal letters, whose chief end is to give pleasure. In the first kind of letter, clearness and accuracy are the chief essentials. Many people believe that a letter to be business-like must bristle with business terms—" Received your favour of the 16th inst." " Yours of the 21st to hand," etc., etc. Such jargon merely obscures what it wishes to make clear. The following letter from T. H. Huxley to Matthew Arnold might serve as a model for clearness and force, though it is of course not a business letter.

26 ABBEY PLACE,
July 8th.

DEAR ARNOLD,

Look at Bishop Wilson on the sin of covetousness and then inspect your umbrella stand. You will see there a beautiful brown smooth-handled umbrella which is not your property.

Think of what the excellent prelate would have advised, and bring it with you next time you come to the club. The porter will take care of it for me.

Ever yours faithfully,
T. H. HUXLEY.

This example shows how a letter should be set out. The first thing to write is the place from which, and the date at which it is written. A date always has a certain value, even when the letter is quite recent : and this value goes on increasing with the years. As to the place of writing, every letter—even those of the most intimate character—should bear at the top right-hand corner the address of the sender in sufficient fulness for postal purposes. If the letter by any chance goes astray, the postal authorities can do nothing with it if it bears no trace of its origin; and the case is no better if the address is some such vague term as Home : London.

The next thing is the address to the person to whom you are writing. The most formal beginning is *Sir*. All letters to Government officials should begin in this way, and should end *I have the honour to be, Sir, Your obedient Servant*.

The more usual form in business is the conventional *Dear Sir*. This beginning implies a relation of friendly equality between the correspondents, but it does not imply that they are acquainted with or have ever even seen each other. The ending for a letter of this kind corresponds to the beginning : *Yours faithfully*, *Yours truly*, *Yours sincerely*, rank in ascending order of friendliness. The first is the most common of all, but the second is almost as colourless. Into the third there creeps a shade of personal friendliness.

My dear Sir marks a certain amount of personal interest in your correspondent. It should not be used in a purely business letter, unless your correspondent is a personal friend as well as a business connection. The natural ending demanded by this beginning is *Yours very truly*, or *Yours most sincerely*. There are many people who dislike these adverbs *very* and *most* at the end of letters. With respect to grammar this dislike is justified : *truly, sincerely* and *faithfully* are not words that admit of comparison. If one is true, sincere, or faithful there is no more to be said. One is either sincere or one is not. The only justifiable qualification would be a time limit. *Yours sincerely on most occasions*, or *Yours at all times faithfully*. After admitting the literal inaccuracy of the forms, we may frankly recognise them as existing, and as useful to indicate certain degrees of friendliness.

The following beginnings of letters addressed to John Smith are arranged in ascending order of intimacy : *Dear Mr. Smith, My dear Mr. Smith, Dear Smith, Dear John*. People who regard themselves as authorities quarrel over the claims of *Dear Smith* and *My dear Smith* to the higher degree of intimacy. The difference between the two really seems to be that *My dear Smith* commits one to a somewhat friendlier relation with him than is implied in the shorter form. The same slight distinction holds between *Dear John* and *My dear John*. We use the Christian name only with relations or with those whom we have known in our childhood. It is safe to avoid this form in all the other cases of mere friendship.

The endings of letters begun on the model of

the John Smith series may end in *Yours truly, or sincerely, or very truly,* or *most sincerely.* As a rule *faithfully* is rather cold for this form. *Yours ever* is a conveniently brief and easy ending to a letter that begins *Dear Smith* or *Dear John.* As a matter of fact, both beginnings and endings in all except purely business letters depend to a great extent on the temperament of the writer. Every one is entitled to follow his own bent in private letters : but the rule in all cases of doubt is to use the colder form. *Dear Sir* and *Yours truly* commit one to nothing. *My dear Sir* and *Yours most sincerely* ought to mean a little more than the recognition of your correspondent as a civilised fellow-creature.

In business letters in which the name of our correspondent does not occur, it is necessary to write his name immediately before the *Dear Sir,* or else in the left-hand bottom corner of the page on which you finish the letter. It is usual and desirable to add his address. We must not depend upon the envelope to tell us to whom the letter was originally sent.

It is literally true that it takes at least two to write a letter. The person you write to has almost as much to do with your letter as you yourself have. If you examine two letters written by the same person describing the same circumstances to two different correspondents, you will find the letters as different as are the correspondents, and the better the letter-writer the more different will the two letters be. The first quality of a good letter-writer, indeed, is this very power of responding easily to the influence of the correspondent. A good letter is always written from the point of view of the person for whom it is meant. Naturally this does not mean that we must always accept the views of those to whom we write, but we must so express our views that they may fit in most easily with the mental habits of our correspondents. Even when we wish to make a man adopt our view, we must begin by looking at the matter from his standpoint.

That we all naturally do adopt the standpoint of our correspondent is proved by the prevalence in letters of a peculiar kind of technical error. We write for example : " I hope to come to you on the 27th at latest ". As a matter of strict accuracy we hope to *go*, not to *come*. But since we unconsciously adopt the correspondent's point of view we speak of coming.

Exercise 27

George Maidenhead, foreign correspondence clerk in a large London office, finds on his arrival at 13 Ingleborough Avenue, Wirencester, where he is to spend a fortnight's holiday, that he has lost the umbrella that his wealthy Aunt Matilda gave him as a birthday present. It is a silk umbrella, with a thin wooden shaft of a green colour : the handle is straight (*i.e.*, there is no hook or cross bar) and silver-mounted. He *thinks* he took it with him from his rooms in Montague Street, kept it beside him in the office all day, took it to Euston Road Station, put it in the rack in a third-class compartment in the 3 P.M. train for Bletchley, where he arrived at 4.58 P.M., and changed carriages for Wirencester, where he arrived at 6.11 P.M. Maidenhead has expectations from Aunt Matilda, who is to be a fellow-visitor with him at the Rushton's in Wirencester. He arrives on the 16th July, 1937. She is to arrive on the 18th. She is jealous about the respect paid to her presents. He must recover the umbrella before her arrival, and has already made fruitless inquiries about the lost umbrella at Wirencester Station.

Write such a letter as he might send to—

(a) The stationmaster at Bletchley, inquiring if the umbrella has been found, offering a reward of 10s., and the payment of all expenses of a search.

(b) To his landlady, Mrs. Hickson, to make sure that he has not left the umbrella in his rooms, and directing how to send the umbrella if found.

(c) To his fellow-clerk, Jerkyns, to inquire whether the umbrella has not been left in the office, and urging immediate despatch of umbrella if found.

(d) To his sister, Violet, living at home in the same town as Aunt Matilda. He encloses P.O.O. for 30s. to buy and send on to him an umbrella as like the aunt's present as possible. Violet has seen the original, and George assumes that it was bought at Akenside's, the local umbrella shop. Violet is not to buy the umbrella unless she receives a wire next day (i.e., the 17th) with the order *buy* : this wire is to arrive before noon, else she is to understand that the lost umbrella has turned up.

LESSON XXVIII

THE ESSAY—HEADS

By an essay is usually understood an attempt to treat a subject in the way most suitable for a given occasion. There is often a didactic tone about the essay, its business seems to be to teach its readers. If we read an essay on Bimetallism or on Bivalves we expect to be instructed. Yet many of our best essayists are read merely for the charm of their style : we read them because we enjoy them, not because we learn from them. The amount of instruction we gather from reading Charles Lamb's " Dissertation upon Roast Pig " would never justify the time spent in reading that charming production. The word dissertation, here used in a whimsical sense, is generally applied to a serious and somewhat long essay. If a subject is discussed at great length the result should be called a treatise : but it is generally felt that *essay* is a more modest name. Accordingly we find some very important works known as essays, notably the most striking book on philosophy in the English Language— Locke's *Essay Concerning Human Understanding*. Though usually written in prose, an essay may take the form of verse, as in Pope's *Essay on Man*.

For our purpose an essay must be regarded as an attempt to express in a brief form our views upon any subject. It implies the selection of the proper matter, and the choice of the best way of expressing that matter. At first, therefore, it is well to write on subjects with which you are familiar. This will save you the excessive labour involved in doing two different things at the same time—discovering what to say and how to say it. The how is sufficient in itself to occupy all your attention.

Suppose the subject to be " My Favourite Book ", you are clearly assumed to know all about the book, yet you may find considerable difficulty in determining how to proceed. You may treat your favourite merely as an object, give a full description of its size, general appearance, type, paper, binding and so forth. You will find that you have material here for a complete little essay. Then you may deal with the question, Why is this book my favourite? Here you will find yourself writing half about the book and half about yourself, and a complete little essay will result. Again you may examine the place of the book in English literature, and give a history of it; or you may treat the matter of the book as subject for criticism; or the style of the book may become your subject.

Each of these would make a complete essay, but very frequently parts may be taken from each and welded into a harmonious whole. It is here that the skill of arrangement is called into play. The essay must not be a thing of shreds and patches. It may treat only one aspect of a subject, and be complete so far as it goes; but if it takes up two or three aspects, these must be so related to one another as to be seen to be parts of one whole.

Assuming that you are dealing with a subject about which you know something, and that you have selected the point of view from which you propose to treat it, you must set about preparing a few " heads " to keep you from mere rambling. It is indeed surprising how many ideas " come out of the ink-pot " when you sit down to write. You may think you have little to say on a subject, but somehow one thing suggests another till you find you have written quite a long essay. This method of following the suggestion of the moment is to be avoided. Some of our best writers no doubt write their pleasantest essays in this way, and when you have formed your style and acquired habits of logical arrangement you too may let yourself go, and follow the lead of association. But at your present stage you must guide your associations.

You should practise writing essays containing about as much matter as two pages of this book. For this kind of essay there should be at least three heads, each head representing a paragraph in the finished essay. Each head again should have sub-heads under it, and in some cases there may even be sub-sub-heads. You will understand this better by examining the following illustration.

Suppose the subject given is *The Style is the Man*, we might draw up some such notes as the following :—

I. In its widest sense this means that we are known by our manifestations.

> By their deeds shall ye know them.
> Manners makyth man.

II. Special meaning limited to a man's manner of writing.

F   165

A. Writing is expression of highest part of man's nature.

B. Style may be the man even though we cannot read the true man in it.

    (*a*) Compare Johnson's style and character.

    (*b*) Compare Rousseau's style and character.

III. Confusion between style and matter.

A. It does not follow that Sterne was kind because he wrote sympathetically. Thackeray the cynical writer was a kindlier man in reality than was Dickens the sentimentalist.

B. Style probably limited to the intellectual aspect of character.
The style is the head rather than the man.

While the beginner should always prepare heads for his essay, he should keep them private. The cupboard is the place for literary as well as for family skeletons. Your methodical student thinks otherwise. As soon as he gets the idea of the scheme of heads and sub-heads he is proud of it, and proceeds shamelessly to expose the scaffolding of his essay. He begins :—

First, let us consider it in its widest sense. . . .
Now let us consider it in its special sense, which may be divided under two main heads. . . .
Finally, let us consider the confusion between style and matter. . . .

Students are led to this display of the inner workings of their minds by the example of public speakers, notably clergymen. But the cases are not parallel. The audience or the congregation require much more help than the reader. He can take his own time, and can turn back at any moment to examine something that has gone before. The audience must take things as they come, and if anything is missed it is gone for ever. It is right, therefore, that the speaker should give them all the help possible by indicating beforehand the general line he is about to follow, and by mentioning anew each important head as he comes to it.

Certain essays too of a severe, argumentative type may have some of their sub-heads boldly stated. For example, the arguments for a given theory may be tabulated and numbered. But even here the whole skeleton need not be exposed : a rib or two will do quite well. With an ordinary essay the heads ought to be there for the seeking, but they should be decently covered up. The essay should read all the more smoothly because of the heads.

Exercise 28

Write a short pleasant essay on " Getting up on Cold Mornings ". (Do not be afraid to treat it from a personal angle.)

LESSON XXIX

THE ESSAY—BEGINNINGS AND ENDINGS

Take up a book of essays, preferably a book of essays selected from many different authors, and turn over the pages, noting carefully the first sentences of each essay. You will find it extremely interesting to observe how each begins, and a second rapid glance through the book will provide an equally interesting study of how each essay ends.

Some writers are fond of beginning with a striking sentence, and frequently call in the aid of somebody else. Augustine Birrell confesses that he likes " to leap-frog into his subject " over the back of a fellow-author, and if not too frequently used, this mode of opening an essay is very effective. Green, the historian, begins his examination of the character of King John with the words of a thirteenth-century writer : " Foul as it is, hell itself is defiled by the fouler presence of John ". Nothing could be more direct or more striking. Sometimes the quotation is indirect, and the point lies rather in the setting. Robert Louis Stevenson begins his essay on " Truth of Intercourse " : " Among sayings that have a currency in spite of being wholly false upon the face of them, for the sake of a half truth upon another subject which is accidentally combined with the error, one of the grossest and broadest conveys the monstrous proposition that it is easy to tell the truth and hard to tell a lie ". This is not so striking, but it arouses our interest by its contradiction of a popular saying. Stevenson is not here brief enough to claim an epigrammatic beginning : but the epigram, especially if it takes the form of a paradox, makes a very effective opening. Thus Charles Lamb begins his essay on " New Year's Eve " with the words : " Every man hath two birthdays ".

A plain, straightforward beginning is a definition of one's subject. Swift begins his essay on " Good Manners " : " Good manners is the art of making those people easy with whom we converse ". This is a literal definition, but sometimes a fantastic description of the subject takes the place of the more exact logical form. Charles Lamb thus introduces his essay on " Poor Relations " : " A poor relation is the most irrelevant thing in nature—a piece of impertinent correspondency—an odious approximation—a haunting conscience—a preposterous shadow lengthening in the noontide of our prosperity— an unwelcome remembrancer—a perpetually recurring mortification . . ." and so on with another score of whimsical equivalents.

A statement of the problem to be discussed makes an excellent start. Stevenson thus introduces his " Plea for Gas Lamps " : " Cities given, the problem was to light them ". But this style of opening in the hands of an ordinary writer is very liable to be dull. The interrogative beginning, as " Is Alpine climbing justifiable ? " is in itself good enough, but it has been so much abused by tired journalists that it had better be avoided.

The exclamatory beginning may be permitted in dealing with suitable subjects, but it must be rigidly kept to its own place. John Wilson may begin his essay on streams : " How delightful even to elders like us to feel Spring breathing once more over air and earth ! " But the ordinary prose writer will find it advisable to begin without the help of the exclamation mark. You must not here confound two totally different things. A beginning is not an introduction. No essay can do without a beginning, but most are all the better for lacking an introduction. If you examine all the beginnings now from the point of view of matter, you will find that in almost every case the first sentence tells us something that is of real importance in the essay. In other words, the best essayists begin at once, they do not require a paragraph to say that they are going to begin. An essay on female education was thus introduced by a student in an examination paper :—

" As soon as my eyes fell upon these words on my paper of questions, my heart misgave me. I know little about education, and nothing at all about female education, since my life-work will not run on these lines; but as the subject is prescribed I must do something, even if I have to adopt the method of the man who wrote an essay on Chinese hieroglyphics, by first of all reading all he could find about China and then all he could find about hieroglyphics, and finally combining the two kinds of knowledge thus acquired."

Clearly all this is irrelevant and must be struck out. It has nothing to do with female education, though it may have a great deal to do with covering a certain number of sheets at an examination.

Compare Sydney Smith's first sentences on the same subject : " A great deal has been said of the original difference of capacity between men and women ; as if women were more quick, and men more judicious—as if women were more remarkable for delicacy of association, and men for stronger powers of attention. All this, we confess, appears to us very fanciful." Here female education is not even mentioned, and yet we feel that we are in the middle of the subject.

However the essay begins it must take an immediate grip of the reader. In order to catch the attention one need not be startling. Many of the essays by our best writers begin in the most unobtrusive way—perhaps the most common beginning of all is the simple impersonal formula *It is*—but they all get at once into their subject. Writers vary in the way they distribute interest throughout the essay. Some begin with minimum interest, go on to maximum interest, and end with medium interest. Others begin with maximum, fall gradually to minimum, and then gradually increase to maximum. When a difficult problem is being dealt with in which point after point is elucidated, there is a steady rise in interest from the beginning to the end. Interest begets interest in essays as well as in old-fashioned bank balances.

Whatever the general distribution of interest, there must be no fall *near* the end, though *at* the end a fall there must be, else the essay is not complete. The end of a good essay is coincident with the dissipation of interest. The interest ceases because the mind is satisfied.

The ending has the choice of most of the forms referred to as possible beginnings—a quotation, an epigram, a broad generalisation, a striking concrete example of some principle expounded in the essay. Yet the purpose of the end is quite different from that of the beginning. The purpose is not now to rouse and stimulate, but to satisfy. One essential characteristic of an ending is that it should be felt to be an ending. This does not mean that the essay should begin towards the end to wind itself up. The closing paragraph may not be recognised as the close of the essay, but the final sentence should leave no doubt on the matter. The ending of the estimate of King John of which we have already quoted the startling beginning is admirable : " The awful lesson of his life rests on the fact that it was no weak and indolent voluptuary, but the ablest and most ruthless of the Angevins who lost Normandy, became the vassal of the Pope, and perished in a struggle of despair against English freedom ". We feel that there is no more to be said.

" Truth of Intercourse " ends : " But the morality of the thing you will be glad to hear is excellent ; for it is only by trying to understand others that we can get our own hearts understood ; and in matters of human feeling the clement judge is the most successful pleader ". Here the wide general statement with its special application produces a feeling that the matter is settled, and we may attend to something else.

It would be mere affectation to pretend to expect anything more about New Year's Eve after Lamb has said, " And now another cup of the generous ! and a merry New Year, and many of them, to you all, my masters ! " His ending of " Poor Relations " is equally pointed.

" This was—a Poor Relation." This repetition of the title—a favourite trick at the end of amusing plays—must be sparingly used in essays.

Exercise 29

Make up a scheme of " heads " and sub-heads for essays on the following subjects—each essay to have at least three main heads.

(*a*) The Renaissance.

(*b*) The Exception Proves the Rule.

LESSON XXX
THE ESSAY—PREPARATION OF MATTER

You must now get some practice in preparing to write on subjects with which you are less familiar. Here you must read before you write. It is well to choose such a subject as may repay this preliminary reading and thinking. If you have no interest in natural history it would be a pity to read up all about insects in order to write an essay on the *Ravages of the Colorado Beetle*. Further, you should choose a subject that admits of complete preparation within a limited time. The preliminary reading for an essay on *The Elizabethan Literature*, or even for one on *The Elizabethan Dramatists* is a matter of several years of hard work. Many of the books on Shakespeare alone, embody the work of a lifetime. But take now a subject like *Shakespeare's Treatment of the Supernatural.* Here the range of preliminary reading is absolutely limited. It is true that if you wish to write an essay exhaustive enough to satisfy Shakespearean scholars you must read all that the critics—English, American and Continental—have said on this subject. But for a first-hand essay by a student all that need be read is Shakespeare himself.

It seems a disproportionate demand that all Shakespeare should be read in order to write an exercise. But if you have not yet read Shakespeare the sooner you begin the better, and if you have read him you will be all the better for looking over again the parts that deal with the supernatural. There is no better exercise in literature than to read over a known author to find his connection with a given aspect of his work.

If you have not read Shakespeare before, there is nothing for it but to read the whole of his plays. No other method will give you the right to treat the subject at all; for even when the supernatural is not prominently introduced it is frequently implied, and Shakespeare's treatment must be held to include indirect as well as direct use of his materials.

If you do not know Shakespeare and are afraid to undertake the whole of his works at once, the next best thing is to read over the *Dramatis Personæ* at the beginning of each of the plays. Your examination will direct you to those that make the most striking use of the supernatural. This will give *The Tempest, A Midsummer Night's Dream, Richard III., Macbeth, Hamlet.*

To these you had better add the first part of *Henry IV.*, the first and second parts of *Henry VI.* and *Julius Cæsar*. Having read these you will have a fair idea of Shakespeare's style, and a first-hand acquaintance with his methods of dealing with the supernatural. It may be convenient to keep separate his use of supernatural agents as *dramatis personæ* from his use of the supernatural as an element in human experience, and therefore an agent in the development and portrayal of character. His supernatural characters fall naturally into three classes : fairies, ghosts and witches.

We have now clearly two main heads : the direct use and the indirect ; and in an essay by a student there can be no doubt that most attention should be given to the direct use. Since this essay should run to about ten or twelve pages of this book, it can stand a short introduction, if this introduction has some real connection with the subject.

The following set of heads gives a fair idea of a suitable way of selecting and grouping the matter for this essay. Examine the different heads carefully, treating each as a hint for further thought and investigation, and then write out an essay embodying the heads and extending to about a dozen pages of this book. When finished, this essay should be compared with that supplied at the end of Part II. This closing essay was written by a student, and represents the level to which you may be fairly expected to attain.

Introduction. " After God, Shakespeare created most." (Victor Hugo) : the two worlds of his creation.

Shakespeare's broad human sympathies are carried over into Cloudland.

> Limitation of supernatural characters—gives reality.

> Modern fairies lacking humanity are mere abstractions.

Direct use of supernatural.

Fairies.

> Contrast of Puck and Ariel—as illustrating Shakespeare's idea of fairy nature.

> Underlying meaning—prominent in *Tempest*, less so in *Midsummer Night's Dream.* Never obtruded.

> Allowed to break down when to keep it up would injure the story.

Ghosts.

> Command our belief more readily.

> No underlying meaning—they do their duty and go.

> Fail on ideal side—mere means to ends.

Witches.

> Rank in interest intermediate between fairies and ghosts.

> Rank highest in probability.

> More scope for underlying meanings—*e.g.*, three tenses, three witches.

> Motif of *Macbeth*—story not sacrificed to moral or theory.

Subordinate use of supernatural.

The supernatural as supplying an atmosphere.

The supernatural in expressing character.

Mere superstition.

SUGGESTIONS FOR FURTHER STUDY

Now that you have progressed thus far in the art of writing, you will profit by reading something of the theory of style. This can best be learnt from those who are accomplished writers themselves, for they discuss the writer's problems in the light of their own experience.

Herbert Spencer has an interesting essay on *The Philosophy of Style*. It is a good one to begin on, for it is short (only thirty-four pages), and very clearly set out. You may not agree with all his conclusions—indeed, it will be better if you do not, for then you will be forced to think the matter out for yourself. Sir Walter Raleigh, who was for a long time professor of English at Oxford, has left a very fine essay *On Style*, and he has some very good things to say in his notes *On Writing and Writers*. He is worth reading not only for what he says, but for his own brilliant style, and for his exact and scrupulous use of words. "Q", who is a novelist as well as a professor, has written a book, *The Art of Writing*, which you will find delightful reading; and, if you are interested in the theory of style, you will like the essays by the novelist, C. E. Montague, entitled *A Writer's Notes on his Trade*. In *The Craft of Fiction* Percy Lubbock discusses the technique of the novel, and illustrates the different methods of constructing a novel. Even though you do not wish to write a novel yourself, Mr. Lubbock's book will give you a keener interest in the novels you read. You are not likely to read all of these, immediately, one after another, but try at least to read Herbert

Spencer's essay and Q's lectures on the *Art of Writing*, and reserve the others for future study. You will find them interesting in themselves, as well as of practical value.

If you have little leisure for general reading, see that what you read is good. Your familiarity with good prose sets a standard for your own, and by steady reading you will keep that standard in mind. It is well to read as widely as possible, for in this way you will widen your vocabulary, as well as your interests and knowledge. Some people find it a good plan to have several books on hand at the same time, each one being of a different character. They will, for instance, be reading a novel, a biography and some more serious book on history, politics or art—all three more or less concurrently, according to their mood. If you find this method confusing, you should at any rate vary the kind of books you read. If you read any foreign language, you should keep up the habit of translating into English, not making a literal translation, but re-casting the material into good idiomatic prose. In this way you will gain readiness in the use of words, which is as important as learning new ones.

At this stage your style will be less easily influenced by reading authors with a highly individual style, whom you were discouraged from reading in the first chapter of this book. From Lamb you can learn very much about the technique of the essay, for in the *Essays of Elia* he has used all his art to produce an effect of ease and artlessness. Read them carefully, noticing the skilful way the style is adapted to the mood and the many changes of style within the compass of a single essay. The essays of Max Beerbohm and G. K. Chesterton will show you how many unusual ways there are of treating a seemingly ordinary subject—you might take Max Beerbohm's essay " An Infamous Brigade ", and Chesterton's " What I found in my Pocket " as especially good examples. Their dazzling style is, of course, beyond imitation.

Robert Louis Stevenson tells how he worked out his own style by deliberately imitating other people's, writing passages now in the style of one, now of another. This is easier than it sounds, for after reading any author for a little time, you will find that, when you write, you unconsciously adopt some of the characteristics of his style. It is a more difficult matter to re-write a passage from one author in the style of another—to reproduce a passage from Ruskin, for example, in the style of Carlyle, or a passage from Johnson in the style of Charles Lamb. It is amusing to attempt this, but extremely difficult to do it well, since it is rarely that form and matter can be easily separated. You will find it easier to practise the first kind of imitation, and you should practise it regularly. After you have read a book by any writer with a fairly pronounced style, set yourself to write a short passage on a subject he might himself have chosen, imitating as far as possible his customary rhythm and balance, and using a vocabulary similar to his own. If, for instance, you have been reading Lamb's essay, " Mrs. Battle's Opinions on Whist ", then try to write a short character sketch of someone you know, modelling your style on the crisp, incisive style of the first three paragraphs of that essay. This practice in imitation will give your style greater flexibility and wider range. The charm of a good style is that it is never monotonous, but offers a continual variety.

Journal-keeping should by now have become a steady habit, and you will have gained from it, not only greater fluency, but greater power of observation. As you gain power to express what you see, so you see more to express. But you must practise other more formal modes of writing, essays, narrative, exact description. If you wish to write fiction, you will be best at first to confine yourself to fact. Fiction is, after all, only the imaginative handling of facts. The imagination creates nothing of itself, but merely transmutes experience, and you will not be able to write well on anything that is outside your experience. If you write stories, let them be about people such as you know yourself, and set them against a familiar background. If you go beyond it, you will not only make mistakes in detail, but you will create characters who are not real people, but dummies in fancy dress.

It is wiser not to confine yourself to one form of composition, or to one style of writing. If you are fond of a poetical diction, a course of writing on exact subjects with plenty of statistics is a good counterpoise. If you are given to bald statements of fact, you should practise on subjects involving a certain amount of feeling. If you tend naturally to abstractions, practise yourself in dealing with the concrete. You aim is to get a grip of language, to master it, to make it obey your will. If you write only in the way you like, and on subjects you are fond of, your grip of language is limited, you become lopsided and can treat a subject only in one way. You become the subject of language, not the master.

A very valuable exercise is to read articles by different authors on the same subject. Opportunities for this comparative method are to be found almost every month in the more serious periodicals. There is usually some subject of general interest treated in two or three of these, and it is very instructive to compare the points of view, the arrangement of matter, the tone, the vocabulary. After reading such articles critically for a month or two you cannot do better than try the experiment of writing an article yourself on some subject that you find in one or two of them, and then compare your work with the printed matter.

One great advantage of the study of articles by competent writers in the more serious periodicals is the training it gives in the perception of the proportions of the various parts of a subject. An inexperienced writer goes wrong more frequently in proportion than in anything else. To treat a wide subject within a narrow compass and maintain the relative importance of the different parts is the mark of an accomplished essayist. An excellent exercise is to make a skeleton outline, such as we used on page 165, to correspond to an article we are examining. You will be surprised to find how interesting this process of analysis becomes when intelligently practised. Many articles that read well, and seem all right on a general view, will be found to fail in proportion and arrangement when the test is applied of reducing them to their skeletons. Here, as elsewhere, we must be on our guard against pedantry. If we are dealing with a light article whose purpose is to produce a certain more or less pleasurable impression, we must not exact just proportion as measured by arithmetical standards. The criterion of success is the impression produced. But in a seriously reasoned-out article proportion must be observed or the reasoning itself must suffer. So important is this matter of proportion that a weekly analysis of a serious article, solely from this point of view, is not too much.

Set aside a definite period for work, and work systematically, not despairing though your progress seem slow. A good style is the reward of long practice. It is not a natural gift bestowed at birth by some good fairy, but is only to be gained by hard work and an infinity of pains. Yet it can be gained if we will spare the time and trouble. Everyone has the power to write well, though to write very well be the prerogative of few.

PART II

KEY TO EXERCISES

Exercise I

(*a*) 1. *Derogatory*. The word *derogative* does not exist. 2. *Observance*. *Observation* means looking at something so as to learn more about it. 3. *Profitable*, or *lucrative*. *Payable* implies that something must *be* paid. 4. *Dissension*. *Dissent* lays stress on difference of opinion : *dissension* lays stress on the resulting discord. 5. *Contemptuously*. *Contemptible* means worthy of contempt, *contemptuous* full of contempt for somebody or something. 6. *Healthful*. 7. *Die*. 8. *Spoiling*. *Spoliation* has become equivalent to plundering. 9. The girl was *homesick*. *Nostalgia* is a big word meaning homesickness. 10. *Imply*. We usually infer *from*, and imply *by*. 11. *Break*. 12. *Luxuriant*. *Luxurious* means given to luxury : *luxuriant* means abundant. 13. *Acceptance*. *Acceptation* has become narrowed down so that it applies to words only. 14. *Act*. Action is not usually applied to a single uncomplicated deed. 15. *Discovery*. We discover what was there already though unknown, for example planets or old manuscripts. We invent something that did not before exist, for example a steam engine. The compound called chloroform was discovered. Its application to surgery may be called an invention. 16. *Human*.

(*b*) 1. Shadowy, translucent, limpid, sparkling, glassy, glittering, dappled, tranquil, placid, rippling, low-lapping. 2. Shining, mysterious, iron-grey, opaque, oily, sluggish, turgid, un-hurrying, majestic, noiseless, slow-sliding. (Many of these adjectives might serve to describe both.)

Exercise 2

(a) 1. *Interesting. Entertaining* originally meant "*holding the attention*" : now it is nearly equivalent to *amusing*. 2. *Wistfully.* This is almost the same as *wishfully*, but is acquiring a connection with things that are unattainable. 3. *Fraud* refers more to the action done, *guile* to the character of the persons acting. 4. *Adjoining* is inaccurate since the islands are not joined, *contiguous* is inapplicable since they do not touch, *neighbouring* is, perhaps, the nearest equivalent. 5. *Determined* implies indifference to the opinions of others, *resolute* indifference to the consequences of our actions. 6. *Delinquents* refers more to sins of omission, *offenders* to sins of commission. 7. *Funeral* is felt to be much less imposing. 8. *Obliged* is usually used of a slight service : we can be *indebted* to things, but obliged only to persons. 9. *Survives* implies *going on living* after something else has gone : *outlives* merely means that we live long enough to see the end of the other thing. 10. *Marriage* refers to the state, *wedding* to the initial ceremony. 11. *Balls.* All globes are balls, but all balls are not globes. 12. *Disgrace* is not quite so bad as *reproach.* 13. *Encroaches* includes *intrenchment* as well as other forms of pushing our way where we have no business. 14. *Detest* applies more to our intellect, *abhor* more to our feelings. 15. *Screamed* is not quite so shrill as *shrieked*, but it may last longer. 16. *Readable* rather implies worth reading, while *legible* refers to the mechanical difficulty of reading manuscript or type.

(*b*) 1. Impassive, immobile, monumental, majestic, wooden, phlegmatic, dignified, solemn, courteous, good-humoured, patient, officious, efficient. 2. Fervent, passionate, eager, intense, scornful, ironic, patient, exasperated, hectoring, shrill, factious, earnest, pathetic, ridiculous.

Exercise 3

1. The Opposition must bestir themselves if they wish to gain anything at the approaching election. 2. The judges had a military escort to their hotel. 3. Omit "religious". 4. Mr. Parkins of this city died last night. 5. It is rumoured that jealousy was the cause of the tragedy that occurred. . . . 6. The distinguished party had a cold supper at midnight. 7. The authorities were shocked when they learned how wildly the newcomers had behaved in the town. 8. The Government was utterly rotten. [Garboard-streak is the name of the plank next the keel—but the general reader cannot be expected to know that.] 9. Open-air meals ——. 10. The Countess is shortly to give birth to a child. 11. Do not work at this exercise till midnight. 12. I drink cocoa regularly every night. 13. In science Einstein is pre-eminent. 14. He suffers from a strong sense of his own inferiority. 15. She declared she loved birds. 16. Uncorrupted conduct is very desirable. 17. A really fashionable child

requires an engagement book in which to record her many social activities. 18. I am astounded (amazed, astonished, confounded, etc.) by the impertinence of the honourable member who has just spoken. (*Honourable member*, as a term of etiquette in the House of Commons, must not be changed.) 19. Now is the fitting moment for the restoration of the monarchy. 20. His book is worth reading.

Exercise 4

(*a*) 1. —— his spirit never wavered. 2. It was bitter to fail —— 3. —— he entered the forbidden territory. 4. It was in your power —— 5. The modern schoolmaster is expected —— 6. —— William proceeded to the Hague. 7. —— the bubble increased for a time, but ultimately burst. 8. The success of the newspaper was not secured —— 9. —— set out for London. 10. It is mortifying ——

(*b*) (i) The cuckoo flies early to the south, leaving her young in another bird's nest. (ii) The town clock marks each hour with a noisy chime. (iii) The silver gleamed in the faint light of the candles.

Exercise 5

The important part of the sentence is, *we came to our journey's end*, and the position of this part really determines the character of the whole sentence. As the sentence stands in Part I. this important part comes first. Herbert

Spencer in his *Philosophy of Style* would put part of it in the middle and the rest at the end :—

(*a*) At last, with no small difficulty, and after much fatigue, we came, through deep roads and bad weather, to our journey's end.

Dr. Whately places the *came* nearer the end :—

(*b*) At last, after much fatigue, through deep roads and bad weather, we came, with no small difficulty, to our journey's end.

The important part may be thrown to the very end :—

(*c*) At last, with no small difficulty, after much fatigue, through deep roads, and bad weather, we came to our journey's end.

(*d*) . . . to our journey's end we came.

It is clear that by rearranging the various phrases we may produce a very great number of variations on the original. Thus we might begin :—

1. At last we came . . . 2. At last after much . . . 3. At last through deep . . . 4. At last through bad weather . . . 5. At last to our journey's end . . . we came.

So we might begin with, *After much fatigue* . . . and ring the same changes, and so with each of the phrases.

(*b*) We started out along the edge of a field. The barley was still grey-green. Then the path twisted through a little coppice. We could hear the churring of wood-pigeons. A rabbit ran across the path a few yards ahead. By the far gate a game-keeper had nailed a dead stoat and a jay to a branch. We supposed it was by way of warning. We stopped for tea at a farm-house.

There were small black pigs scampering about the yard. The farmer's wife gave us eggs and honey for tea. She charged us only a shilling each. We returned to the station by road.

Exercise 6

(*a*) 1. Is this English straightforwardness? 2. Where is a braver man to be found? 3. Who can doubt any longer about the matter? 4. Is there a scrap of evidence against him? [The answer is clearly, *No*. But if the question were: Is there any evidence against him? it would have to be treated as a mere question, and the answer would depend on circumstances. It is the word *scrap* that makes the difference.] 5. Am I a dog that I should do this thing?

(*b*) 1. What a very ugly mouth he has! [Or simply, What an ugly mouth he has! For the exclamatory form more than makes up for the loss of the *very*.] 2. How I dislike babies! 3. How wonderful are the ways of God! 4. What plunder! [Neither *plenty* nor *here* are required. They are really included in the two words of the exclamation.]

(*c*) I woke late. The room was very light. The ceiling had an unaccustomed whiteness. Footsteps outside sounded soft, muffled. On roof and chimney stack, street and garden, snow lay thick. The postman, padding from house to house, left diagonal tracks to and fro across the road. The lawn was patterned with sparrows' foot-prints. Snow began to fall again, softly, softly—white goose-feathers fluttering down.

Opening the window, I picked a snow-flake from the sill. It glittered a moment on my finger-tip, a bright filigree flower. Then it was gone. Faster came the snow, in a swirl and a flurry, out of a chalk-white sky. It twisted and danced in the air. I drew the bedclothes closer. Soon, men would put down salt to melt it. They would sweep it from the streets. But in the country it would lie outspread over field and farm and haystack. The air would be still, and muffled every sound. Under its white counterpane the earth would sleep.

Exercise 7

(*a*) 1. Principal verb : *is*.

> There's a story
> |
> that the river's angry
> |
> when the mill changes hands.

2. Principal verb : *have*.

Nevertheless, we have reason to be thankful that the thing, well or ill, is over.

3. Principal verbs : *love, let*. The clauses are independent and of equal importance. 4. Principal verb : *could give*. The sentence, in spite of its length and apparent intricacy, is Simple.

(*b*) We started out along the edge of a field where the barley was still grey-green. The path twisted through a little coppice where we could hear wood-pigeons churring, and saw a rabbit run across a few yards ahead. By the far gate a game-keeper had nailed a dead stoat and jay to a branch—by way of warning, we supposed. We stopped for tea at a farm-house where there were small black pigs scampering about the yard. The farmer's wife gave us eggs and honey for tea, and charged us only a shilling each. We returned to the station by the road.

Exercise 8

(a) 1. —— I never had a patron before. 2. —— impertinent. 3. —— offered a sacrifice to God. 4. —— presented an epitome of country abundance. 5. —— God disposes. 6. The manuscript was lost and —— 7. The prince himself interceded for the captives —— 8. The prince is merciful—— 9. —— followed his work amain. 10. —— threw an appealing look at Hepzibah. 11. The rumour was false; —— 12. —— he does not love her.

(b) When I woke at last, the room was very light; the ceiling had an unaccustomed whiteness, and footsteps outside sounded soft and muffled. I looked out of the window, and saw that on roof and chimney stack, street and garden, snow lay thick. The postman, padding from house to house, left diagonal tracks to and fro across the road; a sparrow's foot-prints patterned the velvet lawn. Snow began to fall again, softly, softly—white goose-feathers fluttering down. Opening the window, I picked one from the sill: it glittered a moment on my finger-tip, a bright filigree flower, and then was gone. Faster came the snow, in a swirl and a flurry, out of a chalk-white sky. It twisted and danced in the air. Soon men would put down salt to melt it, and would sweep it away; but in the country it would lie outspread over field and farm and haystack; the air would be still, and muffled every sound, and under its white counterpane the earth would sleep.

Exercise 9

1. (*a*) The man that had a widowed mother was exempted from military service. (*b*) The man, who had a widowed mother, was exempted from military service. 2. (*a*) The ship that Jackson & Co. built was wrecked. (*b*) The ship, which Jackson & Co. built, was wrecked : or, The ship was wrecked which Jackson & Co. built. 3. (*a*) The little lamb that Mary had went with her to school. (*b*) Mary had a little lamb which went with her to school. 4. (*a*) The novelist that is conceited and has few friends is despised : or, The novelist that is conceited has few friends and is despised. (*b*) The novelist, who is conceited and has few friends, is despised.

(*b*) Sir William used to show with pride a silver casket which he had received from an Indian prince. He had been able to accommodate him in a small matter which had arisen out of some diplomatic entanglements. These necessarily arise in a country whose rulers are kept at peace only by fear of the force which the government can bring to bear upon those who transgress the limits marked out for them.

(*Princes* can be omitted since it clearly refers to the *rulers* just mentioned. Such a sentence cannot be satisfactorily re-modelled, since its bad construction results from the looseness of the thought, and the attempt to group together ideas that are not closely related to each other.)

Exercise 10

(*a*) 1. Periodic: Edward the Black Prince reverenced the age, the station and the misfortunes of your king when he made him his prisoner; attending him, serving him, consoling him like a son. 2. Loose: If the knight had not called him to his side, complaining that the length and roughness of the roads had shaken his saddle so as to make it uneven and uneasy, the servant would, as became him, have kept behind his master. 3. Periodic: Strewing flowers before the funerals, and planting them at the graves of departed friends, are among the beautiful and simple-hearted customs of rural life which still linger in some parts of England. 4. Loose: When it is excited by the bounty and familiarity of their elders there is something genuine and affectionate in the gaiety of the young. 5. Loose: That the Aristotelians erected their castles upon a basis far less reliable than air is the simple truth. 6. Periodic: We must leave out of sight altogether such nothings as the speed of a cannon ball or of sound, when we attempt to appreciate this interval by the aid of any considerations of velocity, as we did in endeavouring to estimate the distance of the moon. 7. Periodic : They have a spirit indeed, they that pretend to have the Spirit and so turn away from the straight rule of the Holy Scriptures; but it is a fanatical spirit, the spirit of delusion and giddness. 8. Periodic : I am led to imagine that one of Ponto's black Hampshires had been sacrificed a short time before my visit, for the dinner was composed of pig's head mock-turtle soup, of pig's fry and roast ribs of pork.

(b) I love the city for the people in it : the endless ebb and flow of the crowd; the chance encounters, overheard conversations; the friendly bus conductors, the large solemn policeman; the whole gay, ridiculous, ever diverting cavalcade of my fellow-men.

To feel turf beneath my feet instead of dead pavement; clean wind in my face instead of dusty air; to know the changing beauty of trees instead of the monotonous sameness of houses—for this I would give all the luxury of Mayfair in exchange for a cottage in the country.

Exercise 11

(a) It ought to be presumed that a respectable and honourable publisher will wind up his affairs respectably and honourably, however suddenly he may retire from business.

(b) Turning to Friday I said, " Now, Friday, do as I bid thee "; and when he said he would, I said, " Then, Friday, do exactly as you see me do—fail in nothing ".   Note that this change is not for the better. The short sentences, as is explained in the text, are more effective.

(c) A very interesting case is now being treated at St. ——'s Hospital. The patient, the child of poor parents, had stolen from his sister a necklace of large wooden beads. In playing with them, he cut the string and swallowed a bead. Finding it extremely pleasant, he returned next day and swallowed two beads. On the day after he swallowed three, and in this way he went on, until by the end of the week he had swallowed the whole necklace—twenty-five beads in all. His sister was deeply grieved at the loss of her necklace and searched everywhere for it in vain. A few days afterwards, when the family were at dinner, and the child, not being hungry, was playing about the room, a loud rattling was suddenly heard like the sound of a small hailstorm. The father told the child to be quiet, but after a little, the noise broke out again, louder than ever. In annoyance, and by way of punishment, he shook the child. A tremendous rattling ensued. He thereupon declared with an oath that he must have croup in the wrong place, but the child, beginning to cry, confessed he had swallowed the necklace. The father promptly caught him up and carried him to the hospital, the beads in the boy's stomach rattling all the way, so that, as they went by, people looked everywhere to see whence the unusual sound came. He is still in the hospital, and makes so much noise when he walks about that is necessary to muffle him in a watchman's coat for fear he should wake the patients.

Exercise 12

(*a*) Second paragraph begins : Sarah Battle was none of that breed; third paragraph begins : I never in my life; fourth paragraph begins : Pope was her favourite.

(*b*) The fruiterer's shop is easily the gayest in the street. Behind its plate-glass windows rises a hillside of oranges and apples; bananas are festooned above, and the grapes hang in heavy clusters ravishing the eye. What colour is here ! Red-gold oranges, and the paler gold of lemons; tangerines in silver jackets, rosy Jonathon apples polished till they wink with brightness; soberer colours, too, in the freckled pears and pale field mushrooms—someone rose early in the grey morning to gather those ! Most of the fruit has been brought from afar : oranges from Brazil and Africa and Spain, gathered months ago under the warm sun; lemons from Italy; little spotted bananas from the Canaries, and the big yellow ones from Jamaica; prickly South African pineapples, and stranger fruit besides, grenadillas, passion-fruit, persimmons—names out of romance. The seasons are turned topsy-turvy; all the fruits of summer are here in the November dusk. Only the English fruit keeps due season— Bramley's Seedlings, William pears, Cox's Orange Pippins—these shone on orchard trees not many weeks ago. With the brown beech leaves there on the shelf, and the tawny curled chrysanthemums, they are the last reminders of the autumn that is over.

Exercise 13

(a) 1. A man going to sea, his wife desires the prayers of the congregation. 2. The woman that deliberates is lost.

3. Ask where's the north? At York, 'tis on the Tweed;

In Scotland at the Orcades; and there

At Greenland, Zembla, or the Lord knows where.

4. At length Mary died: Elizabeth succeeded; and Cecil rose at once to greatness. 5. "And what did your uncle say to that?" asked the judge. "He said, 'You must never breathe a word of this to a living soul'", was the reply. 6. I go to a convention of philanthropists. Do what I can, I cannot keep my eyes off the clock. But if there should appear in the company some gentle soul who knows little of persons or parties, of Carolina or Cuba, but who announces a law that disposes these particulars, and so certifies me of the equity which checkmates every false player, bankrupts every self-seeker, and apprises me of my independence on any conditions of country, or time, or human body, that man liberates me; I forget the clock; I pass out of the sore relation to persons; I am healed of my hurts; I am made immortal by apprehending my possession of incorruptible goods. 7. If he was an inhumane old gentleman (and I am afraid it is a fact that he was inhumane), he was also perfectly intrepid. 8. He promised to go down first; and boldly he did so; for William, give him his due, had the heart of a lion.

9. " I'm no leech," said Adam. " Let me go."

" No—not yet. I will convict thee of ignorance. Thou dost not even know where the liver is placed."

" I do," answered Adam shortly ; " but what then ? "

" Thou dost—I deny it. Here is a pin ; stick it into this wax, man,[1] where thou sayest the liver lies in the human frame."

Adam unsuspiciously obeyed.

10. " You and I, Master Worthy, have worked hard many years, and think it very well to have scraped a trifle of money together ; you a few hundreds, I suppose, and I a few thousands."

(b) There was a table set out under a tree in front of the house, and the March Hare and the Hatter were having tea at it : a dormouse was sitting between them, fast asleep, and the other two were using it as a cushion, resting their elbows on it, and talking over its head. " Very uncomfortable for the dormouse," thought Alice ; " only, as it's fast asleep, I suppose it doesn't mind."

The table was a large one, but the three were all crowded together at one corner of it. " No room ! No room ! " they cried out when they saw Alice coming. " There's plenty of room ! " said Alice indignantly, and she sat down in a large armchair at one end of the table.

" Have some wine," the March Hare said in an encouraging tone.

" Alice looked all round the table, but there

---

[1] *Man* is here nominative of address : *wax-man* would make equally good sense, though this is not what Lord Lytton meant.

was nothing on it but tea. "I don't see any wine," she remarked.

"There isn't any," said the March Hare.

"Then it wasn't very civil of you to offer it," said Alice angrily.

"It wasn't very civil of you to sit down without being invited," said the March Hare.

"I didn't know it was your table," said Alice; "it's laid for a great many more than three."

"Your hair wants cutting," said the Hatter. He had been looking at Alice for some time with great curiosity, and this was his first speech.

"You should learn not to make personal remarks," Alice said with some severity; "it's very rude."

The Hatter opened his eyes very wide on hearing this; but all he said was "Why is a raven like a writing desk?"

"Come, we shall have some fun now!" thought Alice. "I'm glad they've begun asking riddles—I believe I can guess that," she added aloud.

"Do you mean you think you can find out the answer to it?" said the March Hare.

"Exactly so," said Alice.

"Then you should say what you mean," the March Hare went on.

"I do," Alice hastily replied; "at least—at least I mean what I say—that's the same thing, you know."

(*Alice in Wonderland*: Lewis Carroll.)

Exercise 14

1. Babies rolled and tumbled about. (We have no right to add *in the grass*, since that refers to the fruit.) The metaphor is a pleasant one, and might be kept on that account, even if it is not very necessary. 2. Be silent. (Close your mouth is meant, but the size of the mouth is supposed to be so great that closing it is like closing the whole head.) The metaphor is much more effective. 3. When lovers are together they pay no attention to time. Metaphor is better, because shorter and neater. 4. The ashes of Mr. Foster's note curled up. The metaphor gives a much wider meaning here, for it suggests that the contents of the note were sour also. 5. He had failed in literature; he now turned to law. Literal form perhaps better, for the personification has been rather often used. 6. That shop, which was dark and smelt of Bibles, attracted all boys. Literal form better. It is difficult to think of the smell of the shop and then to imagine it as a loadstone. 7. Habit can be changed only by gentle means persistently applied. Metaphor more effective. 8. The very wood seems as if it sympathised with us in our troubles. This is clearly an emotional passage, and the personification is best suited to it. 9. Plenty of men are willing to abase themselves before those who will supply the good things of life. A very awkward metaphor in which eating truffles and licking blacking seem intended as equivalents. 10. Mrs. Agar ate very little. Metaphor so common as to be almost literal. 11. The lid of the

kettle cluttered noisily. The simile is unnecessary and tiresomely facetious. 12. An Ogilvie's sword could not pierce so deep as that. Metaphor suited to the somewhat elevated tone of the sentence. 13. His evil soul went shrieking down to its place. An effective simile in its context. 14. "No," said his daughter, preparing to combat him with tears. A very awkward metaphor. 15. With these words he withdrew, leaving his furious companion to pace the deck. A very awkward metaphor.

(b) The rocket rose and broke, *flowering* in sudden brightness. It fell *like a silver fountain* out of the black sky.

She *rode* the waves proudly. Then a wind sprang up, and she moved away down the strait *like a great white bird.*

The *greedy* water lapped closer. It advanced slowly, yet perceptibly, *like a stealthy ravenous beast.*

Exercise 15

1. Antithesis : This is a mild epigram, which is literal enough as it stands. 2. Hyperbole : another epigram. 3. Irony : The Duke of Wellington did not write good French. 4. Hyperbole : Some German words are extremely long. 5. Antithesis [also simile]. 6. Epigram. 7. Hyperbole : The hills in the south of Scotland are extremely bare. 8. Epigram. 9. Epigrammatic irony. 10. Metaphor : The people of Paris go mad. 11. Antithesis : All the advantages that age brings cannot equal the advantages which youth possesses. 12. Ironical

epigram : And the verse is very bad. 13. Antithetical epigram : Since we still love those we lose, can we be said to have altogether lost them? 14. Antithesis and antithetical simile. 15. Euphemism : The Prime Minister was dismissed.

Exercise 16

(a) " I more than half guessed that there might be some hanky-panky of this sort, and I have therefore taken such steps as will prevent me from being left out in the cold. I propose to deal with this affair as I deal with matters of politics or of organisation, that is, I shall use plain language and speak out my mind like a man. If a man or a woman behaves straight to me I behave straight to them; if they behave crooked, I behave crooked. That's me all the world over. Further if I were here and now to undertake to write my own epitaph, I would simply take a pen, dip it in the ink, seat myself at the table, and write these words : ' He was as open as the day '."

(b) " Fame is dear to the heart of every man. Poetic fame is dear to the heart of my friend Snodgrass; the fame of conquest is equally dear to my friend Tupman; and the desire of earning fame in the sports of the field, the air, and the water is uppermost in the breast of my friend Winkle. I will not deny that I am influenced by human passions and human feelings (cheers), possibly by human weaknesses (loud cries of ' No '), but this I will say, that if ever the fire of self-importance breaks out in my bosom the desire to benefit the human race in preference effectually quenches it. The praise of mankind is my Swing; philanthropy is my insurance office. (Vehement cheering.) I felt some pride —I acknowledge it freely, and let my enemies make the most of it—I felt some pride when I presented my Tittlebatian Theory to the world; it may be celebrated or it may not. (A cry of 'It is' and great cheering.) I will take the assertion of the [1] honourable Pickwickian whose voice I have just heard—it is celebrated; but if the fame of that treatise were to extend to the farthest confines of the known world, the pride with which I should reflect on the authorship of that production would be as nothing compared with the pride with which I look around me on this, the the proudest moment of my existence. (Cheers.) I am a humble individual. ('No, no.') Still I cannot but feel that you have selected me for a service of great honour, and of some danger. Travelling is in a troubled state, and the minds of coachmen are unsettled. Look abroad and contemplate the scenes which are enacting around you. Stage coaches are upsetting in all directions, horses are bolting, boats are overturning, and boilers are bursting. (Cheers— A voice, 'No'.) No! (Cheers.) Let the [1] honourable Pickwickian who cried 'No' so loudly come forward and deny it if he can. (Cheers.) Who was it that cried 'No'? (Enthusiastic cheering.) Was it some vain and disappointed man —I will not say haberdasher— (loud cheers)—who jealous of the praise which

---

[1] In both these cases we might retain *that*, but since the Pickwickian in each case is clearly pointed out by the relative clause the definite article is sufficient.

has been—perhaps undeservedly—bestowed on my researches and smarting under the censure which has been heaped upon his own feeble attempts at rivalry, now takes this vile and calumnious mode of——"

Mr. BLOTTON (of Aldgate) rose to order. " Does the honourable Pickwickian allude to me?" (Cries of "Order", "Chair", "Yes", "No", "Go on", "Leave off", etc.)

Mr. PICKWICK. " I will not put up to be put down by clamour. I *did* allude to the honourable gentleman." (Great excitement.)

Mr. BLOTTON. " I shall only say then that I repel the honourable gentleman's false and scurrilous accusation with profound contempt. (Great cheering.) The honourable gentleman is a humbug."

(*c*) The atrocious crime of being a young man, which the honourable gentleman had, with such spirit and decency, charged upon him, he would neither attempt to palliate nor deny; but content himself with wishing that he might be one of those whose follies might cease with their youth, and not of those who continued ignorant in spite of age and experience.

Whether youth could be attributed to any man as a reproach he would not assume the province of determining; but surely age might justly become contemptible, if the opportunities which it brought had passed away without improvement, and vice appeared to prevail when the passions had subsided. The wretch who, after having seen the consequences of a thousand errors, continued still to blunder, and in whom age had only added obstinacy to stupidity, was surely the object either of abhorrence or contempt; and deserved not that his grey head should secure him from insults. Much more was to to be abhorred, who, as he had advanced in age, had receded from virtue, and become more wicked with less temptation; who prostituted himself for money which he could not enjoy, and spent the remains of his life in the ruin of his country.

(d) He could not, he assured their lordships, he would not, join in congratulation on misfortune and disgrace. That was a perilous and tremendous moment. It was not a time for adulation : the smoothness of flattery could not save them in that rugged and awful crisis. It was then necessary to instruct the throne in the language of truth. They must if possible dispel the delusion and darkness which enveloped it; and display, in its full danger and genuine colours, the ruin which was brought to their doors. Could ministers still presume to expect support in their infatuation? Could Parliament be so dead to its dignity and duty, as to give its support to measures thus obtruded and forced upon it? Measures, he assured their lordships, which had reduced that late flourishing empire to scorn and contempt ! " But yesterday, and Britain might have stood against the world : now none so poor as do her reverence ! " That people whom they had at first despised as rebels, but whom they had now acknowledged as enemies, were abetted against them, supplied with every military store, had their interests consulted, and their (the Americans') ambassadors entertained by their (Britain's) inveterate enemy ; and ministers did not—and dared not—interpose with dignity or effect. The desperate state of their army abroad was in part known. No man more highly esteemed and honoured the British troops than he did; he knew their virtues and their valour; he knew they could achieve anything but impossibilities; and he knew that the conquest of British America was an impossibility. They could not, he told their lordships, they could *not* conquer America. What was their present situation there? They did not know the worst; but they knew that in three campaigns they had done nothing and had suffered much. They might swell every expense, accumulate every assistance, and extend their traffic to the shambles of every German despot: their attempts would be for ever vain and impotent.

Exercise 17

Mrs. Dash-Blank has always found Susan Liskens careful, honest and willing. Susan has been in Mrs. Dash-Blank's service only nine months, but she came with a four years' character and has done nothing to forfeit it. Susan of her own accord leaves Mrs. Dash-Blank.

Mr. Brown presents his compliments to Mr. Johnson, and will be much obliged if Mr. Johnson will keep his dog on his own side of the wall during the day, and on the side of the house remote from Mr. Brown during the night as neither Mr. Brown nor Mrs. Brown gets any sleep while the dog occupies his present position.

If advertiser R. S., 4,309, will call on Mrs. Spross at 47 Arlington Villas he will find a suite of rooms that fulfills all the conditions he specifies. Mrs. Spross can assure him that nothing will be wanting on her part to make him comfortable. She does her own washing, so the advertiser may rely upon having his linen well attended to.

Exercise 18

1. (a) For do I now persuade God or do I persuade men? (b) For do I now persuade God or do men persuade Him? 2. (a) We know little of his hearers as individuals. (b) We as individuals know little of his hearers. 3. (a) I shall read your verses at once. (b) I shall not waste time reading your verses. 4. (a) Drink to me with your eyes only. (b) Drink to me alone with your eyes. 5. (a) You cannot pass from that place where by His decree you are fixed. (b) By His decree you cannot pass from the place where you are fixed. 6. (a) . . . is a poor thing, a small portrait of, etc. (b) . . . who was sister of Rossetti and a poor thing. 7. (a) . . . character not the profession makes the man. (b) . . . makes the man but does not make the profession. 8. (a) That is either a man's voice or a woman's. (b) If that is not a man, it is the voice of a woman. 9. (a) For sale a fine bulldog which is fond of children and is not dainty about its food. (b) . . . eats anything, particularly children. 10. (a) The timid creatures . . . (b) The terrible creatures . . .

Exercise 19

(*a*) The Honourable Mrs. Jamieson, who has just left me, told me in the course of conversation that she had received a call yesterday from her husband's former friend, Lord Mauleverer. You will not easily guess what brought his lordship to our little town. It was to see Captain Brown, whom it appears he had known in the wars, and who had somehow saved his lordship's life off the Cape of Good Hope. Knowing Mrs. Jamieson's lack of innocent curiosity you will not be surprised to learn that she could not tell me how the thing occurred. I was curious to know how Captain Brown, with his small house, could put up so distinguished a guest; and I discovered that his lordship slept at the Angel but had his meals with the Browns, during the two days he stayed at Cranford. From the butcher's wife I learn that Miss Jessie bought a leg of lamb, but besides this I can hear of no preparation whatever for so distinguished a visitor. Perhaps the entertainment was mainly intellectual, and we who know Captain Brown's sad want of relish for good English may be glad he has had the opportunity of improving his taste by talking with a cultured nobleman. But who is altogether free from some earthly failings?

(*b*) All that I know is that it is a Miss Hawkins of Bath : but I do not understand how you could hear it, Mr. Knightley; for it is not five minutes since I received Mrs. Cole's note, and the very moment she was told it by her husband she wrote to me.

(c) 1. Omit either *annual* or *every year*. 2. The reluctant boy goes to school because he must [*reluctant* cannot be cut out. Though a boy must go to school, it does not follow that he goes reluctantly.] 3. *There's* a type of man that cannot allow that anybody possesses principles for which he is prepared to argue. Such is the base condition of that person standing amongst you that he cannot recognise an honest man when he meets him. 4. Omit *previously*. 5. Omit *downward* or *descending*. 6. Omit any two of the three : *free, gratis, for nothing*. 7. I put on my hat and walked into the Strand. 8. The sentence is useless as it stands. Probably what was meant is : She and her brother are twins. 9. He was mounted on a horse. 10. The defaulter was sent to London by train. 11. This sentence is nonsense. There is no connection between the two clauses. Put a period after *song*. Then add : The air was moist, etc. 12. Omit *elder*. 13. Meaningless as it stands : The sentence means : This picture is beyond comparison the best picture in that gallery. 14. For *make the remark that* substitute *say*.

Exercise 20

1. In every occurrence there are some elements which are recognised by only a few. 2. It would be quite unfair to read party newspapers and form our opinions upon them. 3. Judged from this point of view the picture may present an aspect entirely different from that it presents

to a person without the same knowledge. 4.
We have no universal law to include everything
under its sway [*under its sway* might be with
advantage omitted]. 5. Here *though* suggests
that well-worn grooves are not usually smooth,
which is untrue : *smooth because well-worn* would
be nearer the truth. *Smooth through use* ex-
presses what is meant. 6. The arguments of
each may . . . 7. Omit *without reason* :
mechanism never has reason. 8. *These* data :
data is plural. 9. Omit *and exhaustive*, for
complete includes *exhaustive* 10. Omit *and which
is wrong*. 11. For *them* read *him*. 12. Omit
too much, as these words would imply that we
ought to be somewhat, though not excessively,
prejudiced. 13. *On* or *about* our views. 14.
In thinking or discussion of any sort . . . [The
change is necessary to keep the two important
words together. As the sentence stands *sort*
has too much prominence.] 15. Although two
apparently opposing opinions may be formed
closer examination may show that both are
absolutely correct. 16. The newspaper man puts
in a great many unnecessary details in order to
add to the number of lines, since he is paid at
the rate of a penny per line. [As the sentence
stands it means that the more unnecessary details
he can introduce the greater the number of
pennies paid for each line.] 17. . . . *are* the
same. 18. This sentence is hopeless as it stands.
Observe particularly the vicious repetition of *use*.
Probably the meaning intended may be thus
expressed. The main advantage of political
clubs and literary societies is the practice they
afford in debate. 19. There is no more difficult
thing than to see both sides of a question, or . . .

than to look at a subject from our opponent's standpoint. 20. Seldom do we get any one who thinks exactly like his neighbour, and never do we get many persons who think absolutely alike on a subject. [As the sentence stands it implies that many persons *may* sometimes think absolutely alike, but two persons never.]

Exercise 21

1. Broken construction: omit *at*, or substitute *he* for *there*. 2. Loose participle: After thinking for a long time she hit upon a bright idea. 3. Wrong future: shall I. 4. Wrong sequence of tenses: wished to submit. 5. Since *every* is distributive *health* should be singular: every one may have abilities and live under circumstances, but he can have only one health. 6. Clumsy agreement of verb and noun: It was no joke to feed five score. 7. False reference of other: a fish is not a " beast of the forest ", so omit *other*. 8. Double negative: omit *not*. 9. Loose participle: . . . all turned their thoughts towards supper. 10. Misapplication of word; only creatures having will can be unanimous: There was none that did not admire this poem. 11. Misapplication of word: Through debt he died in poverty. 12. Wrong use of the possessive, and mixed metaphor: We admit the generosity of the gift, but the Town Council in accepting it will, we believe, be found to have made a bad bargain. 13. Lack of proper limitation of statement: Paris is larger than any other city in France. 14. False

agreement : . . . those who cannot describe what they do not see. 15. Wrong order : Three times daily before meals put one of the pills in a little water and swallow it. [Even in this form the *it* is a little ambiguous. The whole sentence should be re-cast.] 16. Tautology : Omit " everything till to-morrow ", or substitute " putting off " for " procrastinating ". 17. Bad arrangement : The sparring with words between Benedick and Beatrice, who says " nobody marks you ", and yet she herself does, makes us wonder how all that will end. [Even when Beatrice and Benedick are brought together the sentence is ill balanced : perhaps " who . . . does " might be marked off by dashes.] 18. Wrong limitation : Little Hop-o'-my-thumb was cleverer than any of his brothers. 19. Misapplication of phrase : We cannot " come between " a marriage . . . she had prevented. 20. Contradiction between the two parts of the sentence : If we let her have her wish there is no need to aid her towards the consummation of it, though we may aid towards the consummation of further wishes.

Exercise 22

(*a*) 1. If this juggler does well I'll get him as high-class an audience as can be attracted here. For my part I always like to praise a poor fellow who does his best, however feeble that best may be ; for there always remains the satisfaction of having done a good turn. To make a poor juggler happy suits my humour more than to see the best juggling in the world. But crowds are ill to please and cruel as the Holy . . . Shall we all go now in company?

2. (A free rendering.) Let but this juggler do well, and I'll get him a first-rate audience. It suits my humour to reward a poor fellow's best. If one has little pleasure in the juggling, one has always the satisfaction of having done a good turn. But crowds are cruel and hard to please. Let us all go in company.

(b) 1. It is worth while repeating the story that old Sir Roger Chamloe, who was at one time Chief Justice, used to tell about himself. When he was Senior Barrister of the Inns of Court he was called upon to deal with some young men who had been guilty of certain misdemeanours. As it was well known that Sir Roger in his youth had been himself a roystering blade, one of the boldest of the culprits pled that they were young fellows, and that wise men before them had sowed their wild oats, and were now none the worse. The knight, however, was equal to the occasion. He admitted that as a youth he had behaved like them, but he pointed out that all his twelve comrades in evil had come to a bad end. Accordingly he urged the delinquents to follow the counsel of his age, rather than the example of his youth, if they had any desire to attain to either his years or his rank, and warned them that their present course was leading straight to poverty, if not indeed to the scaffold.

2. (A free rendering.). Old Sir Roger Chamloe, Chief Justice of England, used to tell how, when he was an official at the Inns of Court, some young fellows were brought before him on a charge of breach of discipline. Their spokes-

man, knowing that Sir Roger had himself had a stormy youth, pled that they were spirited young men and had done no more than many had done before them, without harm to any one. The judge wisely admitted that he himself had erred like them in his youth, but explained that the result in his case was exceptional. He alone of all the band of roystering blades to which he had once belonged had not come to a bad end. He therefore urged the culprits to follow the advice of his mature years rather than the example of his callow youth.

(*c*) During the fortnight we stayed here our amusements were both numerous and delightful; nothing in fact could be more attractive. Before breakfast we both walked on the pier, my master in a blue marine jacket, and I in a grand new livery. We were both provided with marine binoculars with which we carefully examined the sea and all the petty details connected with it, from the fishwives down to the little waves playing leap frog like children and tumbling over one another in their hurry to get to shore as if anxious to enjoy the peace of dry land.

After breakfast we went down to the beach again, each of us to his own place—for in this foreign town my post involved no work—and examined the marine details as before. This lasted till dinner, and dinner kept us busy till bed-time, and bed-time tided us over till next day, with its breakfast, dinner, and marine details as before. Year in and year out all the people here, including as I am told some ten thousand fortunate English people, lead this pleasant life.

(*d*) " Well, let it be the presbytery," said I,

for I saw that my wife's patience, none too firm at the best, was giving way. I know exactly how much it will stand, as indeed I ought to by this time. " Well, the court met and was constituted."

" What does that mean? " asked Rob Adair.

" Faith, I don't know. You must ask the clerk. These were his words," said I. " Then there were reports and columns of figures like children's exercises in arithmetic. But nobody attended much and there was a good deal of general conversation till the clerk called out ' Order '. There was silence for half a minute, and then they were all at it again. Indeed the clerk himself talked when he was off his guard."

" Dear me ! So that's a presbytery. I thought it was like a week of sacraments ! " said my wife.

" Far from that," said I, " for of all fighting creatures pigeons and clergymen are the most quarrelsome."

" Did our minister fight ? " asked my wife pointedly.

" No, he was rather a peacemaker in a way," said I cautiously. " Of course a man must sometimes speak his mind."

" Oh, he never does anything wrong, our minister, I understand," replied she drily.

" You surely are not the man to find fault with your own church," said Rob. Sometimes I fear that old Rob is beginning to dote a little.

Exercise 23

Were it true that, given ideas, words will cause no difficulty, it would follow that the most learned man is the most eloquent—a conclusion contrary to experience. Words, as well as matter, demand our attention. Indeed many eminent authors find the effort of expression greater than that of thought. Frequently the lack of a single word necessitates the reconstruction of a whole paragraph, and when all difficulties have been overcome, the result seldom pleases the author.

Exercise 24

Material for essay on Railway Station (arranged according to second method in Lesson XXIV).

1. What does it look like? What general impressions have you? High, murky, smoke-encrusted roof, network of gleaming rails below, trains, great engines vomiting smoke, long grey platforms, porters with trucks, high piles of luggage, waiting taxis, hurrying people, bookstalls, newspaper-boys, chocolate-sellers, perambulating tea-urns, endless crowds, continuous bustle, etc., etc.

2. What is its character and use?

Centre of communications, focus-point of great network of lines, beginning and ending of journeys, home of the engines, importance in commerce and organisation of transport, for the traveller a starting-point of adventure, for the little boy a lasting fascination, etc., etc.

3. What special associations has it for you? (It is only possible here to suggest some associations that may be general.) Starting holidays: luggage, clothes, odd parcels, picnic baskets, excited children, etc.

Returning from holidays : as children, bringing back beloved possessions—spades and buckets, damp seaweed, twisted shells, smooth pebbles, sticky pink rock. The whole family sunburned and somewhat shabby.

Seeing friends off : Embarrassment of finding conversation for the last five minutes, last messages, repeated good-byes, waving of handkerchiefs, etc., etc.

(*Note.*—It is worth while to see how G. K. Chesterton has treated the subject in his essay " On Railway Stations.")

Exercise 25

(*b*) " This must be the place," said Ann as, turning a bend in the lane, they came in sight of a white-washed cottage by the edge of the wood. A straggling hedge screened it in front, and a rusty gate opened on to a gravelled path, leading between empty flower-beds to a faded green front door. It was locked and bolted, but through the uncurtained windows they could peer into a little low-roofed parlour. Plaster, fallen from walls and ceiling, lay thick upon the floor, and a spider had built his web across the empty grate. They tip-toed round to the back. Grass stood high where once the lawn had been, and the lily pond was thick with fallen leaves. The kitchen door stood ajar, for the latch was broken, and brown leaves had drifted in across the floor. A narrow creaking staircase led out of the kitchen, and ended in a dusky passage. There were three small attics and in one of them a long coffin-shaped bath. Ann gazed doubtfully at the cracked, greying paint, the ancient geyser. " H. & C.," said William gloomily. " It's very old-world," said Ann.

(In this description, the details are selected to emphasise the air of dereliction, the rest omitted.)

Exercise 26

In order to see how the subject is treated by a master, turn to Addison's " Adventures of a Shilling " as told by him in the *Tatler*. To begin with, he takes off the edge of the unreality of the composition by making it the outcome of a reverie which " cannot be so properly called a dream as a delirium ". The actual adventure should be read in the original.

Exercise 27

13 INGLEBOROUGH AVENUE,
WIRENCESTER, 16*th July*, 1937.

The Stationmaster,
    L. & N. W. Railway,
        Bletchley.

DEAR SIR,
            To-day I travelled in a third-class compartment in the train leaving Euston at 3 P.M. and reaching Bletchley at 4.58 P.M. Be-

tween these two stations I have lost a silk umbrella. The stick is thin and green; the handle is straight, widening gradually into a silver top, which is not a knob. If it has not turned up at Bletchley, will you please wire to the terminus of the train in question to find whether the umbrella has been found there. I shall be glad to send a postal order for 10s. by way of reward if the umbrella is sent to me at the above address. A note of your expenses in the matter will have my immediate attention.

Yours truly,
GEORGE MAIDENHEAD.

13 INGLEBOROUGH AVENUE,
WIRENCESTER, 16*th July*, 1937.

DEAR MRS. HICKSON,
Please would you look all through my rooms to make sure that I have not left that new umbrella—with the green stick and the silver top—that came to me by parcel post the other day. If you do find it, make it up into a parcel, and send Susan with it to the Globe Parcel Express in Worcester Road. She knows the place. I enclose an addressed label which you will stick on the parcel. If you do not find the new umbrella do *not* send any of the others.

Yours truly,
GEORGE MAIDENHEAD.

13 INGLEBOROUGH AVENUE,
WIRENCESTER, 16*th July*, 1937.

DEAR JERKYNS,

Would you mind taking a look round
in my corner to see if I have left my green-
handled, silver-topped silk umbrella anywhere
about? It is a present from my " expectations "
aunt, who is due at the Rushtons' here on the
18th. I remember that I did not put it in the
stand along with the others, so anxious was I
not to forget it, when I set out for the train in
the afternoon. I have an impression that I had
the wretched thing with me in the train, and that
I put it in the rack. I have written to the railway people, but I write you also as there is no
time to be lost if I am to make a respectable
impression on the 18th. If the thing is lurking
in the neighbourhood of my desk make it worth
Billy's while to send it here by passenger train,
and charge the damages to me.

Yours ever,
G. MAIDENHEAD.

13 INGLEBOROUGH AVENUE,
WIRENCESTER, 16*th July*, 1937.

MY DEAR VI.,

I wonder if you remember the gamp
Aunt Matilda gave me on my birthday—thin
green stick, straight top, silver-tipped (just like
yours, only thicker and less silver), silk stuff.
Well, so far as I can make out, it is now lost.
Of course she bought it at Akenside's. There

221

must be others of the same kind in stock. If you get a wire from me to-morrow with the message *buy*, then go straight to Akenside's, buy as near a match to the lost umbrella as you can get, and get him to send it to me here by passenger train (Midland). If you don't get a wire by noon, that will mean that the lost umbrella has turned up.

The enclosed P.O.O. for 30s. is all I can afford to send. I am sure the wretched thing did not cost more, but at any price I must have a duplicate before I can face the old lady on Thursday.

Now, *don't* buy an umbrella or do anything more in the matter unless you get a wire. If the thing turns up you may keep the 30s. for your honesty.

Yours ever,

GEORGE.

In these letters there is a difference in tone corresponding to the relation between Maidenhead and his correspondent. The station-master and the landlady are not at all interested in Maidenhead's reason for recovering the umbrella; so no mention is made of the aunt. Inexperienced writers often expose themselves to ridicule by putting unnecessary details into letters to strangers. Jerkyns himself should not be told about the aunt unless Maidenhead and he are on very friendly terms. Even here, however, it is well to avoid naming her. In writing to the sister, Maidenhead might have omitted the slang term " gamp "; but in familiar letters we must not be pedantic so long as clearness is not sacrificed. It is a wise rule, all the same, to avoid any expression about the propriety of which you have any doubt. The very fact that you question the fitness of an expression should condemn that expression. Note too the different directions about how the umbrella is to be sent, if found. The stationmaster gets no instructions at all; Jerkyns merely gets the hint to send it by passenger train. The clerk is supposed to know how to despatch a parcel, but the landlady gets minute directions, while the sister is told to get the shopman to send the umbrella.

Exercise 28

See Leigh Hunt's essay on this same subject, which he treats from a very personal standpoint.

Exercise 29

(a) THE RENAISSANCE.

I. New birth of the world beginning about middle of fifteenth century.

Two previous but minor Renaissances.

(1) Time of Charlemagne.
(2) Thirteenth century.

II. Causes—

A. Immediate—Taking of Constantinople and scattering of Greek scholars.

B. Ultimate—

  (1) Invention of printing and consequent spread of inquiry.
  (2) Invention of gumpowder and consequent fall of feudalism.
  (3) Progress of geographical discovery and consequent breadth of view.

III. Results—

  A. Broadening of interests.
  B. Recognition of the solidarity of humanity.

IV. The passing of the new spirit—end of Renaissance.

  A. Mistaking the letter for the spirit.
  B. Reformers became bigots, and scholars became pedants.

(b) THE EXCEPTION PROVES THE RULE.

I. As commonly used this proverb is false. Example : the rule *No quadruped lays eggs* is disproved by the exception *Crocodiles lay eggs*.

II. Distinction between two ways of regarding proverb.

  A. Inductively : Passing from examples to the rule.
    Here the proverb is false.
  B. Deductively : Passing from the rules to examples.
    Here the proverb is true.

III. Deduction does not express the exception
as such.

> Good boys die young—adjective *good*
> excepts all other boys.
> Therefore we have the rule proved—bad
> boys do not die young.

IV. Silliness of the proverb as usually used.
> When used inductively very misleading.
> When used deductively tends to clear
> expression.

Exercise 30

SHAKESPEARE'S TREATMENT OF THE SUPERNATURAL

" After God, Shakespeare created most."
For once, an epigram speaks true. Hugo's
phrase conjures up an infinite company—Hamlet sad-coated, Lear " fantastically crowned ",
Falstaff and Prince Hal sauntering arm-in-arm,
Shylock and Antonio, Beatrice, Benedick, Bottom the Weaver. . . . They are shadows, yet
more real than life ; their vitality is greater than
our own. And what of the other creatures of
his creation—ghosts and witches haunting the
confines of darkness, Warwickshire fairies, brutish
Caliban, delicate Ariel ? In the supernatural
world, Shakespeare's imagination moves most
freely. So long as men and women are the
subjects of his art, the dramatist is limited by
all the imperfections of humanity ; but in fairyland and the dread domain of the weird sisters
he can give full scope to his imagination. It has
been complained of Shakespeare that he makes

his characters of every age and country express themselves in the forms of his own time, and there is of necessity an element of truth in the objection. But in the supernatural world all this is changed. Nature is jealous of the copyright of humanity, but the poet may evade her claims by crossing Styx, just as the publisher evades the poet's by crossing the Atlantic.

Living in the world Shakespeare was emphatically of the world. He had none of your philosopher's contempt for mere earthly things, yet he dearly loved a flight into cloudland. In such flights he carried with him his broad human sympathies, and imparted to the airy nothings just so much of human nature as rendered them intelligible to ordinary men. It is true that there are some men who do not consider themselves " ordinary ", to whom all that is not tangible or demonstrable is folly. For such matter-of-fact philosophers is the apologetic tone of *A Midsummer Night's Dream* intended. But Shakespeare has his revenge, for the dullards who could see nothing but childishness in the fairy gambols were led to laugh at their own reflection in " sweet bully Bottom " and his friends.

In giving a kind of reality to the supernatural agents, Shakespeare has, as elsewhere, seized upon the universal side of his subject. " In literature as in love," says Heine, " the secret of success is to dare." Who would now dare to introduce a real live fairy into poem or novel? Yet now, as in Shakespeare's time, men have a hungering after the supernatural. Every one with imagination enough " to raise the ghost of a fishwife " would like to believe in fairyland,

and secretly resents the cold insensibility with which Reason explains away Titania and all her train. On this point modern writers have made a compromise, which, as is natural, satisfies neither reason nor fancy. Who does not remember the rude shock which his credulity—the charm of childhood—received on first reading at the end of a thrilling tale of enchantment the depressing sentence—" And I awoke ". Heine himself, daring as he is in other fields, often thus falls asleep over his lyrics. Shakespeare, however, introduces us to no mere shades. Titania and Oberon are as real to us as Joan of Arc and Hotspur. In *A Midsummer Night's Dream* the fairies are but human beings whose smaller growth is compensated by increased powers. They must use means to attain their ends, and though the means be powerful they sometimes bungle their application. Oberon sets himself up as a kind of Providence to " human mortals ", and is sadly perplexed at the peculiar results of his good intentions. Puck confesses that " fate o'er-rules ", and thus establishes a bond of sympathy between the spirits and those mortals at whose folly he laughs. The fairies do not derive their interest merely from their influence on the other characters, they are in themselves attractive. Shakespeare lets us into the secret of all the intrigues of fairyland, but the disclosure of the hidden springs which move the natural and supernatural world of Athens, far from destroying the interest, lends a new charm to the whole.

A Midsummer Night's Dream marks the highest point to which the mere fairy of literature ever attained. Before this play, the fairy had too close a connection with the hobgoblin; after it the progress of higher education not only predisposed men to disbelieve in fairies, but actually corrupted the fairies themselves. When we find them singing Latin songs,[1] we are in some sort prepared for the shock of recognising Oberon's legitimate descendants in the monstrosities in " ism " and " ation " which tantalise the readers of " instructive books for the young ".

By as much as the ethereal Puck transcends the gross Robin Goodfellow of popular superstition with his coarse Ho ! ho ! ho ! by so much does Ariel transcend Puck. Puck may be said to be, in the language of popular novelists, founded upon fact, Ariel is a pure creation of the fancy. In however short a time Puck can girdle the earth, he is but an agent to carry out the directions of his master, and blunders even in that. Ariel has merely to be told what Prospero wishes, and it is accomplished with " no mistakings ". Yet Ariel is but Puck caught, tamed and educated. The spirit now " tricksy " in his master's interest was formerly mischievous enough in his own, and his true nature is shown in the use he makes of his liberty. He lapses into the fairy life from which Prospero's art had for a while withdrawn him. *The Tempest* is indeed the converse of *A Midsummer Night's Dream.* Man and fairy change places. Prospero dethrones Oberon and himself assumes the part of Providence. This combination of natural and supernatural forces is powerful but not all powerful. Charles Lamb is disappointed that Prospero went quietly into the boat without at least raising a storm or two; and certainly it

[1] Randolph's *Amyntas* (1640 A.D.).

seems strange that nearly twenty years should be allowed to elapse before the " so potent art " was put in operation against the usurper. But it must be remember that had Prospero been omnipotent there would have been no tale to tell.

Perhaps there is no other play of Shakespeare's in which the ideal meaning is so conspicuous as in *The Tempest*. Ariel represents the imagination of man in its widest sense—scientific as well as poetic. We have here man triumphing over nature, as in *A Midsummer Night's Dream* we have man subject to nature. It may be said that the liberation of Ariel spoils all these fine theories, and in a sense this is true. But the breakdown in the hidden meaning arises from the harmony of the story, and is really one of the beauties of the play, illustrating as it does one of the finest characteristics of Shakespeare. He is an artist first, a moralist or a philosopher only in the second place. The " dainty Ariel " would have been utterly out of place in the civic life of Milan, hence he was liberated, and the moral was left to take care of itself. In fact Shakespeare's hidden meanings were intended only for men with intelligence enough to take them in as a whole. To such minds hints are sufficient, the details can be easily filled in. Some characters in the plays indeed seem to have many meanings which may be read in them, to say nothing of those which may be read into them. Caliban represents the untutored savage drinking the " water with berries in it ", brutalised humanity, and evil forces as opposed to the good in Ariel. All these points are hinted at in the play, but none of them is brought into such prominence that the unity of the story is at all marred.

The simple man reads it as a story, and is satisfied.

Even this subordinate degree of undermeaning detracts from the artistic value of the work. The highest poetry is that which combines reality and ideality : the poem must be perfectly ideal and yet accepted as true. This is recognised even in the nursery, where the question, " Is it true ? " must be answered in the affirmative before the promised story has much chance of success. A boy by a strong effort of the imagination can realise to himself Swift's Lilliputians and Yahoos. Explain the satire, and the boy's mind becomes divided between real Yahoos and shadowy abstractions, and finally falls back upon his faithful Crusoe, of whose existence he has no doubt. In the same way, though in a less degree, we are disturbed in our belief in the reality of Prospero and his powers.

All this is changed when we consider Shakespeare's ghosts. They have no secret meaning, they come for a definite purpose, accomplish it, and are gone. Again they appeal to a more universal instinct than do the fairies. It is a part of man's nature to seek to pry into futurity, to seek to know something of that great unknown land to which we are all journeying. Besides, Shakespeare's ghosts no more resemble those of our churchyards than Titania the fairy of common superstition. The ghost in *Hamlet* is no white-sheeted spectre, but a majestic warrior wearing a well-known suit of armour. Banquo's ghost is but Banquo invisible to all save Macbeth. It is true that in the interest of reality the former is subject to the insulting power of chanticleer, and is condemned " to walk the night ", though why he should object to a cool walk on a breezy night after a day spent in "sulphurous and tormenting flames" is not set forth. Such ghosts, and those that appear in *Richard III.* and *Julius Cæsar*, are quite conceivable. They represent persons who once lived upon this earth, and moreover their common purpose is distinctly human—revenge. They all come of their own accord, at any rate, no human influence calls them up. Though they come, however, with a common purpose, they do not seek it by a common method. Hamlet's father hands over the business to his son. Julius Cæsar merely intimates disaster, but he appears personally to his enemy; the ghosts in *Richard III.* simply give utterance to their good and bad wishes; Banquo alone says nothing, yet he has most effect. Only in *Hamlet* and *Macbeth* is the ghost of paramount importance, in the other two cases it is a mere incident.

Compared with the fairies the ghosts command readier belief, but they fail on their ideal side. Like photographs they are too true to life—to real life, not to ghost life—but this is compensated for by the use made of them. Unlike the fairies they are in themselves unattractive, and we are interested in them only in so far as they affect the characters in the play. They are but means; the fairies are both means and ends. The ghosts are placed before us with no character save that which they carried with them from this life, with no apparent relation to spirit-land, or at least none that they are allowed to explain; in short they merely appear in order to finish off those tag ends of life which their hurried departure prevented them from attending to. They act on the same principles as those on which we should expect them to act were Shakespeare, like Scott in a notable case, to call back any of them from the dead. Hamlet could have been made to discover for himself the treachery of the new King, yet there is no waste of spiritual energy in the play. Whatever else the author wished to express he certainly intended to draw a picture of the most pronounced irresolution, and for this the ghost was a most useful instrument. Hamlet disbelieved in the ghost till he saw it : even after seeing it he doubted the truth of its utterances, and this doubt is at the root of the movement of half the play. Banquo's ghost has no such outstanding part to perform, it merely takes its place in a whole world of horrors.

The witches occupy an intermediate place between the fairies and the ghosts : they are in themselves more interesting than the latter and less interesting than the former. In *Macbeth* the witches have some system of organisation the exact nature of which is artistically suppressed. Philosophy is mingled with the loathsome gibberish of their rites, and their aims are higher than to crook an arm or waste a liver. They hunt not bodies, but souls. It has been ingeniously suggested that the witches are three in number because they represent past, present and future time—Glamis, Cawdor, King; and there is nothing against the hypothesis. Three is a convenient number, a mystic number, an odd number, and " Witchcraft loveth numbers odd ". In a tragic work like *Macbeth* it is important to introduce the supernatural in its most plausible form, and nowhere has Shakepeare been more successful than here. The English nation were prepared to believe in fairies and ghosts, but they felt bound to believe in witches. To deny their existence was blasphemy: were they not mentioned in Scripture? In 1584 Reginald Scot in his *Discovery of Witchcraft* maintains that people would have believed as strongly in fairies as in witches were it not that "it hath not pleased the translators of the Bible to call spirits by the name of Robin Goodfellow".

With these awful powers, then, Shakespeare opens *Macbeth*. Whence they come and wherefore is left untold. All that we know is that they are seeking to obtain the soul of the honourable and courageous general, Macbeth. The weird sisters may be regarded at the beginning of the play as the fates, at the end as the furies. Yet with all their power they are not absolute: "amen" is not the only word with which man may reply to their machinations. Nor can they be even said to fight unfairly against humanity: they tell no lies. If Macbeth fall he must blame his interpretation, not their statements. Like Mephistopheles in Marlowe's *Faust* they seem to be compelled, however much against their will, to speak the truth, even at the risk of breaking the fifth commandment. The subordinate apparitions are in perfect keeping with traditional witchcraft, and with the *motif* of the play. It would be rash to assert dogmatically what Shakespeare meant to express in *Macbeth*; yet to a mind like his, delighting to toy with intellectual edge-tools, nothing could be more attractive than the ever-present question of fate and freewill. Instead of trying to solve the insoluble problem by a quarrel with some neighbour, he quietly writes a drama of thrilling interest for every one, in which is contained an example of the harmonious action of fate and freewill. Macbeth is quite evidently doomed from the first, yet at no point can we stop and say that here he was forced to act thus and thus. This may seem rather a frivolous view of a very solemn question, but it certainly is in keeping with Shakespeare's character. He knew too well the difficulties of a question to answer it absolutely one way or another.

Be this as it may, it is certain that the play does not suffer for the sake of the moral. But besides this artistic indifference to " leading ideas ", which we have marked throughout, there is another peculiarity in Shakespeare's treatment of the supernatural—it is always used in an organic relation to the development of the plot.

A very effective use is sometimes made of the supernatural in supplying a suitable setting for certain incidents. A notable case is found in *Julius Cæsar*, where Casca's description of the weird sights he has seen prepares a fitting atmosphere for the events that are to follow. So with the comet brandishing its crystal tresses in the sky " importing change of times and states ". Full well Shakespeare knew the power of the materials he used :—

" Look how the poor world's people are amaz'd
At apparitions, signs and prodigies ".

Still more important is the use Shakespeare makes of the supernatural in developing character. In few ways can we get more directly at a man's character than by a study of his superstitions. The fiends that appear to Joan of Arc in the first part of *Henry VI.* are really symbols to express the popular estimate of her character, and of the English gallantry which could overcome both man and devil. Shakespeare does not make her a witch in revenge for her victories over the English, but because she was burned as a witch, and that—in the popular opinion of his time—justly. The spirit raised by Bolingbroke in the second part of *Henry VI.* is a counterpart of the " juggling fiends " of *Macbeth*. Throughout this play there runs a thread of poetic cursing that reminds one of Gray's " Bard ". The curse and its effect are skilfully varied as speaker and hearer change. The wild Celtic egotism of Owen Glendower is developed in a special kind of superstition which glorifies himself and ruins his fellow rebels. The same fitness in the supernatural relations of men and shades is maintained through all the plays. The King, cut off in his sins, is " doomed" to walk. Banquo's ghost has a kind of ghastly enjoyment in shaking his gory locks at his murderer, but the gracious Duncan is too good to be compelled to return from the spirit world, and too gentle to return of his own accord to increase Macbeth's misery.

INDEX

236

ADVERTISING & PUBLICITY   ALGEBRA   AMATEUR ACTING   AN
BOOK-KEEPING   BRICKWORK   BRINGING UP CHILDREN   BUSIN
CHESS   CHINESE   COMMERCIAL ARITHMETIC   COMMERCIAL
COMPOSE MUSIC   CONSTRUCTIONAL DETAILS   CONTRACT BRIDG
SPEEDWORDS   ECONOMIC GEOGRAPHY   ECONOMICS   ELEC
ENGLISH GRAMMAR   LITERARY APPRECIATION   ENGLISH RENA
REVIVAL   VICTORIAN AGE   CONTEMPORARY LITERATURE   ETC
FREELANCE WRITING   FRENCH   FRENCH DICTIONARY   FRENC
LIVING THINGS   GEOLOGY   GEOMETRY   GERMAN   GERMA
GOOD CONTROL OF INSECT PESTS   GOOD CONTROL OF PLANT DI
GOOD FARMING BY MACHINE   GOOD FARM WORKMANSHIP   GO
GOOD MARKET GARDENING   GOOD MILK FARMING   GOOD PIG
GOOD ENGLISH   GREEK   GREGG SHORTHAND   GUIDEBOOK TO
GREAT BOLIVAR BOTHA   CATHERINE THE GREAT   CHATHAM CL
LIBERALISM   HENRY V   JOAN OF ARC   JOHN WYCLIFFE   LENIN   LOU
ROBES   HASTIN
HOUS   EPAIR
WRITE   **GIVE INSTRUCTION**   ND TO
MECH   LCRA
MOTO   **TO A WISE MAN···**   FICIEN
PHYSI   DESI
ADMI   NG
PHRA   OOK   SAILING   SALESMANSHIP   SECRETA   ACTIO
DEBATE   SPELLING   STAMP COLLECTING   STUDE   DE
TYPEWRITING   USE OF GEOGRAPHY   WAY TO POETR   W
COOKERY FOR GIRLS   DOGS AS PETS FOR BOYS AND GIRLS   K
PHOTOGRAPHY FOR BOYS AND GIRLS   RADIO FOR BOYS   RIDIN
SOCCER FOR BOYS   STAMP COLLECTING FOR BOYS AND GIRLS   V
ACTING   ANATOMY   ARABIC   ASTRONOMY   BANKING
CHILDREN   BUSINESS ORGANISATION   CALCULUS   CANASTA
COMMERCIAL ART   COMMERCIAL CORRESPONDENCE   COMM
CONTRACT BRIDGE   COOKING   CRICKET   DRAWING   DR
ECONOMICS   ELECTRICITY   ELECTRICITY IN THE HOUSE   ELO
ENGLISH RENASCENCE   ENGLISH RENASCENCE TO THE ROMAN
LITERATURE   ETCHING   EVERYDAY FRENCH   TO EXPRESS YOU
DICTIONARY   FRENCH PHRASE BOOK   GARDENING   GAS IN
GERMAN   GERMAN DICTIONARY   GERMAN GRAMMAR   GERM
CONTROL OF PLANT DISEASES   GOOD FARM ACCOUNTING
GOOD FARM WORKMANSHIP   GOOD FRUIT FARMING   GOOD C
GOOD MILK FARMING   GOOD PIG KEEPING   GOOD POULTRY K
GREGG SHORTHAND   GUIDEBOOK TO THE BIBLE   HINDUSTANI
CATHERINE THE GREAT   CHATHAM CLEMENCEAU   CONSTANTINE
ARC   JOHN WYCLIFFE   LENIN   LOUIS XIV   MILTON   PERICLES   PETER
USE OF HISTORY   WARREN HASTINGS   WOODROW WILSON   HOO
HOUSEHOLD ELECTRICITY   HOUSE REPAIRS   ITALIAN   JOINE
MANAGEMENT   MATHEMATICS   HAND TOOLS   ENGINEERIN
DRAUGHTSMANSHIP   METEOROLOGY   MODELCRAFT   MODERN D
MUSIC   NORWEGIAN   PERSONAL EFFICIENCY   PHILOSOPHY   P
SHORTHAND   PLANNING AND DESIGN   PLUMBING   POLISH

A Comeback Begins in Earnest

It was old-fashioned training, the way it used to be—no crowds, no frills, just riding and more riding. Lance went out every day and rode in all kinds of weather. The experience brought Lance back to earlier days and he began to just enjoy the act of riding hard, of feeling his body tire, of working against the elements and pressing on. In the evenings the men ate and talked and laughed about old times, all the things that had brought Lance so close to the pinnacle of his sport before his illness had struck. Going to North Carolina was almost like going back in time, when things were much simpler, when Lance would get on his bike and attack, just one man against everyone else. . . .

Books by BILL GUTMAN

Sports Illustrated: Baseball's Record Breakers
Sports Illustrated: Great Moments in Baseball
Sports Illustrated: Great Moments in Pro Football
Sports Illustrated: Pro Football's Record Breakers
Baseball Super Teams
Bo Jackson: A Biography
Football Super Teams
Grant Hill: A Biography
Great Quarterbacks of the NFL
Great Sports Upsets
Great Sports Upsets 2
Michael Jordan: A Biography
NBA High-Flyers
Pro Sports Champions
Tiger Woods: A Biography
Shaquille O'Neal: A Biography
Brett Favre: A Biography
Ken Griffey Jr.: A Biography
Sammy Sosa: A Biography
Marion Jones: The Fastest Woman in the World

Available from Pocket Books

Lance Armstrong: A Biography

Available from Simon Pulse

LANCE
ARMSTRONG
A BIOGRAPHY

BILL GUTMAN

Simon Pulse

New York London Toronto Sydney Singapore

First Simon Pulse edition June 2003
Copyright © 2003 by Bill Gutman

SIMON PULSE
An imprint of Simon & Schuster
Children's Publishing Division
1230 Avenue of the Americas
New York, NY 10020

Designed by Ann Sullivan
The text of this book was set in AGaramond.

Printed in the United States of America
10 9 8 7 6 5 4 3 2 1

Library of Congress Control Number 2002115625
ISBN 0-689-86242-3

To all those people battling a serious illness or
other seemingly insurmountable adversity:
There is always hope.

Table of Contents

Introduction

Every now and then there will be a story from the world of sports that earns the label of "feel good." The feel-good story might be about an underdog team that bucks enormous odds to emerge as champions, such as the New England Patriots in 2001. It might be about a player who comes back after a serious injury to show his critics that his career is not over, something that has happened numerous times in various sports through the years. Or it might even be a once great athlete turning back the clock and creating a moment of greatness everyone had thought long past, such as when an aging Jack Nicklaus won the Masters golf tournament in 1986. These feel-good stories are usually embraced by both press and public alike. In a sense, they humanize sports, taking them out of the realm of money, marketing, and business—elements that have dominated the sports world over the last decade.

Under these circumstances, it's not surprising that feel-good stories always make news, but as heartwarming as they can be, the aura usually fades before long as new heroes and new events unfold. There is, however, one sports story which has been unfolding since 1999. It has undoubtedly been described as "feel-good" many times over, but in reality, it is much more than that. In fact, this may be the most miraculous sports story of the last century. This is rather a far-reaching description, but it would be difficult to find someone to say it is an exaggeration. What makes the story even more amazing is that it just won't go away, and that's because the athlete creating the story continues to remind everyone of what he has accomplished for the last four years.

The athlete is Lance Armstrong and his sport is cycling. If he were just a top cyclist and nothing more, his accomplishments would probably elicit no more than a passing yawn from the majority of the American public. Cycling is a sport that has never been considered major in the United States; it has simply not caught the fancy of a sports-watching populace. But Lance Armstrong has accomplished something that no one—sports fans or otherwise—can ignore. Not only has he won the Tour de France, the world's most prestigious and grueling cycling event, for four straight years, he did it after overcoming a severe case of cancer which, by the time it was diagnosed, had spread to his lungs and brain. Doctors had given him just a forty percent chance of survival.

Someone just hearing this scenario would probably think it came from a disease-of-the-week TV movie rather than from real life, and who could blame them? The odds of an athlete rising from the brink of death to reach the pinnacle of a sport, especially one that takes tremendous strength and endurance, are literally off the scale.

Why is the Tour de France considered by many the world's most grueling sports event? For argument's sake, let's compare the Tour, briefly, with another event that takes tremendous conditioning and endurance—the Ironman Triathlon. The Ironman Triathlon is a one-day event in which competitors begin by swimming 2.4 miles. As soon as they come out of the water, they jump on a bicycle and pedal 112 miles. Once they complete that phase, they jump off the bike, change their shoes, and commence to running 26.2 miles, a marathon-distance run. Top competitors finish the three phases in something over eight hours. The Ironman is certainly a test of conditioning, endurance, and will. But does it really compare to the Tour de France?

The annual Tour de France is not only the

world's most prestigious cycling event, it is also the most physically demanding. The race takes place in stages over a three-week period and covers more than two thousand miles. Some of the stages are time trials, with the riders sprinting from start to finish against the clock. Other stages take place in the Pyrenees and Alps, exhausting mountain climbs that require strategy, strength, and a strong will, not to mention cooperation among teammates. But only one individual can win the Tour, the rider who covers the entire distance in the shortest amount of time.

In the 2002 Tour, for example, the riders were on their bikes for twenty days, with just two rest days in between. Each stage brings the riders to exhaustion, but they have to be ready to go again the next day, ready to climb steep hills and mountains, ready to keep their bikes stable on curving, narrow roads while others ride all around them. It can be dangerous as well as physically draining, and there is no other athletic competition in the world like it.

This is Lance Armstrong's sport of choice, and the event that he has made his own. An American winning four straight Tours in a sport traditionally dominated by Europeans, where cyclists are national heroes, would be a huge story in itself. Before his near-fatal illness, however, Armstrong was not a dominant Tour rider. In fact he was told by his own advisors, early in a promising career, that he didn't have the body type to win the Tour. He was too big, too muscular. In a strange and perhaps ironic way, it was Lance Armstrong's dramatic bout with testicular cancer that would totally change his life for the better, both on and off his bike.

Before being stricken with cancer, Lance was a top cyclist, but not a man considered a threat to win the Tour de France. He simply wasn't a good enough climber and couldn't keep up with the top riders in the mountains. When he returned to racing, his body had changed. He was some twenty pounds lighter, about 160 compared with the 180 pounds he weighed before, and climbing became his forte. In the mountains, no one could keep up with Lance Armstrong.

"When I came back [from cancer]," Armstrong explained, "I said, if I ever get a chance to do this, I'm going to give it everything. I'm going to train correctly, eat right, and not going to mess up. That's why I say all the time that the illness is the best thing that ever happened to me. I would never have won one Tour de France if I hadn't had [cancer]. No doubt."

Perhaps because of his illness, Lance

Armstrong has been able to keep his life in perspective more than most athletes. He has learned to handle adversity, focus on his goals, and achieve them. Despite having won the world's most prestigious cycling race four straight times, he considers himself first and foremost a cancer survivor. To that end, he has been able to inspire countless others, both directly and indirectly, and because of that has become a true American hero. Ironically, had he been a champion cyclist and nothing else, America would hardly have noticed.

1

The Beginnings
of an Athletic Life

There was very little about Lance Armstrong's
beginnings that would suggest a future Tour de
France champion. But then again, there is very
little about any young American boy that
would suggest that. Sure, nearly all kids ride
bicycles, but more of them will gravitate toward
riding BMX bikes and doing tricks than going
out-of-bounds on mountain bikes. Racing generally isn't an option unless it's BMX racing
over rough terrain, full of bumps and jumps.
Add that to the very difficult circumstances
Lance was born into, and there wouldn't have
seemed to be any kind of blueprint for athletic
success.

He was born on September 18, 1971, in

Oak Cliff, Texas, a suburb of Dallas, to a single mother. Her maiden name was Linda Mooneyham and she was just seventeen at the time Lance was born. His father had already left; Lance wouldn't even know who he was for many years. Even after he found out, he said he had no interest in meeting him because there had never been any kind of connection between them. Fortunately, Lance's mother was a very special kind of person who could overcome hardship and was determined to raise her son to the best of her ability. They forged a close bond early on, a bond which remains very strong to this day.

Linda Mooneyham and her son lived in a one-bedroom apartment in Oak Cliff while she worked several part-time jobs and also finished high school. When she finally got a secretarial job, she began making more money and moved with her young son to another suburb north of Dallas called Richardson. She continued to work hard trying to make a better life for herself and Lance, and would later get a job with a telecommunications company and eventually obtain a real-estate license on the side. She is living proof that, through hard work and perseverance, a single mother can make a good life for herself and her child.

When Lance was three, his life changed

again. His mother married a man named Terry Armstrong who would soon legally adopt his stepson, giving him his last name. But Lance wasn't always happy with his stepfather. Terry Armstrong was a tough disciplinarian who wasn't averse to punishing Lance, sometimes for little things. He also used a paddle on occasions, something Lance doesn't remember too fondly. Because of these things, he never forged any kind of close bond with his stepfather.

Then when he was seven, he got his first bike. The family was still living in Richardson then and there was a store across the street from their apartment called the Richardson Bike Mart. The owner was a man named Jim Hoyt who often sponsored bicycle races. Hoyt loved the sport and also took pleasure in introducing young riders to racing. He got to know Lance and his mother, liked them, and finally gave her a deal on what Lance would call his first serious bike, a Schwinn Mag Scrambler. Lance loved it from the first.

He said having the bike represented "independence . . . freedom to roam without rules and without adults." So, if things weren't so good at home with his stepfather, Lance had his bike and could ride. Around this time the family moved again. Doing well at her job, and with a second paycheck coming in from her husband, Linda Armstrong was able to buy a house in nearby Plano, Texas, which was considered an upscale suburb of Dallas.

Even then, Lance had the ability to see things as they were. At first glance, he said it appeared to be the perfect American suburb, but he felt the place had no tradition and that nothing was real. People were very conscious of their status and the poorer people were looked down upon. Like so many other places in Texas, when it came to sports in Plano, football was king. As Lance said, "If you didn't play football, you didn't exist."

Naturally, any kid trying to fit in would try to play football. Lance tried, but soon found he didn't have the proper coordination for the sport. He admitted that he simply wasn't good at any sport that involved a ball, hand-eye coordination, and moving from side to side. Yet he had an athletic mentality, the tenacity needed to compete, and he desperately wanted to find something at which he could be successful. His first taste of athletic success came in a sport where nothing was needed but his own ability to move his body—running.

It began when he was in the fifth grade. That's when his elementary school announced a distance-running race and he entered. Before it started, Lance told his mother he was going to win. Sure enough, he got out front and, with all the determination he could muster, held on and crossed the finish line first. Winning was a new kind of feeling for him, and he liked it. Soon after, he joined a local swim club. At first, he wasn't very good and had to practice with younger kids. It didn't come easily. He worked and worked, and by the time he was twelve, he was a member of the City of Plano Swim Club.

Suddenly, Lance was becoming a very good swimmer. He had a fine coach in Chris MacCurdy, who worked very hard with him, and within a year of joining, he finished fourth in the state in the 1500-meter freestyle in his age group. He seemed to take to sports that required endurance and tenacity. In fact, it was with the Plano Swim Club that he began to develop his tremendous work ethic. He would work out with the swim club from five-thirty to seven A.M. before going to school, and work out again in the afternoon. To add another kind of training, he always rode his bike to and from school, a distance of ten miles each way. So he was swimming some six miles a day and biking twenty. Not bad for a young kid trying to get into shape. And all the while, he was becoming more and more of a quality athlete.

Soon after that, he discovered a sport that seemed a natural for his talents. He was about thirteen when he spotted a flyer for a competition called IronKids. It was a junior triathlon, and combined swimming, bike riding, and running. Young Lance couldn't believe his eyes.

"I had never heard of a triathlon before," he said, "but it was all the things I was good at, so I signed up."

It seemed a natural for him, a combination of three sports, all requiring great endurance, and all sports at which he had practiced or simply taken to, and at which he had begun to excel. He got himself the proper clothing and his first racing bike—a Mercier—which he described as a slim, elegant road bike, and jumped into his first triathlon with no previous experience or specific training. He won the event easily. Soon after, he entered a second triathlon in Houston and won again. Suddenly, Lance felt very good about himself. He had some athletic success at swimming, but had never been the best at anything. Before long, he was the best junior triathlete in the entire state of Texas.

"I liked the feeling," he said, simply and definitively.

What he found out about himself during those first triathlons was that the sport was almost a battle of attrition. Several athletes might have the same skill level, but the one with the will to win, the one willing to push himself with total disregard to how he felt and the strain he was putting on his body, would win. Lance Armstrong soon felt that in this type of event, one where he could grit his teeth and absorb the punishment, he could outlast anyone and win.

A short time after finding his first real sports success, Lance had to deal with another crisis. When he was fourteen, his mother told him she would be asking Terry Armstrong for a divorce. Lance had never really liked his stepfather and didn't hide the fact that he was very happy about it. He made it clear a short time later that he didn't want to continue any kind of relationship with the man who had given him his name. He and his mother now grew closer than ever. No matter what else had happened, they always had each other.

Soon Lance began to concentrate even more on his growing athletic prowess. When he was just fifteen, he entered the 1987 President's Triathlon in Lake Levon, California, where he would be competing against many older and more experienced athletes. There would be no Cinderella-story finish here; Lance didn't win. But he still got a great deal of publicity by finishing 32nd in an experienced field. He was a kid competing against men; he had held up well. In races against competitors his own age, he was already picking up significant prize money. He was really beginning to feel his oats and went so far as to tell a reporter: "I think in a few years I'll be right near the top, and within ten years I'll be the best."

For young Lance, triathlons were a way to achieve the kind of success he craved, as well as a way to make some money that would help his mother. He began entering both events for his own age group and events where he competed against men, even if it meant fudging his birth-date on the entry forms. Competitors in men's events had to be at least sixteen. He won many of the age-group races, and sometimes placed in the top five in the other events. Either way, he was earning money and a reputation as a young triathlete on the rise. It seemed, at this point, that Lance Armstrong had found his sport.

Because he was a youngster with boundless energy, Lance soon began competing in some local bicycle races as well. He rode for his old friend Jim Hoyt, the man from whom he had bought his first bike. Hoyt sponsored a club team that competed in multi-lap road races around the fields that encircled the Richardson Bike Mart. Before long, Lance was winning those races. As with triathlons, he always gave it everything he had, pedaling until he felt his lungs would burst and his legs would move no longer. If there was another competitor to pass or a finish line in sight, he simply wouldn't quit or slow down.

Lance was so good that he quickly advanced to the age groups above his. When he was sixteen he was already riding against cyclists in their mid to late twenties. At sixteen, he also became the National Rookie of the Year in sprint triathlons and was earning some twenty thousand dollars a year. Even his mother now felt he had a future as an athlete and helped him every way she could. Lance continued to train in earnest, sometimes entering ten-kilometer runs just to improve his overall conditioning and endurance. When school was in session, he would run six miles right after school and in the evening hop on his bike for a long ride. On Saturdays his long rides would sometimes take him nearly to the Oklahoma border, and his mother would have to get in the car and go get him.

Riding all over the area on his bike wasn't always the safest situation for Lance. One time, after being run off the road by a truck, Lance made an obscene gesture. The trucker came after him, forcing Lance off his bike. He took off by foot only to see the trucker trashing his bike. Because he got the license number, Lance and his mother were able to take the trucker to court and win the case. Meanwhile, he got himself a new bike. This one was a Raleigh with racing wheels. A short time after getting the Raleigh, however, Lance wrecked it and almost got killed in the process.

He recalls riding in town and doing the dangerous practice of running stoplights, going through them one after another in an attempt to beat the timers. He had gone through five without incident when he came to an intersection that had six lanes. The light turned yellow and Lance started through at full speed. He remembers getting across the first three lanes but as he raced across the fourth, he saw a Ford Bronco out of the corner of his eye. The driver didn't see him and accelerated. The Bronco slammed right into the bike, sending Lance flying out of the seat and flying headfirst across the intersection. He landed on his head in what had to be a very frightening sight for those who witnessed it.

As unbelievable as it sounds, Lance was not wearing a helmet. In addition, he didn't even have identification with him. These are two things bike riders should *never* be without. The ID is especially needed when a rider is alone. Lance was taken to a hospital where it was determined that he had a concussion, plus he needed stitches to close gashes in his head and foot. He also had a sprained knee and, of course, a trashed bike. Needless to say, once his mother found out what had happened, she was extremely upset.

Lance, however, was upset about something else. He had been training for a triathlon that was to be held in six days at Lake Dallas, in Lewisville. His heart sank when he heard the doctor say there was absolutely no way he could compete. "Don't do anything for three weeks," the doctor ordered. "Don't run. Don't even walk."

The next day Lance was out of the hospital. He was limping badly and his whole body was sore from the impact of the crash. Within a couple of days, however, he had cabin fever and had to get out of the house. He played some golf, took the brace off his knee and felt pretty good. Just four days after the accident, Lance signed up to compete in the triathlon. He arranged to borrow a bike from a friend, actually took the stitches out of his foot himself, cut holes in his shoes so they wouldn't rub on the cut, and went to work. He was leading the race in the water and still leading when he got off the bike. In the 10K finishing run, he faded a bit and was passed by two other competitors, eventually finishing third.

Yet he got plenty of publicity for his accomplishment. There was a big newspaper story about how he had competed successfully so soon after being seriously injured in an accident. His determination turned a lot of heads, including that of the doctor who had patched him up. A week after the race, Lance and his mother received a letter from the doctor, which said, in part, "I can't believe it."

It wouldn't be the last time that Lance Armstrong would amaze the sporting world and doctors alike.

2

A Champion
in the Making

Lance was pretty much a wild guy during his high
school years. Though he didn't play football,
he was still popular and had plenty of friends.
Just as he liked fast sports, he also liked fast,
"muscle" cars, and often drag-raced with his
buddies. Like any athlete who seems to revel in
speed, there was an element of danger in much
of what he did. The accident he had while running yellow lights proved that, but he enjoyed
the risks and wasn't about to slow down. It was
life in the fast lane, and Lance felt he was head-
ing toward something special.

That feeling soon became the primary
motivation in his life. He had reached a point
where he wasn't about to skip training to attend

a football rally or even to hang out with his friends. Training, competing, and improving in the sports he had chosen—sports still considered "weird" by many of his peers—had become more important than anything else. It wasn't long before Lance's dedication began to pay off. In the fall of 1988, his senior year in high school, Lance really began to give the cycling world a glimpse of things to come. He entered a time-trial race in Moriarty, New Mexico. It was considered a very big race for young riders.

The race was twelve miles over a very flat course along a highway, in an area with very little wind. It was tailor-made for speed. In other words, it was the kind of race where riders could record fast times and hope that potential sponsors and others within the cycling world would notice them. In that sense, it was a very important race, and Lance, like the other entrants, wanted to excel. The race was held in September. The weather was still hot in Texas, but when Lance and his mother arrived in New Mexico, the air was cold, almost frigid. Because he hadn't packed any cold-weather clothing, Lance wasn't sure he could ride.

He took a forty-five-minute warm-up ride wearing his mother's thin windbreaker, but when he reached the starting area to wait his turn, he was still cold. In a time trial, riders are staggered so that each has a chance to make the ride by himself. It's strictly a matter of the rider against the clock; no strategy, no chance of colliding with another rider—just an all-out sprint for twelve miles. So Lance began waiting for his turn. He knew that if his body was cold when he started, chances were it would cost him valuable time. Instead of waiting outside, he got in his mother's car and had her turn the heat up. He sat there until his name was called. Then he jumped right on his bike and went.

Lance rode with the single-mindedness that would always characterize his style in this type of race. He was focused on one thing, going as fast as he could for as long as he could. He worked as hard as he could, ignored the pain, gave away nothing. When he finally crossed the finish line, exhausted, he had not only won the race, he had also broken the course record by an amazing forty-five seconds!

The victory in the Moriarty time trial seemed to complete his metamorphosis. Lance was now fully focused on becoming a world-class athlete, and cycling was becoming the sport in which he felt he could really excel. He began training even harder. Most everything else had become secondary, which was quite unusual for a high-school-age athlete. High schoolers who feel they have a future in baseball, basketball, football, or other sports may work hard, but they know they will get more experience at a higher level in college or in the minor leagues, so their lives in high school are often pretty normal. Cycling is different. It is up to the athlete to make it happen. There is no high school team, no college scholarship waiting, and no minor league. The athlete has to do it on his own. That was the way Lance saw it; in his mind, that was the only way it could be viewed.

Lance was now taking long, solitary bike rides. There wasn't a lot of time for fun and games with his friends. Then, after the first of the year in what would be his final semester in high school, another opportunity came along. Word of his growing talent had spread, and the United States Cycling Federation invited him to travel to Colorado Springs to train with the U.S. Junior National Team and then travel to Moscow in Russia for the 1989 Junior World Championships. It was an incredible opportunity, but it didn't take long for a problem to develop.

Plano East High School had a policy regarding long absences. Lance was told if he went to Moscow he might not qualify to graduate with his class. Though he was disappointed at the stance the school had taken, Lance knew he couldn't pass up the opportunity. He had to go. The trip turned out to be a learning experience in more ways than one.

Up to this point, Lance knew only one way to ride. Attack! That was his credo. Go as hard as you can, pass other riders, look to take the lead and hold it—an all-out attacking style. Going to Moscow and competing against other top riders, he soon learned that his tactics didn't always work. To put it bluntly, he admitted, "I had no idea what I was doing." He took the lead, and held it for several laps. Suddenly, he found himself running out of gas. This wasn't a time trial in New Mexico or a race around the Richardson Bike Mart. The other riders knew what they were doing, bided their time, and finally passed the tiring Armstrong. Though he finished out of the money, a disappointment to him, he had nevertheless made an impression on others.

U.S. Cycling Federation officials saw tremendous potential in the hot-spirited young rider, while a Russian coach said, flat out, that Lance was the best young rider he had seen in a long time. So there were plenty of positives to take away from Moscow.

Back in Plano, however, there was one big negative. School officials gave Lance an ultimatum. Unless he made up all the work in each subject that he had missed during the six weeks he had been gone, he wouldn't graduate with his class. Lance sucked it up, attended a private academy, made up the work, and graduated with his class.

Finally school days were over and Lance had to make some decisions. College wasn't an option because there was simply no way he could pursue a cycling career at an American college. While trying to decide, he just stayed around Plano for a few months; in the fall, he watched most of his friends go off to various colleges. During this time, however, he was also competing in local bike races and traveling a bit with a sponsored team. In addition, he was competing in 10K runs and triathlons, and beating adults regularly. But he wasn't happy in Plano, especially with his friends gone. As a cyclist, he already knew the place to be was Europe. He did some riding for his old friend, Jim Hoyt, but the two had a falling out when Lance got into a fistfight with another rider. Finally, he knew it was time to leave town.

After his trip to Moscow, Lance had been named to the United States National Cycling Team and finally received a call from the team's new director, Chris Carmichael. Carmichael was well aware that cycling was a go-nowhere sport in the United States and hoped to change that. His objective was to develop a group of exciting young American riders. He had a list of the top kids and Lance was among them.

At the age of eighteen, Lance left Plano, Texas, and didn't look back. He was going head-first into cycling, an all-or-nothing rider whose idea of strategy was to get on the bike and go as hard as he could for as long as he could. It was not the way to win international races. Chris Carmichael knew immediately that there was a great deal to teach this young upstart, a Texan with attitude, but he also saw the great potential in the strong, young rider. He began getting Lance ready for his first big international race, the 1990 amateur World Championships in Utsunomiya, Japan. This was a 115-mile road race, held over a difficult course that included a long climb. On race day, the temperatures went into the nineties, making conditions even more difficult for the riders.

Chris Carmichael laid out the strategy for Lance. He told him he expected him to stay back in the pack for a good part of the race, and to watch for his signal before Lance made a move to the front. He explained that the heat made it imperative for Lance not to take the lead. The lead racer has to deal directly with a headwind, while the riders in the pack can draft behind the lead rider and avoid some of the tiring effects of the wind.

"I don't want to see you near the front catching the wind," Carmichael said, with absolute certainty. "Stay back and wait."

Did Lance listen? Does a wildcat hold back when it sees its prey? He followed instructions for one lap, then decided to test his wings. On the second lap he took the lead and sprinted way out ahead of the field. For the next three laps he pedaled like mad and built a lead of nearly a minute and a half. That's when the heat began to get him. At the halfway mark, Lance was hurting, and about thirty riders had already caught him. The heat and the climbs took their toll and, while Lance didn't quit, he finished the race in eleventh place.

Despite ignoring instructions and wilting in the heat, Lance had still managed the best American showing ever in the race. Chris Carmichael wasn't really angry. He understood Lance's desire to win and the way he preferred to attack a course. It wasn't always the right way, but Carmichael felt that if Lance's talents could be properly channeled, he would not only succeed, but excel. He told Lance again that he felt Lance could have taken a medal if he had conserved his energy and made a late move. Then he added, "I'm convinced you're going to be a world champion, but there is still a lot of work to do."

Much of the work seemed to involve making Lance understand the total nature of the sport. He had to learn strategy and realize that he couldn't always attack, though his instincts told him to do just that. Even though Lance had fared better than any American rider ever in the amateur championships, Chris Carmichael pulled no punches when he told the young rider that the top guys in the world were all as strong or stronger than he was. He explained that it was often tactics that separated riders of equal or near-equal ability. Lance had to listen to those who had been there, and he had to ride. The more experience he got, the better off he would be.

So he raced, spending more than half the year in Europe with mixed results. When he returned to the States he moved to Austin, Texas, where he found a more relaxed atmosphere than in Plano. People weren't as interested in status, or who you were, what you wore, and what you did. Lance enjoyed training there because there were so many bike trails and back roads where he didn't have to battle traffic. He got himself a small house not far from the University of Texas campus. His goal was to race as an amateur through the 1992 summer Olympic Games, which would be held in Barcelona, Spain. Then he would turn professional. Until then, he continued to race for two teams. In the United States, he was part of the Subaru-Montgomery team, while in Europe he rode under the banner of the United States National team.

Besides tactics, Lance had to learn about the politics of cycling. This may sound strange, for in most sports this kind of thing doesn't exist. Good sportsmanship, yes; politics, no. But in cycling, things are different. Lance also learned that while it's an individual who wins a race, the sport is a lot more about *team* than most people think. Within a team of riders, each individual has a particular job because many of the riders are simply not expected to win. The slower riders, for example, are called *domestiques,* or servants, because they do what can be considered the grunt work. They often lead for a time up hills, pulling the faster riders behind them. In other words, they are blocking the wind for their teammates, making the climb easier for them so they can go hard at any time. They also protect the team leader during various danger zones in a stage race. The team leader, obviously, is the cyclist with the best chance to medal or win.

During some races, spectators will see a huge pack of riders moving as if they were one big group. This pack is called the *peloton*. The speed of this large group of riders can vary from around twenty miles per hour to perhaps forty. If there were no unwritten rules within the peloton, a helter-skelter situation might result, with riders bumping, pushing, falling, and perhaps even fighting. In other words, the peloton could easily become a dangerous mess. Instead, riders often help each other in a kind of one-hand-washes-the-other situation. If you help, someone will help you. If you don't, enemies can result. A rider who gets a reputation for being ruthless and reckless within the peloton may soon find himself in trouble, despite the efforts of his teammates. It isn't always easy, but the smart rider will observe a certain etiquette and political correctness within the pack.

These were not easy lessons for someone with Lance's temperament. He always wanted to win so badly that it was difficult for him to give anything, even in the peloton. But he gradually learned that discretion was the better part of valor and, as much as possible, did what was necessary to keep from being labeled a rebel. As was his plan, he rode in the 1992 Olympics as an amateur and finished fourteenth in the Olympic cycling road race. Yet despite the disappointment of not even approaching a medal, Lance's obvious natural talent caught the eye of someone who would help take him to the next level.

The man's name was Jim Ochowicz, who was the director of a professional racing team sponsored by Motorola. The team was made up of mostly American riders, and Ochowicz was constantly on the lookout for new young riders who he felt would improve the team while having a good chance to excel as individuals. After watching the Olympics, Jim Ochowicz made it a point to set up an appointment with Lance.

He told him straight out that his goal was to find an American rider with the ability to win the Tour de France. Only one American, Greg LeMond, had ever won the Tour, and he had done it three times. None of Ochowicz's riders had ever won. When Ochowicz asked Lance about his goals, the answer he got was short and to the point.

"I want to be a professional rider," Lance said, "and I don't want to just be good at it. I want to be the best!"

That was the kind of answer Ochowicz was looking for. He offered Lance his first professional contract. The immediate plan was for Lance to race in Europe with the Motorola team. His first event was the 1992 Classico San

Sebastian, and it would be a rough one. It was a one-day race that covered more than one hundred miles in Spain. The terrain was difficult and the weather often bad. Sure enough, on race day the weather lived up to its reputation: It was raining very hard, and it was cold. That makes it extremely difficult for riders. They can't wear a lot of clothing, so they get cold easily. It's extremely difficult to dress lightly and ride well in bad weather.

The icy rain really affected Lance and he soon found himself at the back of the pack, dropping further and further off the lead. As the race wore on, riders began dropping out, too exhausted to continue to battle the elements. As Lance saw the field moving further and further ahead of him, he thought about dropping out as well. But he simply couldn't do that, not in his first professional race. He didn't want Jim Ochowicz and his new teammates to think he was a quitter. He would finish the race, no matter what.

Finishing was almost as embarrassing as quitting. Lance crossed the finish line dead last in a field of 111 riders. As he finished, he had to endure laughter and some hissing from the spectators standing by the finish line. He would call it the most humiliating and sobering race of his life, to the point where he actually thought about quitting the sport. Self-doubt had crept into his head; maybe he couldn't compete with the big boys, after all. It was his old friend Chris Carmichael who convinced him to stick with it, to use the race as a learning experience. The positive thing that he had to grab onto was that he didn't quit, that he had shown his new teammates that he was tough. Build from there, Carmichael advised him.

That's just what Lance did. Two days after the disaster at San Sebastian he was competing in the Championship of Zurich in Germany. With much to prove to himself, his teammates, and all the other riders on the tour, he went back to the tactics that had always served him well. He attacked the course like the demon; no holding back, no strategy. He just pedaled his tail off and crossed the finish line in second place. What a difference! In the space of two days, he had gone from being a last-place finisher with a ton of self-doubts to a rider standing on the podium and getting a medal for a second-place finish. There were no thoughts of quitting now. In the often ebb-and-flo world of sports, Lance's confidence soared.

3
On to the
Tour de France

It's one thing to tell an American about a largely European sport, its traditions, politics, and rules of etiquette. It's totally another thing to get him to understand and adopt them. In effect, Lance was still an aggressive young rider who grew up with American sports traditions. Right or wrong, he was filled with attitude and approached his sport with an in-your-face philosophy that said, *Attack, ride hard, take no prisoners.* So while he was moving forward as a top cyclist, he was moving backward in the eyes of many European fans and riders.

Lance himself admitted that he would often ride with a chip on his shoulder and, in effect, look for trouble. He would holler at other riders in the peloton, almost ordering them out of the way, not realizing he was going against the team concept. What he didn't realize was that in the tightly packed peloton, other riders could easily keep someone they didn't like from moving up or breaking out when he chose. More and more riders didn't want to see this arrogant Lance Armstrong win a race. Even his Motorola teammates told him to keep his emotions under control, that he was making too many enemies. Fortunately, his teammates pretty much understood him. They slowly convinced him that he had to put some of his natural instincts on hold and adopt the European racing ethic.

In one race, Lance insulted a highly respected, top Italian rider, Moreno Argentin. Again, it was his temper that got the best of him. He was racing in the Trophee Laigueglia in Italy, a tough, one-day race. The heavy favorite was Argentin. During the stretch run, it turned into a two-man race between Lance and Moreno Argentin, with two other riders close behind. Lance, as always, gave it all he had and crossed the finish line first. Argentin was behind him, but just yards from the finish line he hit his brakes, slowing enough to let the other two riders pass him. Then he crossed the finish line fourth.

Argentin was sending a message. By finishing fourth, he wouldn't have to share the medal podium with Lance. It wasn't so much that Lance had won, but that he had disrespected Argentin in his own country and in front of friends and fans. By stopping his bike and finishing fourth, Argentin was showing he had no respect for Lance and was returning the insult in his own way. Ironically, Lance and Moreno Argentin would later become close friends. All it took was some understanding of the need to play by both the written and unwritten rules, and Lance was finally beginning to learn.

Once Lance realized he couldn't go out there on his own and be the rebel with the perpetual chip on his shoulder, he began listening more to other riders, as well as his advisors, Chris Carmichael and Jim Ochowicz. It was even difficult, however, for Lance to adjust to life in Europe. Everything was different—the food, the accommodations, the climate, and the lifestyle. As much as he loved cycling and winning, he was finding that there was a lot more to being a successful professional rider than just jumping on the bike and pedaling. It would take some time, yet slowly but surely it all began falling into place.

The 1993 season was a real breakthrough for him. He would win ten titles that year, as well as finally tasting the kind of money a top cyclist could earn. That summer, Thrift Drugs, a major sponsor of American cycling, offered a one-million-dollar bonus to any rider who could win the Triple Crown of Cycling, which meant all three of the most prestigious races in the United States. When Lance learned of the bonus money, his competitive juices began to flow, but the money wasn't a slam-dunk by any means. All three races were distinctly different. The first was a difficult one-day race in Pittsburgh, Pennsylvania. Next came a six-day stage race in West Virginia. The last race was the United States Pro Championships, a one-day road race of 156 miles through the streets of Philadelphia.

Each race demanded a different riding style. Most riders were stronger at one kind of racing than another. For example, someone who excelled in a one-day road race might struggle to come back day after day in a six-day stage race. A sprinter who could eat up the pack on flat surfaces might well wilt on the steep hills of a climbing stage. Many felt that the Thrift Drugs bonus money was safe. There wasn't a rider good enough to win all three. But they didn't count on the determination of Lance Armstrong.

He won the first race in Pittsburgh, then

surprised a lot of people by winning the stage race in West Virginia. Up to that point, he wasn't considered a stage racer, yet his determination and strength wore the other riders down. Now, with the U.S. Pro Championships looming, the buzz throughout the cycling world was whether Lance could complete the triple play and win the million-dollar bonus. It was the first time he had attracted so much attention, and it was happening in the United States. The final race in Philadelphia would have 120 competitors, each trying not only to win the race, but to knock Lance Armstrong off the pedestal he was climbing. The race received so much publicity that nearly half a million people lined the streets to watch, an incredible turnout for a bicycle race in the United States.

A much smarter racer now, Lance vowed not to get caught in his old trap of going too fast at the beginning and burning himself out. He wanted to be fresh and fit in the final miles so he could handle any challenge that might arise. Listening to his head and not his heart, he paced himself, staying close enough to the front so he could catch the leaders. With about twenty miles remaining, a little alarm clock went off in his head, the one that said, *Attack!*

He made his move on the steepest part of the course standing up on his bike and pedaling.

But it was no ordinary Armstrong attack. He would later say that he felt a new emotion, rage, and when he made his move he also began to scream. The crowd loved it, but his competitors didn't. A few tried to go with him, but just couldn't keep up.

Within an incredibly short amount of time, Lance had opened up a huge lead. It was now apparent that barring an unforeseen catastrophe, he was going to win the race. When he crossed the finish line, he had won the race by the largest margin in its history. He immediately got off his bike and ran to his mother, giving her a huge hug. They both realized now that all the hard work and sacrifice was paying off.

Later that summer he accepted the ultimate challenge. He would compete in the Tour de France for the first time. For a young cyclist, this should have been a daunting proposition, but confidence was something Lance never lacked. Early in the Tour, Lance made news again. He surprised everyone by winning a stage victory, on the 114-mile ride from Chalons-sur-Marne to Verdun. He did it in typical fashion, sprinting away from the others over the final fifty yards. At the age of twenty-one, he had become the youngest rider ever to take a Tour stage. Only this time, the euphoria over winning a stage was short-lived.

For one of the few times in his career, Lance was unable to finish. After the twelfth stage of the race he could continue no longer. He dropped out, finding that he couldn't keep up with the world's top riders in the mountains. There was no shame in what he did. The mountain stages of the Tour de France had humbled many riders over the years. Lance simply wasn't ready for the arduous climbs, both physically and mentally. However, he had come a long way. While not yet a major Tour de France challenger, in the other races he was proving to be one of the best in the world.

He showed that again later in the season. Though he still tended to revert to the old Lance at times and go out so fast that he would burn out, or *bonk,* as they call it in cycling, he was still a threat to win most major races. The World Championships were held in Oslo, Norway, in 1993, a one-day race that featured most of the top cyclists in the world, including Miguel Indurain of Spain, who was fresh off his third straight victory in the Tour de France. On race day, it was raining. Rain probably creates the worst possible conditions for a major road race because the roads become slick and it's easy for riders to lose control and fall.

Once again Lance hoped he would run a smart race and not burn himself out. Maybe the rain helped in that respect because it wouldn't allow him to go all-out at every turn. In fact, he fell twice that afternoon, but fortunately was able to get back on his bike and continue. The race was a lap race held on an 18.4-kilometer course. With fourteen laps left, Lance was riding in the lead pack, as were Indurain and several other top cyclists. Lance felt it was almost time, and on the second-to-last climb of the race he began his attack. In typical Armstrong fashion he leaped out in front, pedaling as if his life depended on it. He continued down the other side, then attacked the final climb. A number of other riders stayed with him and he knew he couldn't let up, not for a second.

On the final descent he had opened a gap. He just hoped he wouldn't fall victim to the slick roads, not now. When the finish line was in sight he knew he had done it. He had won the World Championships, once again the youngest rider ever to do so. At twenty-one, he had become an international star, and with his natural talent augmented by growing experience in all kinds of racing, it appeared that the sky was the limit. A few years later, however, he would look back at that World Championship with a rather different view.

"In retrospect, perhaps I was too successful too soon," he told a reporter. "The rider crowned

World Champion comes under tremendous scrutiny and at the time I probably wasn't prepared. Of course, I really wouldn't change a thing."

At twenty-one, Lance was a full-time professional cyclist. He would now spend about eight months of the year racing on the European circuit, then come home to Austin, Texas, where he would again see the familiar faces of old friends. There were still many times when he was the sole American in the European races, and that was sometimes lonely for him. However, he was no longer the pesky kid that so many European riders resented. He now had friendship and respect from many of the competitors.

Lance's 1994 season wasn't quite as successful as the previous year, but he began 1995 with a victory in the Tour du Pont, the biggest stage race in the United States. He also spent a great deal of time working on his riding technique, trying to find ways to get the maximum effectiveness from his body. That year he met the great Belgian rider, Eddy Merckx, who had won the Tour de France five times between 1969 and 1974. Merckx and Lance became friends, but when Merckx began to evaluate Lance as a rider, he said something that Lance knew he would have to consider.

Merckx told Lance that he certainly had the

ability to win the Tour de France, but that his body type was holding him back. At 180 pounds and with a thick neck and heavily muscled chest, Lance was a big man, too big for a Tour rider. Merckx felt that unless Lance lost some weight, he would always falter in the mountain stages of the Tour. The more weight a rider has to carry up steep inclines and mountain roads, the more difficult it is, no matter how strong he might be. The trick, Merckx said, was for Lance to lose weight without losing strength, and that isn't always easy.

Though Lance was having a good season in 1995, his coaches felt it was important for him to not only compete in the Tour de France, but to finish it. At twenty-three, he still had plenty of time to win it, but it was important for him to get a taste of the entire race and to cross the finish line, no matter what his final standing. The coaches knew he wasn't ready to win and they told him so. His job was to ride all the stages as best he could, to pace himself and not burn out so he couldn't continue. He still had a reputation as a one-day racer, a guy who could muster all his energy and adrenaline, and even his anger, into one day of manic riding. The stage race was a whole different thing, especially the Tour de France.

The 1995 Tour would be a showcase for

Miguel Indurain, who would set a record by winning the race for the fifth straight time. While Indurain occupied the attention of the press and the fans, Lance was toiling in near anonymity, working hard, pacing himself, and learning more and more about competing in the Tour. Then, late in the race, something happened that had a profound effect upon him. One of his Motorola teammates, Fabio Casartelli, who had won a gold medal in the 1992 Olympics, crashed and was killed while making a descent at high speed. It was a chain-reaction crash in which some twenty riders went down.

Most Tour crashes are relatively minor. Riders often get up and continue in the race. In the more severe crashes, the rider might suffer injuries that prevent him from continuing, but deaths are relatively rare. Fabio Casartelli had the misfortune of going down hard, then striking the back of his head on a curb. The news of the accident and Fabio's death hit Lance hard. Not only was he Lance's teammate, but Fabio was a rider with great potential. He was also a husband and the father of a month-old infant. It was a terrible tragedy, both personal and for the world of cycling.

That night, the entire Motorola team met to discuss whether they should continue in the race or not. Lance's first reaction was to abandon the race, but he and his teammates decided to continue. The final decision was made when Fabio's wife came in and asked them to continue, saying her husband would have wanted it that way. The next day they simply rode together as part of the peloton, no one breaking out or attacking. It was a tribute to Fabio, and the team was given a ceremonial stage victory. Lance called it "another long, terrible day—eight hours on the bike, with everybody grieving."

The next day the team again began to race. The day after, the stage was a run into the city of Limoges. Jim Ochowicz told the riders that this was a stage that Fabio wanted especially to win. Hearing that, Lance immediately set a goal for himself. He wanted to win the stage for his fallen teammate. For the first half of the race he rode within the lead pack, close to Indurain, who was wearing the traditional yellow jersey always worn by the overall leader of the race.

With about twenty-five miles left and a downhill section approaching, Lance suddenly attacked as only he can. Pedaling as if his life depended on it, he bolted to a thirty-second lead in no time flat. Because he had attacked so early, probably too early, the other riders were caught by surprise. The element of surprise worked. Lance lengthened his lead and none of the other riders got close. He won the stage by a minute over his nearest competitor and said it was the most meaningful and special victory of his life. He still was far from winning the Tour, but winning the stage race in honor of his fallen teammate gave him a very spiritual feeling.

"I know I rode with a higher purpose that day," he would say.

This time Lance would finish the entire Tour de France. He knew there was still plenty of work to be done before he could win the overall title. The Tour, he felt, was more than just the longest bicycle race in the world. It required a combination of body and mind to be successful. All the training and strength in the world wouldn't help if you weren't ready for it mentally. He wasn't yet, but felt he was approaching that level step by step.

Later in the 1995 season, Lance would win the Classico San Sebastian, the same race he had finished dead last three years earlier when he made his professional debut. And when he returned to the United States, he established the Lance Armstrong Junior Olympic Race Series, which was designed to promote cycling and racing among young American riders. He was now fully immersed in his sport and wanted to see more American kids become involved.

At the outset of the 1996 season Lance was widely considered one of the best overall cyclists in the world, a rider with the potential to be one of the very best. He looked forward to the upcoming year with unbridled optimism. However, fate had something else in store for him. Though he didn't know it then, his world and his life were about to change in a way that neither he nor anyone around him could ever have expected.

4

A Devastating Diagnosis

The 1996 season started off as if it were going to be one of more success as well as the continued growth of Lance's status in the cycling world. Over the winter, however, he began to notice his right testicle had become slightly swollen. His first reaction, not surprising for an athlete, was that he had somehow injured it on the bike. Most athletes live with some kind of pain, often on a daily basis, and tend to pass off a newfound ache as part of the business. Football and hockey players, participating in what are known as collision sports, don't know a single day during their seasons when something doesn't hurt, often quite badly. Basketball players also push their bodies to the limit, running, jumping, banging under the boards. They, too, experience aches, pains, and soreness almost on a daily basis. It's also important to remember that the American ethic has always been to be tough and play through the pain. You don't complain.

Individual sports are really no different. Runners, triathletes, cyclists, even tennis players go so hard, often to exhaustion, that their bodies sometimes break down. Being on a bike all day on varying terrains and in all kinds of weather isn't an easy task. As Lance himself said, everything hurts—back, feet, hands, neck, legs, and butt. So he paid little attention to the swollen testicle and continued to compete. It certainly wasn't affecting his performance. In early spring he won a race called the Flèche-Wallonne in France, another that no American had ever won before, then finished second in the Liege-Bastogne-Liege, which was a 167-mile course that had to be covered in a single day. So he continued to excel in the major races and then returned to the States to defend his title in the Tour du Pont.

Since no rider had ever won it two years in a row, Lance wanted to win the Tour du Pont very badly. Though it wasn't comparable to the Tour du France, the Tour du Pont was still a tough stage race, covering some 1,225 miles over twelve days, with much of it taking place in the mountains of North and South Carolina. Lance won the race and appeared as strong as ever in doing it. But those who knew him might have seen something different this time. Instead of pumping his fists in victory as he usually did, he crossed the finish line and appeared utterly exhausted. He was. He also noticed that his eyes were bloodshot and his face flushed.

Again, a young athlete coming into the prime of his life and career isn't going to think about a serious illness. He just felt he was run down and needed some rest. He was already pointing to a pair of events later in the summer, the Tour de France and then the 1996 Olympic Games at Atlanta, so he continued to train and race, taking five second-place finishes following the Tour du Pont. In fact, he was poised to crack the top five in international cyclist rankings for the first time. There was still no hint of a major problem.

But once Lance began riding in the Tour de France, it took just five days for him to realize he didn't have it. He had ridden in the rain early in the race and came down with a bad case of bronchitis and a sore throat. He was coughing so much and also had so much lower-back pain that he couldn't even get back on his bike.

After five days he dropped out. He told the press, "I couldn't breathe," something he would say that, looking back, should have served as more of a warning.

He went back to Austin, rested, felt recovered, and began working toward the Olympics. He competed in both the time trial and the road race, finishing sixth and twelfth, way below his expectations. Once again, he just didn't feel right. Back in Austin, he found himself sleeping a lot, and felt achy and drowsy much of the time. He was still rationalizing, passing his problems off on the long season. But it just wasn't like Lance to feel this way. In his own mind, he couldn't imagine anything derailing his career now. He had recently signed a huge, two-year contract to ride with a major French team, Cofidis, for $2.5 million. He had a girlfriend that he was crazy about and had built a new home alongside Lake Austin. He seemed to be close to having it all.

Then, a few days past his twenty-fifth birthday, he had a group of friends over to his house before going to a concert. At the concert, he got a terrible headache that just wouldn't leave him, despite his taking some over-the-counter pain medication. Though the headache was gone in the morning, the strange sequence of symptoms should again have told him something was wrong. Several days later, something finally happened that he couldn't ignore. He began coughing up blood. His doctor in Austin was also a good friend and next-door neighbor. He came over immediately. Because Lance had often complained about his sinuses, the doctor thought they might be the cause of the bleeding.

Again Lance relaxed, not imagining there could be a serious problem, but within a week he awoke to find his right testicle incredibly swollen, almost to the size of a baseball. He called his doctor again, and this time the doctor said Lance had to be checked out immediately, without hesitation. He recommended that Lance seek the opinion of a urologist. The urologist didn't like what he saw and recommended a test called an ultrasound. Once that was done, Lance was immediately sent to have a chest X-ray. By that time, a nervous sense of foreboding was beginning to creep over him. He was told to take the X-rays back to the urologist's office. His doctor friend joined him as the urologist looked at the X-rays. When he finally spoke, his words hit Lance like a thunderbolt.

"This is a serious situation," he said. "It looks like testicular cancer with large metastasis to the lungs."

At first, Lance couldn't believe it. He was

twenty-five years old, a world-class athlete, a guy who always took great care of his body. How could he possibly have cancer? The urologist told Lance he had every right to get a second opinion, but added he was confident his diagnosis was correct and that Lance should proceed to step one, having the cancerous testicle removed immediately, as in the next day.

Lance was understandably shocked by the grave diagnosis. He realized he had been sick with a number of symptoms for quite some time. As an athlete, he just didn't want to give into it. He had been trained to overcome adversity, and for a long time viewed his various symptoms as just another bump in the road. What he didn't know at the time was that testicular cancer is the most common form of cancer in men between the ages of twenty and forty, though it's still rather rare. There are only about 7,500 new cases diagnosed annually, with about 90 percent of the cases completely curable. In fact, it is one of the most curable of all cancers if found early. In Lance's case, however, he had ignored his symptoms for months, allowing the original cancer to metastasize, to spread to other parts of his body. That's why his case was so serious.

The morning after the diagnosis, Lance underwent surgery to remove the cancerous testicle. It was then recommended he see Dr. Dudley Youman, a well-known oncologist based in Houston. Lance was told that speed was all-important. Because the cancer had spread, treatment had to begin immediately. His doctors assured him that cancer treatment had improved tremendously and that he could be cured. His immediate reaction was to get on with it, to do whatever it took. In other words, attack, just like he would when he was racing.

Suddenly, Lance wasn't worrying about the next race, about winning the Tour de France or capturing an Olympic medal. He had another battle to fight now and he knew the consequences if he lost. Win or lose, one thing was certain in his mind at that moment: His career as a bicycle racer was over.

Lance's surgery to remove the testicle went well. The next morning, he met with Dr. Youman for the first time. Lance, like most people, knew what chemotherapy often meant—becoming violently ill and very weak, losing all your hair. It was as if the doctors almost had to kill the patient in order to kill the cancer. One way or another, he knew that a real ordeal lay ahead of him. The doctor told Lance he was in the third stage of the disease, the worst, and that the cancer was now spreading rapidly. He would have his first chemo treatment in a week.

To administer the drugs, a Grosjean catheter would be implanted in his chest and would probably remain there for at least three months. Even to a tough-minded athlete like Lance Armstrong, the prospects for the immediate future had to be extremely frightening.

Because he was a world-class athlete, Lance knew he couldn't hide his illness. On October 8, he held a telephone press conference so that the story would be broken correctly and everyone would have it at the same time. His statement said, in part:

> "On Wednesday, October 2, I was diagnosed with testicular cancer . . . A CT-Scan revealed that my condition has spread into my lungs and abdomen. In terms of degrees of the disease, my condition is considered to be advanced and, thus, yesterday, I began my first day of chemotherapy treatment. I will undergo chemotherapy for at least nine weeks and then, depending on how I respond to treatment, may have to undergo more chemotherapy or other procedures to fight this disease.
>
> "I have the utmost faith in all the doctors with whom I am working and

I am determined to fight this disease and to prevail . . . My oncologist, Dr. Dudley J. Youman, was unable to be here today. However, he has told me that the cure rate for testicular cancer in the advanced stage is between 60 percent and 85 percent. Further, if I do beat this disease I have been assured that there is no reason that I cannot make a full and complete recovery.

"For now, I must focus on my treatment. However, I want you all to know that I intend to beat this disease, and further, I intend to ride again as a professional cyclist. I am unable to say today when I will be back in the peloton but hold out hope that I might still participate in the 1997 season."

In many ways, it was a mixed message to those who heard and then read it. Advanced cancer was never an easy foe, and statistics showed that many people had lost the battle. While everyone was pulling for Lance, many probably felt his chances were slim. And virtually no one thought he would ever return to world-class racing. His friends, however, all rallied around him. Led by his mother, they would provide him with endless hours of support throughout his ordeal.

At his press conference, Lance also announced his intention to become a spokesperson for testicular cancer. "Had I been more aware of the symptoms, I believe I would have seen a doctor before my condition had advanced to this stage. I want this to be a positive experience and I want to take this opportunity to help others who might someday suffer from the same circumstance I face today."

Jim Ochowicz, speaking for Motorola, echoed his thoughts. "All the staff and members of the Motorola cycling team extend their full support to Lance and his family, and will be at his side to support him throughout this difficult time," Ochowicz said. "We now know that Lance is facing the biggest battle of his life, but knowing him as we do we feel sure that he will face this new challenge with all the strength and character that has made him one of the top cyclists in the world. Lance's efforts to beat this illness and his desire to bring awareness to this form of cancer to men around the world reflect the courage of this young man to turn his situation into a positive one. We hope that we can help him raise the worldwide understanding about this illness."

Lance Armstrong celebrates as he wins the first
mountain stage of the Tour de France in 1999.

Lance cycles to win the individual time trial and seventh stage of the Tour of Switzerland cycling race in 2001.

In 2002 Lance leads the pack during the fifteenth stage
of the eighty-ninth Tour de France cycling race.

Lance addresses the National Press Club during a luncheon in Washington, D.C., after winning the Tour de France in 1999.

The eleventh stage of the Tour de France in 2001

Lance wins the fifty-kilometer individual time-trial nineteenth stage of the Tour de France in 2002.

Here is Lance on his way to winning the seven-kilometer individual time-trial prologue of the Tour de France in 2002.

His mother, Linda, celebrates Lance's win of the
nineteenth stage of the Tour de France in 1999.

©AFP/CORBIS

Lance holds his son, Luke, high as he smiles
at his victory of the 2000 Tour de France.

The winner of the 1999 Tour de France carries the U.S. flag during his honor lap on the Champs Elysées in Paris.

So all the support pieces were in place, as well as plans for the day when Lance was once again healthy. In the months that followed, it would sometimes be difficult for Lance to keep his optimistic outlook. The fight he was facing would turn out to be much more difficult than anyone had anticipated.

5

A Profile in Courage

Originally, Lance's chemotherapy was supposed to begin one week after his surgery. But the schedule had to be pushed up when tests showed that Lance's cancer had spread even more in just twenty-four hours. It was a rapid progression that obviously had the doctors worried. With chemo set to begin, it was suggested to Lance that he might consider one other thing. Chemo would make him temporarily sterile, a condition that might not reverse itself. If he recovered but was still sterile, he could never father a child. Before starting his chemo, Lance went to a sperm bank in San Antonio so that a sample of his sperm could be stored for possible future use.

It was all unnatural and unnerving. That done, Lance had to begin his treatment. He was told he would be taking a cocktail of three drugs—bleomycin, etoposide, and cisplatin. Though the names are probably meaningless to the average person, just strange medical terms, cancer patients learn them quickly. The most important of them was cisplatin, made from platinum and developed by Dr. Lawrence Einhorn. It had saved the lives of many testicular cancer patients since its development. Lance was told that had he gotten the disease some twenty years earlier, he would have been dead in six months. Now, it seemed, with the modern drugs, he did have a chance to recover.

Because the treatment was so toxic and could make him feel very sick, it would be administered for one week, then he would have two weeks off so his body could recover and develop more red blood cells. Oddly enough, the first treatment didn't make Lance feel very sick. Because of his nature, sitting still wasn't an option. Feeling good enough, he got up every morning and walked. Then, in the evening, he confounded everyone by going for a ride on his bike. Riding was not only therapy, it gave Lance a sense of normalcy, a sense that he was still somehow in control of his life. Though he was acutely aware of his condition, riding made him feel less like a patient and more like a man who was in a race, this time a race to save his own life.

At first, Lance's body tolerated the chemo very well. He even felt at one point that maybe they weren't giving him enough. At the same time, Lance began to read everything he could find about cancer. He wanted to understand everything that was being done and why. If there were any decisions to be made, he wanted to be educated enough to make them correctly, and not leave everything to others. Then one evening, Lance was opening the mountains of mail he was receiving and found a letter from a Dr. Steven Woolf at Vanderbilt University Medical Center. In the letter, Dr. Woolf urged Lance to explore all treatment options and also suggested strongly that he consult with Dr. Lawrence Einhorn, who had developed the use of cisplatin. Dr. Woolf felt there were treatments that would minimize any side effects that might hamper Lance's ability to race if he were to make a full recovery.

That was something Lance had not considered. Without going into all the medical ramifications and technicalities, Dr. Woolf was concerned about one of the drugs Lance was taking, bleomycin. Apparently, bleomycin had a toxic effect on the liver and lungs. The doctor felt that prolonged use of the drug would permanently affect Lance's lung capacity and thus his ability to race. He felt there were other choices and that Lance should look into them. There were facilities to consider in Houston, New York, and at Indiana University where Dr. Einhorn continued his work.

Lance's decision to seek other opinions almost immediately led to yet another complication, a very frightening one. He faxed his medical records to both Houston and Indianapolis, and there was an almost immediate reply from Houston. After reviewing the records, the oncologists asked why Lance had not yet had an MRI done on his brain. When his mother asked why that would be necessary, she received a shocking reply. The doctors said some of the numbers on his recent tests indicated to them that the cancer might very well have spread to his brain.

Once again Lance underwent a test that was frightening in that the results could be devastating. They were. As soon as the results came back Dr. Youman told him, "You have two spots on your brain."

How could it be any worse? Whenever anyone hears something is in his brain, a myriad of thoughts must go through his head. Is this going to affect my mind, my ability to think, to see, to talk? Am I going to have seizures? Will I be able to recognize my family and friends? Lance undoubtedly went through this whole process. The only positive he made out of it, if you could call it a positive, was that he had now heard all the possible bad news. That done, it was time to fight back.

He knew the odds for recovery were dropping. Not only was the cancer in his lungs, but it had now spread to his brain. At this point, he decided he had to find the place that would give him the best chance for recovery. He told his doctors that he wanted to go to Houston and they told him that was a good idea. Once in Houston, the doctors outlined a program that was at once frightening and something that he would have to consider carefully.

The Houston oncologists said they would continue using the drug bleomycin, the one that could damage his lungs. They also told him his treatment would be so caustic that he would *crawl* out of the room after treatment. The way the doctor described it was, "Every day, I'm going to kill you, and then I'm going to bring you back to life." They admitted the bleomycin would tear up his lungs and that even if he recovered, he would likely never be able to race again. They told him he would be in terrible pain. When he asked why the treatment was going to be so radically harsh, they told him point-blank that his was a worse-case scenario and that what had been described to him was his only chance of survival . . . if he opted to be treated there.

While Lance was still taken aback by what had been described to him, the doctors added that they wanted to begin treatment immediately because each day that he waited, his condition would worsen. Lance and his mother drove around Houston trying to decide what to do. His mother was plainly horrified by the picture that had been painted and what her son would have to endure. Lance, while able to accept the fact that he was terribly ill, had a difficult time dealing with the image of being reduced to a shell of a person who could barely move or walk during treatment. They called the doctors back home to get their opinions and it was suggested they make one more stop: Indianapolis. Go see Dr. Lawrence Einhorn, who had been the pioneer for the successful treatment of testicular cancer, the doctors suggested. One phone call and Lance and his mother were told to come to Indiana University immediately. They learned that the staff there never turns away cases, no matter how bad they might be.

The first doctors to consult with Lance and

his mother were Craig Nichols and Scott Shapiro, who was a neurosurgeon. Lance liked them immediately. Dr. Nichols had already gone over Lance's medical records and was candid and up-front. He was also optimistic, telling Lance that they felt good about his chances of recovery, adding that they had seen even worse cases that had been cured. But the doctor also admitted the brain lesions had complicated things. Chemo couldn't be used for them. The options were radiation or surgery. But just when things seemed as if they couldn't be worse, Dr. Nichols would say something that would give Lance hope. He told him they would set up a course of treatment designed to eventually get him back to his cycling.

Lance just wanted to live. That was obviously his first priority. Dr. Nichols said they certainly wouldn't compromise his chances for a full recovery. But if he did recover there was no reason he couldn't race again, so it was important to alter the drugs to preserve his lungs. The combination of drugs they would use would not include bleomycin. He would be taking a treatment tagged "VIP" for the drugs it included. These drugs were vinblastine, etoposide, isofamide, and cisplatin. The isofamide would cause Lance more nausea and vomiting, and perhaps more immediate discomfort, but it wouldn't damage his lungs.

The doctors also suggested surgery for the brain lesions. Again, they were looking to his recovery. If they used radiation he might be left with a slight loss of balance, which might not bother the average person too much, but could be deadly in a high-speed bicycle race. The doctors also pointed out that the lesions appeared to be on the surface of his brain, which would make the surgery much easier. After hearing everything the doctors had to say, Lance and his mother decided quickly that Indianapolis was where they would stay. He would opt for the treatment Dr. Nichols had described. This was where he would roll the dice and hope for the best.

Step one was the surgery. Dr. Shapiro told Lance that the lesions, while on the surface of the brain, were in difficult locations. One was over the part of the brain that controls the field of vision, the other over the center of coordination. Both these faculties, of course, have to be 100 percent for a racer. Brain surgery is always extremely frightening because any kind of damage to the brain can result in some sort of diminished capacity. The doctor did tell him, however, that if the surgery went well, he would recover from it quickly.

The surgery took six hours. Dr. Shapiro was

able to successfully scrape away the lesions. As with all such procedures, tissue samples were sent immediately to the pathologist, and when Lance awoke he finally received a piece of positive news. The lesions were composed of necrotic tissue. In other words, they were dead cells, which meant they weren't spreading. The doctors weren't sure what had killed the cells, but it was the first stroke of good fortune since Lance's ordeal had begun. Maybe, just maybe, it was a sign of things to come, though the worst still lay ahead.

Now it was time for the serious chemo. Lance described it as "one long IV drip." The side effects were nasty. As he said, when he wasn't in pain, he was vomiting. He lost all the hair on his body. When the chemo was dripping into his veins there was always a burning sensation. He was coughing constantly and spent a great deal of time in the bathroom. This routine, the drugs and the side effects, had taken full control of his life. To a cancer patient undergoing this kind of treatment, it seems like there is nothing else.

Lance underwent four cycles of treatment over three months. The side effects became worse with each cycle because of the buildup of toxins within his body. By the time he had the fourth cycle, he would be spending a great deal of time just laying in a fetal position and retching. It was a terrible ordeal, but the only chance Lance had to get well.

Chemo doesn't just kill cancer cells. It kills healthy cells as well, and also attacks bone marrow, muscles, the linings of the throat and stomach, and even the teeth. The patient is susceptible to many infections, bleeding gums, and loss of appetite. But as difficult as it was, Lance still had the full support of his friends and the unending devotion of his mother. Someone was always there for him, though he sometimes had a strong sense of being alone in his battle. He tried to keep as much control over his life as he could by always monitoring his medications, asking questions, and visualizing the chemo driving the cancer cells from his body. Still, too often, when he was feeling at his worst from the medication, he would feel as if things were slipping away, either because he couldn't stay awake or felt disoriented. The gamut of emotions he experienced must have put him on a roller-coaster which was going up and down between life and death.

The chemo and the tests to monitor its effects continued. Finally, in November, the numbers coming back began to look more favorable, and a short time later Dr. Nichols said the words Lance wanted to hear.

"You're responding to the chemo," he told

Lance. "In fact, you're ahead of schedule."

Each week the readings were better than the last. Finally, the doctors could say it: He was recovering. The telltale number, Lance's HCG level, had dropped all the way to ninety-six. Earlier in November it had been at 92,000. It looked as if Lance was going to make it. In fact, he was almost well. Needless to say, he started to feel optimistic again. In fact, he told one friend that "when [cancer] looked around for a body to hang out in, it made a big mistake when it chose mine."

He was also beginning to think about riding. During chemo, Dr. Nichols didn't want him to stress his body, even when he was home between treatments. He didn't say no riding, but he implied it. But riding still made Lance feel good, even if he just got on the bike for a few minutes, which was about all he could manage. By the time his treatments had ended, he would ride loops around his neighborhood for about thirty minutes or so, but it was difficult. This was not racing. In fact, it was barely riding. But at least he was back on the bike.

Lance's final chemo session was on December 13, 1996. He would soon be going home for good. With the worst hopefully behind him, there were suddenly other considerations. Dr. Nichols, who had always been totally honest with Lance, said that all signs were pointing to a recovery, that he was one of the lucky ones who had cheated cancer. He also had another suggestion. Because of Lance's high profile in the athletic world, Dr. Nichols suggested he become an activist and help encourage others who were battling the disease. Lance saw it that way as well. He was thankful for the doctors and for the dreaded chemo, which despite the ordeal it had put him through, seemed to have done its job and done it well.

Besides talking to and encouraging other cancer patients, Lance would also form the Lance Armstrong Foundation. It began as an international, nonprofit foundation established to benefit cancer research and promote urologic cancer awareness and the importance of early detection. It would later evolve into a world leader in the concept of "cancer survivorship," helping people manage and survive the disease.

Lance had quickly made the transformation from cancer patient to cancer survivor. He knew firsthand that cancer didn't have to be a death sentence, and that was a message he wanted to get across to others. It probably didn't dawn on him then that perhaps the best way to show this to the world was to get on his bike and become a champion again.

6

On the Road
to Recovery

Lance remained in the hospital for just a few days after his final chemo session. Though he appeared to have beaten the disease, his doctors reminded him that he would need monthly tests to make sure there were no traces of the disease in his system. As a rule of thumb, cancer survivors can only consider themselves cured if they remain disease-free for five years. The first year is usually the most crucial. If Lance's cancer was going to return, it would likely happen within twelve months.

So there would still be a little doubt lurking in the back of Lance's mind. As he said, "I wanted to be cured now. I didn't want to wait a year to find out." But once back home, Lance was able to relax more. He played golf with friends and worked on plans for his foundation. He went to Dr. Youman's office in Austin every week for tests, with the results sent to Indianapolis. A few weeks later he got the word that, as of that moment, there wasn't a trace of cancer in his body.

For a cancer patient, even one like Lance who is pronounced cancer-free, there are still issues. The body may be cancer-free, but the mind is always wondering whether it will remain that way. Lance was officially in *remission,* which meant the cancer was gone, but he still had to be checked to make sure it didn't come back. That can prey heavily on the mind, especially in the early months, and Lance often found himself wondering if the cancer would come back, or if it already had. Each time he waited for the results of a test he held his breath. And when he received the news that he continued to be cancer-free, he breathed a huge sigh of relief.

Of course, he couldn't be a cancer survivor and nothing else. He knew that in the coming months he would have to make some big decisions about what to do, if not for the rest of his life, then for the immediate future. Lance was thinking about riding again in the spring of 1997. One of the reasons was financial. The

Cofidis team that he had signed with for $2.5 million had voided his contract when he became ill because he was unable to race. He felt that if he went into training and at least tried to come back, he could lock the sponsors back in to the second year of the contract.

Once again, Lance began to train on the bike. It must have seemed as if he were starting all over again, riding the familiar roads in and around Austin. He would sometimes ride for four hours at a time, covering over a hundred miles. Other days, however, he would be exhausted after just an hour. It was an up and down scenario, good one day, not so good the next. For awhile he felt run down and then caught a cold. Still worrying about cancer, he felt it might be back and quickly went to Dr. Youman. But he was reminded that the chemo had compromised his immune system; because of that, he was susceptible to infection.

When Lance spoke to Dr. Nichols in Indianapolis, the doctor suggested he take it easy and not consider any real training for the rest of the year. His system simply hadn't had the time to recover from the hit it had taken from the chemo. Now there were two things to worry about—a recurrence of the cancer, and whether or not he would ever be a world-class racer again. In a way, it was a Catch-22. Lance was ready to train hard, but he felt if he did train hard, it might trigger a return of his illness. There was a great deal up in the air when it came to his future.

The best thing that happened to Lance that year was meeting Kristen Richards. In fact, he had met her when he announced the formation of his foundation. She was an account executive for an advertising and public-relations firm that was helping to promote the event. At the time, Lance was still seeing a longtime girlfriend, but when they broke up, he began seeing Kristen. Soon the two would become inseparable. Kristen knew Lance's situation, but it didn't seem to bother her a bit. They just hit it off, simple as that.

Since he was no longer training, Lance had time to relax. He and Kristen traveled to Europe and just had fun. Lance realized that he had begun training as a professional athlete before he was twenty years old. This was one of the first times he could just hang out without worrying about his next race or training session. By the end of the summer Lance was looking healthier than he had in some time. His hair was back and his weight was nearly 160 pounds. He was still twenty pounds lighter than he had been as a racer, but he also remembered being told that he would never win the Tour de France at his previous weight. Finally, the new, leaner Lance Armstrong decided he would try to race again. This time he would make a serious effort to come back.

One problem was a sponsor. He and his representative tried to revive their deal with Cofidis, but the company refused. They felt that Lance would never ride at a world-class level again. Apparently, they also felt it would reflect badly on them if Lance were to become ill again while a part of their team. On September 4, 1997, Lance and his reps called a press conference to announce his return to racing for the 1998 season. At the same time, they made it known that he was no longer with Cofidis and would welcome overtures from other teams. None came.

In the fall, Lance approached a relatively new cycling team, one created in 1996 and sponsored by the United States Postal Service. It seemed a strange idea, the U.S. Postal Service sponsoring a competitive cycling team that would race at the international level. One of the reasons the team had been put together was the Tour de France. Because it was an international event watched by millions, it provided the Postal Service with great public relations and advertising benefits.

At first, Lance couldn't come to an agreement with the team. He felt the base salary was too low. Finally, after negotiating a series of incentive clauses into the contract, he signed. He was now a member of an American racing team, the U.S. Postal Service, and he wanted to make them proud. Then, before the year was out, Lance and Kristen Richards became engaged to be married. His life seemed to finally be falling back into place.

On October 2, Lance officially became a cancer survivor. That was the one-year anniversary of his diagnosis. Doctors told him there was now just a minimal chance the disease would return. You can't get much better news than that. Now he could concentrate on returning to competitive racing. Whenever he talked to the press, however, the subject of his illness was almost sure to arise.

During an interview in December of 1997, he was asked point-blank if he worried that the hard work needed to become a world-class racer once again would lower his resistance and possibly cause him to have a relapse.

"Now I don't have those thoughts," Lance said. "After I passed the one-year marker, and my doctors became more optimistic, I became less frightened. My doctors feel as if I can continue as I did before, and so do I."

Lance was also asked why a country as large as the United States hadn't produced more cycling champions. "Our society just doesn't support and reward our potential [cycling] champions," he said. "Our kids are more interested in football, baseball, and basketball."

In answering another question, Lance admitted that he hadn't been totally prepared for his early success, especially winning the World Championships at the age of twenty-one.

"Cycling is a traditional sport and the rider crowned World Champion comes under tremendous scrutiny, and at the time I probably wasn't prepared. But also, I wasn't paying much attention, either. In retrospect, perhaps I was too successful, too soon."

It was apparent that Lance had been doing a great deal of thinking about his early career and his relationship to his sport. Perhaps his reflections were due to the fact that he thought it had all been taken from him. Now, he was on the brink of getting a second chance. It was still way too early to tell if that second chance would be successful. But if it was, there were many indications that Lance would handle things differently this time. Now, it was up to him, and also whether his body would respond to intense training.

In January of 1998, Lance and Kristen moved to Europe with the U.S. Postal team. He began training in earnest. It wasn't easy. There were good days, and days when nothing seemed right. The problem was that Lance was still wary of his illness, and when he didn't feel good on the bike, he began to worry. He worried that the cancer might return, and also that his body had taken too much of a beating with the chemo treatments to simply bounce back. If that was the case, he would never be a world-class cyclist again.

In addition, he wasn't getting any new endorsements. Endorsements are always a big part of a cyclist's income, not to mention an important way to get him out in front of the public. In a way, Lance was a forgotten man, a former top cyclist who almost reached the top but had the misfortune to be struck down by illness. He knew the only way he would reverse his fortunes was to win. He began his come-back in February of 1998 in the Ruta del Sol, a five-day race through Spain. It was his first race in some eighteen months. Lance worked hard but didn't have the old magic. He finished in fourteenth place.

Sure, there were positives. First of all, he had done it. He finished, and he finished ahead of a lot of riders. In addition, he returned to the sport he loved only a year and a half after being made weak, sick, and almost helpless during his rounds of chemo. Yet he found himself depressed after the race, for an old, familiar reason. Simply put, Lance Armstrong was used to winning. He was used to attacking and blowing other riders away with his speed and determination. He also hated all the media attention his first race back had generated. But that goes with the territory. The entire event, with all the emotions involved, probably just overwhelmed him a bit.

Lance said he wished he could have just been another anonymous rider that no one noticed. "I just wanted to ride in the peloton and get my legs back," he said.

Two weeks later he was back on the bike, racing in the Paris-Nice, a difficult, eight-day stage race with a reputation for being run in difficult weather. It may not have been the best choice given the circumstances. Before the race began, there was a time trial that was used to determine which riders would be in the front of the peloton. Lance again gave it all he had and finished nineteenth. While people congratulated him on his showing, he again felt disappointment. His desire to win was the one thing that had not been diminished by his illness.

A day later the first stage of the race began. Not surprisingly, it began in brutal weather, with a cold rain pelting down on the riders and a nasty crosswind making it more difficult to ride. The wind made the rain feel even colder. The weather brought back memories of other difficult days on the bike, but this time it seemed worse. Lance remembered almost using the bad weather to his advantage in the past, continuing to push until the other riders gave in. Not this day. When one of his teammates got a flat, they all stopped. Once they resumed, they were some twenty minutes behind the leaders. All seemed lost already.

Finally, as another gust of wind whipped across his body and almost made him lose control of the bike, Lance lost control of his resolve. He pulled over, stopped, and removed his jersey. He had quit. At the end of the stage, when the entire U.S. Postal team returned to the hotel, they found Lance packing his bags.

"I quit," he told them. "I'm not racing anymore. I'm going home."

Once again he had done something that was considered very "un-Lance-like." Lance Armstrong had never in his life been a quitter. He showed that in his racing and he showed it all over again in his battle against cancer. But racing through the streets of France in the wind and rain had triggered a new emotion. It wasn't so much his performance. He said he felt strong. Suddenly, he just didn't want to be there sitting atop a bike and racing. He said he didn't know anymore whether this was what he wanted to do for the rest of his life.

The conflicting emotions he was experiencing undoubtedly had much to do with his illness. It's not likely that anyone who endured what Lance did could have the same priorities, the same values, the same aspirations as they did before. Advanced cancer, the constant thought that you might not make it, and even your ultimate recovery has to change you. Realistically, it was probably too much to expect Lance to just resume racing with the same singlemindedness he had shown before. It wasn't as if he had recovered from a broken leg. He had recovered from an advanced case of testicular cancer from which he originally had a "coin-flip" chance of making it. That in itself could qualify as a miracle.

At the Paris-Nice race, all these things and more were going through his mind. Besides his recovery, he was engaged to a woman he wanted to marry. His health was once again good, but in the back of his mind he still feared the possibility of relapse. It's not surprising that while riding a bicycle through the cold, rainy, windy streets of France, it all seemed suddenly insignificant, a place he simply did not want to be. Though he was fit, he couldn't have expected to win right away. That probably wasn't the problem. It was simply of matter of rethinking priorities. He just found he didn't have a passion for racing anymore.

"I don't know how much time I have left," he would tell Kristen, "but I don't want to spend it cycling."

Back in Austin, Lance admitted to his friends and advisors that he simply didn't love racing anymore. Because it's such a demanding sport, riders *must* love it. He also said that because his illness had turned his life upside-down, nothing was the same. What he had to do was find himself all over again. If it turned out that racing was what he wanted, then he could go back. If not, he was done and there would have to be something else.

What Lance might have overlooked was the fact that he had always been an athlete, a competitor. That had been his mindset since he was a teenager, and it would be a difficult mindset to lose, especially at the age of twenty-six. But once home, Lance began to play a lot of golf and hang out with old friends. Finally, Kristen, Chris Carmichael, Jim Ochowicz, and other members of Lance's support team told him it was too early to announce his retirement. Why not ride, they suggested, in the U.S. Pro Championships in

Philadelphia in May? Then, if he still wanted to call it quits, he could announce it after racing one last time in the United States. Lance thought about it and agreed.

7

A Comeback Begins in Earnest

It was time for some serious training, but in an environment of Lance's choice, one in which he felt he could thoroughly enjoy himself. He decided to go to Boone, North Carolina, in the Appalachian Mountains. Lance liked the area, and it brought back good memories because it was on the route of the Tour De Pont, a race Lance had won twice. Chris Carmichael was there, as was a former teammate from Motorola, Bob Roll, who would ride with him. Lance would almost be starting over. The hiatus in Austin had seen him gain a few pounds and lose some muscle tone. He was already out of shape.

It was old-fashioned training, the way it

used to be—no crowds, no frills, just riding and more riding. Lance went out every day and rode in all kinds of weather. The experience brought Lance back to earlier days and he began to just enjoy the act of riding hard, of feeling his body tire, of working against the elements and pressing on. In the evenings the men ate and talked and laughed about old times, all the things that had brought Lance so close to the pinnacle of his sport before his illness had struck. Going to North Carolina was almost like going back in time, when things were much simpler, when Lance would get on his bike and attack, just one man against everyone else.

The real turning point came when the group decided to ride up Beech Mountain, which was a five-thousand-foot climb and part of the Tour Du Pont. Lance rode the mountain as if he were again racing in the Tour. He left Bob Roll in his wake and continued to drive hard, thinking of his many victories and the satisfaction he had always gotten from riding. When he finally reached the top, Chris Carmichael pulled up behind him in his car, ready to load Lance's bike on top for the drive down.

"Nope," Lance said. "I'm riding down."

Once again Lance Armstrong realized how

much he loved being on a bike, how much he loved competing, against both himself and others. He felt his life was once again beginning to fit together and he now made plans for another comeback, one he wouldn't abandon. In May, he further solidified his life by marrying Kristen Richards in Santa Barbara, California. There was no real honeymoon, because Lance didn't want to take time away from his bike. This time he was intent on trying to regain his former status in the cycling world, and if he could do that, to go beyond it.

He was ready in time for the target race, the U.S. Pro Championships. This time he was far from embarrassed. He rode a strong race and finished fourth. Even though he didn't win, he felt good about his effort and had no doubts about continuing his comeback. The next logical step was a return to Europe to compete against the best. Lance and Kristen moved to Nice, France, and he continued to compete in select races. He began with the four-day Tour of Luxembourg and surprised a lot of people by winning. It was the first victory of his comeback and, he said, erased the last vestiges of self-doubt that he might have had about racing. Now, he knew he could win again.

He still wasn't ready to win them all. He finished fourth in the week-long Tour of

Holland, then made the decision to skip the 1998 Tour de France. He felt he wasn't ready for the rigors of a three-week stage race, especially the biggest in the world. But by September he felt he was ready for bigger fish and entered the Tour of Spain, called the *Vuelta a Espana*. It was similar to the Tour de France in that it was a three-week stage race of more than 2,300 miles. Not only did Lance finish, but he finished fourth, just missing a third-place medal by six seconds and riding only two minutes and eighteen seconds behind the winner. This wasn't just a big step in his comeback; it was monumental.

Up to this point, Lance's reputation had been based mostly on his ability to win one-day races, to dig down deep and outsprint his competitors to the finish line. Because of his track record before his illness, he was never considered a threat in the longer stage races, especially those the length of the Tour de France. Now, he had come in fourth in the Vuelta. Not only had he served notice to everyone else in the cycling world that a new stage-race force was on the scene, but he realized something about himself, something just a short time earlier he never thought possible.

"Not only was I back," he said, "I was better. I felt I was now capable of winning any race in the world."

After finishing fourth in the World Championships in Holland, a race run in brutal weather conditions where only sixty-six of 152 competitors managed to finish at all, Lance knew he was ready for bigger and better things. He returned home to more good news. His cancer foundation was receiving its first two grants for cancer research, which totaled more than three hundred thousand dollars. These gifts were a direct result of monies raised from the 1997 and 1998 Ride for the Roses weekends.

That winter, there was another milestone for Lance and Kristen. They decided they would like to have a child. Because he was infertile from the chemo, the only way they could do it was to use the sperm he had stored before being treated for cancer. Kristen had to undergo in-vitro fertilization, a process that would use Lance's sperm to fertilize her egg. The process was successful, and nine months later Luke David Armstrong was born. It was something everyone who knew Lance and Kristen called yet another miracle.

Though the 1998 cycling season had to be considered a great success for Lance, there was one big trophy that was noticeably missing. He was reminded of it when he received a congratulatory telegram on finishing fourth in the

Tour of Spain from Johan Bruyneel, the U.S. Postal team director. In it, Bruyneel told Lance that he would "look great on the podium at the Tour de France next year."

The message kind of took Lance by surprise. Then he began to think more seriously about it. His recent strong finish in the Tour of Spain had certainly changed his thoughts about stage racing. Now the self-doubts were gone, both about his ability to come back and about his health. Slowly a new and ambitious goal began seeping into his mind. He decided that he wanted to win the Tour de France!

The Tour de France is not only the granddaddy of all European stage races, it is by far the most difficult and demanding. The first Tour was held way back in 1903, when a French newspaper issued a challenge to all riders of bicycles. There were some sixty riders in that first race, with twenty-one of them able to finish a race that was not as long or demanding as it is today. But it must also be remembered that the bicycles were nothing like the high-tech, lightweight racing machines made today. At any rate, with upwards of one hundred thousand people lining the course during that first race, the Tour quickly became a tradition that was there to stay.

Mountain stages were included in the race for the first time in 1910 because the bikes now had brakes capable of slowing and stopping the riders during the steep downhill descents. The bikes in those days had just two gears and the brakes were operated by the feet. Today, the race has evolved into a marvel of modern high technology. The bikes are light enough to lift with one hand, while the riders can be equipped with computers, heart monitors, and two-way radios. But that doesn't stop the race from being a more than two-thousand-mile trek through the Alps and Pyrenees mountains, along narrow roads with steep falloffs, and finally through the streets of Paris. It is a race of attrition, with riders punishing themselves for three weeks with little rest. If you're exhausted at the end of one stage, you had better find a way to be fresh for the next stage the following morning.

Riders who win the Tour de France become instant heroes in their home countries. To the Europeans, the Tour is every bit the equivalent of their other showcase sporting event, the World Cup of soccer. But that only happens every four years. It's also every bit as big as the American Super Bowl or World Series. Those who manage multiple wins become heroes not only in their home countries, but all over Europe. The record is five, shared by Jacques

Anquetil of France, Eddy Merckx of Belgium, Bernard Hinault of France, and Miguel Indurain of Spain. Indurain is the only rider who has won his five races in succession.

Prior to 1999 only one American rider had ever won the Tour. Greg LeMond won the race in 1986 and again in 1989 and 1990. LeMond's story was also dramatic, since after his 1986 victory he was shot and seriously wounded in a hunting accident. Three years later he was back to win another pair of Tours and to solidify his reputation as America's greatest stage racer. LeMond was one of three riders who had won the Tour three times, and eleven riders had won it twice, the earliest being Lucien Petit-Breton of France way back in 1907 and 1908.

The Tour's long and glorious history wasn't always untarnished. Even in the very first race in 1903, some riders resorted to tactics that were decidedly less than reflective of good sportsmanship. They would actually throw tacks and broken bottles onto the roads to try to stop the riders behind them. Drinks were sometimes spiked to make riders sick. Over the years, some competitors have continued to try to think of ways to take unfair advantage of the rest of the field. In recent years, the biggest worry has been athletes who use performance-enhancing drugs. There is testing, but some athletes always try to get around it. That's because the Tour remains cycling's biggest event. It's held during the hottest part of the summer, so the athletes have to be in extraordinary physical condition, especially in the mountain stages.

Prior to his illness, the mountains were always a huge stumbling block for Lance. He was told that at 180 pounds, he was too heavy. Since his illness, however, his body had changed. He was now a sinewy 160, still muscular and strong, but a lot less bulky. That, in itself, augured well for his next foray into the mountains. He had already proved his mettle in the Tour of Spain. Now, it was just a matter of pointing his season toward the Tour de France and hopefully peaking physically at just the right time.

Though the course is never exactly the same, all the riders know what to expect: the biggest test of the year and the race of their lives, no matter how many times they enter. What made Lance's quest more meaningful was the fact that no American team had ever produced a tour winner. When Greg LeMond won his three races, he was a member of a French racing team.

Ironically, while Lance was pointing toward a July date in Paris, he opened the 1999 season in terrible form. There was a crash in the second race of the year that resulted in a shoulder injury that necessitated a couple of weeks off his bike. He was sideswiped by a car in France while on a training run, then had mediocre finishes in the Paris-Nice and Milan-San Remo races. He just wasn't in good form and needed some remedial work on his technique.

Also ironically, Lance noted that now that he was pointing toward winning the Tour de France, he wasn't as effective in the one-day races. He said he didn't have the anger and intensity that always drove him before his illness. But while he might not have been seen by his peers as the overly aggressive rider he had once been, he had developed a single-minded purpose in his riding, and that was to win the Tour de France. For a rider like Lance, who relied so much on emotion, the one-day races suddenly ceased to have the same importance to him. They were more like training for the Tour de France. In fact, Lance said he was willing to sacrifice his entire season to be better prepared for the Tour.

The fact that he was skipping races raised a lot of eyebrows among riders and journalists. Many began to question him about it. Lance didn't mask his intentions.

"I'm putting all my focus into winning the

Tour," he would tell them, in a half-dozen different ways. "All my training and racing decisions are based on that one event."

The entire U.S. Postal Service team had rallied around Lance and was equally committed to helping him win. Though cycling, by its very definition, is an individual sport, in major stage races the entire team is very important to the lead rider. As mentioned earlier, they protect him in the peloton, draft for him to cut down on the wind, and pace him during certain portions of the race. So while it is always an individual who gets the glory for winning the Tour, his team always plays a major role in the winning effort.

At the end of April, Lance entered a one-day race called the Amstel Gold Race. Though he hadn't been focusing on one-day races during the 1999 season, he felt very strong on this day and decided this was one he really wanted to win. Lance was riding at the head of the pack with Holland's Michael Boogerd. With ten miles remaining, Lance continued to lead with Boogerd, also a world-class rider, staying with him. In the final sprint, the point of a race where Lance was rarely caught, Boogerd managed a final push and beat Lance by less than the width of a tire, an incredibly close finish. Lance took the loss hard, as he had in the past.

In addition, because Michael Boogerd was one of the early favorites to possibly win the Tour de France, his loss had a little more bite to it.

Lance returned to his intense, arduous training. He trained in all kinds of weather conditions, on days when no one else would go out, and usually did even more work than he had planned. He was willing to push and punish himself to achieve his goal, which had now almost become an obsession. This was a race the old Lance was told he would never win. And, indeed, before his illness he never thought he could. Now, however, things were different. He knew he had the ability and the heart to win. It was just a matter of putting in the work and then being ready for the biggest three-week push of his life.

By July, Lance felt he was ready. In France, however, he wasn't considered one of the favorites. Maybe there was something of the old feeling that an American team just couldn't cut it in the Tour. The Europeans were simply too experienced. Heck, the experts said, even Greg LeMond had to be part of a European team to win the Tour. Some of the names being thrown around as potential winners were the aforementioned Michael Boogerd, world champion Abraham Olano, Alexander Zulle of Switzerland, and Fernando Escartin of Spain.

Then, a short time before the race was to begin, a reporter asked the legendary champion Miguel Indurain which rider he thought had a good chance of winning. Indurain looked at the reporter and then gave a one-word answer.

"Armstrong!"

8

The 1999
Tour de France

Before the first stage of the Tour there is a short time trial called the Prologue. In 1999 it was held on July 3. It is used to determine where the riders begin in stage one, a kind of seeding system. It is also the first opportunity for the riders to establish themselves to some degree. Because the Prologue is only about eight kilometers long, the riders have to sprint all-out from beginning to end. Even if they let up for just a few seconds, it can cost them dearly at the end. Before the 1999 Prologue, the record for the sprint was 8:12, set by the great Indurain.

The riders started one at a time, as they do in all time trials. The starts were staggered, three minutes apart. That way, there were no head-to-head strategies involved, just a mad-dash sprint with the rider and his bike. On this July day, conditions were good and so were the times. First Olano broke the course record with a time of 8:11. Then, minutes later, Alexander Zulle did even better, crossing the finish line in 8:07. One of Lance's U.S. Postal teammates rode before him and experimented with the gears going up the one hill on the course. That is one way teammates can help each other. The experiment cost him time, but he was able to give Lance some solid advice just before he began.

Finally, Lance took off, riding hard and concentrating on one thing—getting to the fin-ish line as fast as he possibly could. His form was perfect as he sped through the streets, then charged up the hill. He still felt good when he crossed the finish line. He looked up at the clock. When he saw 8:02, he could barely believe it. Then it was confirmed. He had set a new record, beating the record Zulle had set just minutes before by five full seconds and smashing Indurain's old mark by an amazing ten seconds. What was more important was that he would get to wear the fabled yellow jer-sey, emblematic of being in the lead of the Tour de France. He said the feeling of putting on that jersey was utterly amazing.

Of course, the real race hadn't yet begun. Lance knew it was much more important to be wearing that yellow jersey at the end of the final stage. After the time trial there was one more sweet moment. Lance found himself walking past members of the Cofidis team and their organization. They were the ones who had turned their backs on him when he was so ill and even when he had recovered, didn't think he would ride at a world-class level again. Wearing the yellow jersey after his victory in the time trial, Lance walked by them and couldn't resist.

"That was for you," he told them, with a smile.

But there was still a very long way to go. The race in modern times is a little bit more than rider and bike against the elements. Two cars and a van usually follow each team. The coach can direct his riders through two-way radios. There are earpieces in each helmet and a radio cord wired to a heart monitor so the coach and trainers can watch how the racers are reacting to the various kinds of stress at different stages of the race. In addition, there are spare bikes on top of the vans, a mechanic available if a rider gets a flat, and water and food that can be handed to the riders as they go.

The opening stages of the race always

favored the sprinters, as these stages took place on flat roads across flat countryside. Here, the two hundred or so riders would play a chess game of positioning, the teams trying to help their lead rider. Everyone would be thinking about strategies that would give them an advantage as the race wore on and neared the telltale mountain stages.

The rest of the U.S. Postal riders were there to protect Lance. In the peloton they surrounded him, shielding him from other riders and potential crashes and drafting in front so he had minimal wind. There was one massive crash, but fortunately it happened behind Lance. Still in the early stages, a couple of the favorites, Boogerd and Zulle, began falling behind. Big deficits are difficult to make up— it began to appear it wasn't their year.

Lance just wanted to stay near the leaders. He had to give up the yellow jersey after several stages, but that didn't matter. He just wanted to be in striking distance of the leaders when the race went into the mountains. His strategy included an all-out effort at the time trial in Metz, the final leg before the mountain stages began. An Italian rider named Mario Cippolini tied a Tour record by winning four straight stages and taking over the yellow jersey. The other challengers weren't concerned, though.

Everyone knew Cippolini always faltered in the mountains and because of that, simply wasn't a threat for the overall title. That's the kind of strategy that's used. A rider gets almost a week of glory by winning four straight stages, but none of the other riders really care. They are too busy watching each other.

The time trial at Metz was unlike the opening Prologue. This was a longer run of some fifty-six kilometers; the riders would have to go hard for more than an hour. It was a real test of their endurance and determination. It was also a chance to pick up valuable time in the overall race. It was a course that favored the strong riders, and in the early going, Alexander Zulle had the best time, coming in with a time just over one hour and nine minutes. This time the riders were going off in two-minute intervals.

Abraham Olano was the favorite in this particular stage. He started directly ahead of Lance. As Lance was waiting in the start area, the word came back that Olano had crashed on a curve and lost maybe thirty seconds. He was back on his bike, but it would be difficult to make up the time. That's how quickly fortunes can change in the Tour. One slip, one crash, one flat tire, and the rider loses seconds, maybe minutes. If the crash is bad enough, he might have to drop out of the race.

Lance went out fast, working hard as always and attacking the course. He was flying, maybe too fast. By the third checkpoint his time was a full minute and forty seconds ahead of Zulle. He even caught and passed Olano, something that doesn't usually happen in a time trial. Then, a short time later, he passed another rider who had started a full six minutes ahead of him. But Lance had, indeed, gone out too hard. He started to pay the price in the final portion of the race. His legs began feeling heavy, almost as if they wouldn't move. There was also a head-wind and no one to draft. He began to feel he was losing precious time, and wished he had paced himself better.

When he crossed the finish line he was almost afraid to look at the clock. When he did, it read 1:08:36. He had won the stage and beaten Zulle by fifty-eight seconds! Though he was exhausted and concerned he might not recover in time for the next stage, he had regained the overall lead. As he put the yellow jersey on once more, he felt good, very good. Though the race was barely half over, he felt he was in a great position to win and decided he wanted that jersey remaining with him until he crossed the finish line.

Now the Tour was ready to move into the mountains. Lance held a lead of 2:20 over his nearest competitor. But that would mean nothing if he fell apart in the mountain stages. On those steep hills, leads could evaporate as fast as boiling water. This is where the old Lance Armstrong had faltered early in his career. It was the reason he wasn't considered a major threat in stage races. But this Lance Armstrong was different. He already had the lead. Now, if he could control the race in the mountains, he would definitely have a good chance of winning.

Strategy now became even more important. It didn't matter if a rider who wasn't really in contention won a stage. Lance's job was to stay ahead of those who were closest to him and try to increase his overall advantage. In other words, if a rider who was twelve minutes behind him beat him by four minutes in a mountain stage, it wouldn't really matter, if at the same time Lance finished two minutes faster than his closest rivals. Lance would still be increasing his overall lead as well as his chances to win the race.

While all this was happening, word began trickling back to the United States. Normally there was very little interest in the Tour de France in America. There wasn't even much hoopla when Greg LeMond won the race three times. But Lance's story was special. People just couldn't believe that a man who was literally at death's door less than three years earlier was now threatening to win arguably the most demanding and grueling sports event in the world. His agent, Bill Stapleton, expressed the thought that was being highlighted in most of the stories in the American press.

"This guy was on his death bed, and we were more worried about having him live than having him race again," Stapleton said.

Reporters and journalists who normally didn't even cover sporting events were now digging deeper into the story, looking for people to talk about Lance, his battle with cancer, and his amazing comeback. One of his oncology nurses, Janice Thompson, told reporters that it was Lance's fierce determination that helped him in his fight against cancer.

"He had a 'can do' attitude from day one," she said. "He was going to beat this disease; it wasn't going to get him. He's beaten the ultimate competitor—he's beaten cancer. Now I'm sure nothing or no one can intimidate him. He's living large."

And he was riding large, as well. The first mountain stage was a 132.7-kilometer ride that ended in the town of Sestriere. Two of Lance's teammates were climbing specialists and would help draft for him. The two riders that Lance and his teammates would watch would be Alexander Zulle and Fernando Escartin. They were closest to him in overall time. Riders often like to break away on the climbs. Since some are not even in contention, it's the job of the leaders and their teammates to know who to chase and who to let go. The stage featured three major climbs and could be a killer to a lot of riders. For poor climbers, this was where the race would effectively end.

The final ascent of the stage was a long and difficult thirty-kilometer climb to Sestriere and the finish line. The riders had already been pedaling for more than five and a half hours. Add almost constant climbing to that time and it becomes a nearly inhuman task. From this point on it became a matter of will, of who wanted it the most. With just eight kilometers left, Lance was some thirty-two seconds behind the leaders, riding in a second group of five riders, all exceptional climbers. That's when Lance made his move, jumping out in front of the second pack and opening up some distance. He felt strong, like there was more gas in the tank. He continued to work hard as he moved up on the leaders.

Suddenly, Lance was just eleven seconds behind the two leaders and still moving up. When he pulled alongside them they didn't react, so he surged again, taking the lead and opening a slight gap. Still no response from the other two. He accelerated once more, in total control. It's a situation every rider loves to be in, making a move to the front and the other riders not responding. It's a real feeling of power, that you can do it and they can't. When Lance was told that Alexander Zulle was chasing him, he worked even harder, driving toward the finish, not letting up for a second. As he crossed the line he thrust both fists into the air.

What Lance had just done was basically to destroy the rest of the field mentally. He not only proved he could now climb with the best of them, maybe better than the best of them, but he also had won another stage. What's more, he had opened up a gap of six minutes and three seconds over the rest of the field. With that kind of lead, Lance was looking so strong and in such a commanding position that it seemed he would now just have to maintain a consistent pace to win the Tour. Of course, there was always a chance of a crash, illness, or some kind of physical breakdown. But up to this point there were no signs of anything but continued success.

In the next mountain stage, Lance didn't win. He finished fifth. But in doing so, he managed to continue to increase his lead, since the four riders who finished in front of him weren't challengers. Those right behind him, Olano and Zulle, fell farther back. He now had a lead of 7:42 over Olano and 7:47 over Zulle. But just when it seemed only a formality for Lance to finish the Tour at the top, a new controversy arose.

As was the case with other sports in the late 1990s, there were always athletes looking for an edge. One of the ways some athletes tried to do this was to use illegal substances tagged generically as "performance-enhancing drugs," which include but are not limited to muscle-building anabolic steroids. There is a list of banned substances, and athletes in some sports are randomly tested to make sure none of these substances are in their system. The Tour de France, with its status and prestige, has often been a magnet for athletes looking for an edge. Then along came Lance Armstrong, a cancer survivor who was close to death just three years earlier. There was no legal way, many reasoned, that this guy could be blowing away the field in the Tour de France. After all, before his illness he was never remotely a threat to win the Tour, even with all the other titles he had taken. Rumors that Lance was on something began to spread, with some help from the French press.

The most ridiculous allegation was that the

drugs used to battle Lance's cancer had somehow enhanced his ability to race. That was a total joke. Chemotherapy is one of the most debilitating combinations of drugs in the medical world. The drugs weaken and sicken a patient long before they cure him. Had anyone making those accusations seen Lance during his chemo treatments and the aftermath, they would have known how silly they were being. But some found it hard to believe that this man who had been so sick was winning the Tour de France with relative ease. There must be some kind of explanation, people reasoned. It just didn't make sense.

But the drug tests proved that it did. Every one came up negative. Lance didn't like the idea of having blood drawn after nearly every stage, but he couldn't avoid it. They were supposed to be random tests, but he seemed to be the one U.S. Postal Service team rider they always picked to be tested. All the tests showed, however, was that Lance was clean. There were no illegal substances in his system.

"My life and my illness and my career are open," Lance told the press, also citing again that all his drug tests were negative. Yet some members of the French press continued to raise the issue and Lance was forced to stop talking to them for awhile. There was still plenty of racing left and he didn't want any distractions. Because he was the leader, other teams and other riders would try to break him, often by attacking early in a stage and trying to force him to alter his strategy. But Lance and his teammates, for the most part, held true to form. Once, he made an ill-advised charge after the lead pack, but when his coaches told him he was making a mistake, he listened and dropped back. The old Lance might have just continued to attack.

As Lance continued to hold a firm lead on the field, the allegations of drug use continued, despite the negative tests. Finally, he decided to hold a press conference and try to put the allegations to rest, once and for all.

"I have been on my deathbed," he told reporters, "and I am not stupid. I can emphatically say I am not on drugs. I thought a rider with my history and my health situation wouldn't be such a surprise. I'm not a new rider. I know there's been looking, and prying, and digging, but you're not going to find anything. There's nothing to find . . . and once everyone has done their due diligence and realizes they need to be professional and can't print a lot of crap, they'll realize they're dealing with a clean guy."

If nothing else, logic should have told

everyone that a rider who had experienced the horror of chemotherapy would simply not put any substance into his body that had even a remote chance of doing damage or harming him. Yet the speculation continued as he continued to lead the race. There were just so many people who couldn't believe what they were seeing. They just didn't think it was possible.

After the sixteenth stage the riders were finally out of the mountains and Lance still had a lead of 6:15 over Escartin and 7:28 over Zulle. Yet he had to endure another two-hour press conference, one once again dominated by questions about drugs. He began to feel as if the press wanted to break him mentally because none of the other riders could do it. That same day, the International Cycling Federation released the results of all his drug tests so everyone could see everything had come up clean. It was only then that Lance received a glowing testimonial from Jean-Marie Leblanc, the organizer of the race. Fed up from watching what Lance had to endure from the press, Leblanc said, "Armstrong beating his illness is a sign that the Tour can beat its own illness."

The nineteenth stage of the race was another time trial. Lance had such a big lead that his advisors told him to take it easy, not to take any chances, and simply to maintain his position. They didn't want him to risk the one thing that could keep him from winning, a major crash. Lance listened, then shook his head. No way was he going to play safe. He said he was going out hard and was planning to kick butt.

"I'm going to put my signature on this Tour," he said.

With that, Lance went out and gave it all he had once more. Even though he had pretty much wrapped up the overall victory, the other riders didn't want to hand another stage to him. So they all pushed. But when the dust cleared, Lance had won the time trial by a scant nine seconds. With that victory, he became only the fourth rider in the history of the Tour to win all three time trials in one race. The other three were among the greatest ever—Hinault, Merckx, and Indurain. Lance had not only put his signature on the Tour, but on Tour history, as well. Now he just had to ride through the largely ceremonial final stage to make it all official.

At this point, the excitement was also building in the United States. Again, it wasn't so much that an American was on the brink of winning the Tour de France. No, it was the bigger picture, the so-called "feel-good" part of the story, that a cancer survivor was making this miraculous comeback and was on the brink of winning the Tour de France. American journalists were flying to France, while the word came that all the prime-time talk shows in the United States were already scrambling to book Lance once the Tour ended. It's a tradition that the Tour winner travels around Europe and participates in a series of races simply to show off the yellow jersey. Lance felt that was important to him. His agent, however, wanted him to fly to the United States, even if it was just for a day.

But there was one more piece of business to finish. The final stage of the race was an 89.2-mile ride from Arpajon to Paris. Because the race was all but over, the peloton would ride at a relaxed pace until the Eiffel Tower came into view. Then, when the group reached the Arc de Triomphe, the U.S. Postal team would ride in front of the peloton down the Champs-Elysées. Finally, a sprint would take place for ten laps around a course in the center of the city. After that, there would be a final victory lap. It was a longtime tradition for a race that was nearly one hundred years old.

Lance even did interviews from his bike during the ride. When the peloton finally neared Paris, he could feel the emotion building. It further warmed his heart when someone held up a large cardboard sign that said simply TEXAS.

Because there was absolutely no chance of anyone catching Lance, the final ten-lap sprint wasn't highly competitive; Lance was simply careful to avoid any kind of unexpected crash. Finally, as he rode his bike across the finish line, it all sunk in. He had done it. He had come all the way back to win the Tour de France.

Lance was swept up in a myriad of emotions as he stood on the podium for the trophy presentation. His family was there, as were many old friends from Texas. Once the presentation was complete, he leaped off the podium, ran to his wife and hugged her. Then he sought out his mother and hugged her. When a reporter asked his mother if she thought he had bucked the odds to win, she said, "Lance's whole life has been against all odds."

Then Lance and his team got back on their bikes and rode a ceremonial victory lap along the Champs-Elysées. It was a moment for all of them to savor, for each and every member of the U.S. Postal team had played a major role in his victory. When he returned to the press area to answer questions, he told everyone there just how he felt.

"I'm really in shock," he said several times, then added, "I would just like to say one thing. If you ever get a second chance in life for something, you've got to go all the way."

9

A Champion Doesn't Quit

It's virtually impossible to imagine the elation
Lance must have felt, the confluence of emotions in winning the Tour de France. To simply say his life had come full circle was an understatement. It would be extremely difficult in the entire annals of sport to find a story as dramatic and fulfilling. As close as his support group had been, including his wife and mother, only Lance could possibly comprehend the full meaning of what he had done. Yet he wasn't going to hog the glory. He made sure that everyone knew he couldn't have won the race without the selflessness of the entire U.S. Postal Service team.

Lance took the advice of Bill Stapleton, his

agent, and flew from Holland to the United States for one whirlwind of a day. Reporters from all over the country had come to New York for just a precious few minutes with him. He began his day by appearing on *CBS This Morning* at five forty-five A.M. and ending it with *The Late Show with David Letterman* at nine P.M. In between, there was barely time for him to get his breath. He went to Wall Street to ring the opening bell at the New York Stock Exchange, then returned for a series of interviews. At one point a producer from NY1 in New York was still signing off as another reporter from KTBC in Austin began asking questions. At the same time, a producer from KCBS Sports Central in Los Angeles was setting up so he could be ready for his station's eight minutes with Lance.

Diana Nyad from *Fox Sports News* waited her turn, as did Jim Rome of *The Last Word*, and many others. It was like an assembly-line of interviews, with Lance essentially telling the same story over and over again.

"I feel almost guilty doing this to him," said Mike Leventhal, a producer for the Bader TV News, where Lance sat for all the interviews. "I usually space things out, give somebody a rest between interviews, but with Lance there just isn't time, just thirty seconds or so to get a drink of water and on to the next."

For Lance, the message he had to send was important, and that was one of the main reasons he had made this overnight trip halfway around the world.

"If I can save five lives by going on some show, it's worth it," he said. "If I can save one life by going on all the shows, it's worth it. I'm prouder of being a cancer survivor than I am of winning the Tour de France. Believe me. I'm aware of the cancer community wherever I go. I could feel it at the Tour. People would come up to me before races or after races. I could feel it during the races. It's a community of shared experience. If you've ever belonged, you never leave."

Lance also knew that having cancer had changed his life in many ways, not the least of which was his ability to win stage races.

"If I never had cancer, I never would have won the Tour de France," he said, many times during his interviews. "I'm convinced of that. I wouldn't want to do it all over again, but I wouldn't change a thing, either. I'm talking to you today, but I'm not sure how. I know some things about cancer now. I know you have to pay attention, to watch for signs on your body, then react. I know you have to do research, go on the Internet, look for the second opinion, then the third, find out all your options. I also know you have to be lucky. That's probably as important as anything. I was very lucky."

Lance wasn't about to make a long and tiring trip home just to talk about winning a race. He felt he had a more important message to get across to the American public, while hopefully sparking more interest in cycling at the same time. In a strange way, the two distinctly different topics would always intersect with one another. He would continue to say that being a cancer survivor was the most important thing in his life, and he would continue to be the world's best stage racer. His good friend Jim Ochowicz confirmed what Lance had said—that in an unexpected way, having cancer and conquering it had also made him a better racer.

"The doubt about him had always been the climbs in the mountains," Ochowicz explained. "He always could sprint well, and he always was capable of winning a stage in the Tour. The mountains were his downfall. But with his weight loss—if you lose five pounds, that's a large weight loss for the mountains. It was all he needed. He became very good in the mountains."

Back in Europe, Lance continued to celebrate his victory in the traditional European way. He was feted wherever he went, and when he finally returned to the States for a much-deserved rest, he knew he had just begun his second career as a racer. Winning the Tour de France was the obvious pinnacle, but it didn't mean there were no more worlds to conquer. The Tour was a new world in itself each year, and almost as soon as he won the race, Lance knew he had to win it again. For one thing, he wanted to show that his 1999 victory wasn't a fluke. He also decided to make it a kind of anniversary. Each time he won the Tour it would mark another year as a cancer survivor.

For Lance, there was certainly newfound celebrity, endorsements, sponsors, people who wanted him for one thing or another. While Americans still didn't have an all-consuming interest in cycling, they seemed to have a special interest in Lance Armstrong. His story of survival, triumph in Paris, good looks, and commanding personality gave him a star quality reserved for a special few. Some felt he would get caught up in so many activities and demands for his time that his cycling would take a back seat. Those people didn't know the real Lance. From the moment he crossed the finish line at the Tour and raised his arms in triumph, he knew his goal would be to come back again. There were some important things, however, that his newfound status would allow him to do. If those things involved helping other cancer victims, then he would always take the time.

In early January of 2000, he wanted to set the record straight about something else. The whispers about the possibility of his using performance-enhancing drugs had never completely stopped. Though he knew there would always be skeptics, he still wanted to have his say. Nike and Lance got together to produce a documentary-style commercial called *Body*, which explored what was called his "steely resolve." There was footage of Lance riding, undergoing blood tests for drugs, and performing cardiovascular tests, as well as participating in a wind tunnel experiment to measure his cycling efficiency. His own voice-over allowed him to comment on everything taking place. During the footage, he said, in part, "This is my body and I can do whatever I want to it. I can push it, study it, tweak it, listen to it. Everybody wants to know what I'm on. What am I on? I'm on my bike, busting my ass six hours a day. What are you on?"

James Selmon, the director of *Body*, said he really got a sense of what Lance was like while putting together the footage. The essence of the shoot was to recreate Lance's drug-free ethic of hard work. "Yes, he's physically gifted as far as his lung capacity and all that," Selmon said, "but it's that extra hundred-and-ten percent that puts him over the top, as far as his ability to win [is concerned]."

In February of 2000, Lance launched the Cycle of Hope™, a national cancer-education campaign for both those with cancer and those at risk for developing the disease. To create the campaign, Lance teamed up with his non-profit foundation and the Bristol-Myers Squibb Company, the maker of the drugs that success-fully treated his disease.

In effect, the Cycle of Hope was designed to support early cancer detection, reduce the fear associated with the disease, encourage a team approach to treatment, and foster hope in patients and their families. To help spread the word, Lance was featured in a national public service announcement that encouraged people to call a toll-free number or visit the campaign's Web site for the Cycle of Hope information packet. There was little doubt that Lance was committed to giving back to the community by helping other people cope with fighting the dis-ease. His work in this area was extremely important to him.

"I ignored my symptoms until it was almost too late," he said. "I am dedicated to the Cycle of Hope campaign because I want to help oth-ers break out of their cycle of misunderstanding and fear, and empower themselves through the Cycle of Hope."

Even when he was giving time to his public service work and his foundation, Lance didn't stay off the bike for long. A world-class rider has to stay in training, keep his condition, then be ready to peak for the most important races. For Lance, that now meant the Tour de France. Yet despite his incredible victory in 1999, there were still naysayers. He wasn't even being spoken of as one of the favorites for the 2000 Tour. Many were focusing on two riders who had missed the race in '99: Germany's Jan Ullrich and Italy's Marco Pantini. Since they hadn't been in the race, people felt Lance still had to prove he could beat them. Other favorites were France's Richard Virenque and veterans Abraham Olano and Alexander Zulle, who had chased Lance for most of the race last year.

Lance knew it wouldn't be easy. Now everyone would be gunning for him. He would once again need his teammates on the U.S. Postal Service team. The team went to Europe in the spring to begin training in earnest and Lance entered some early-season events. He had mixed results, though he finished second at the Paris-Camembert race in April. Throughout April and May, he and his teammates trained in

the mountains of France. Then, on May 5, his bid to become a two-time winner of the Tour almost came to a premature end.

He was training in the Pyrenees mountains, riding on the Hautacam, which would be one of the more difficult mountains climbs in the 2000 Tour. On the descent, Lance was traveling at high speed when his front tire hit a rock and popped. The bike hit a brick wall and Lance was thrown off the bike and into the wall. He hit headfirst. Even worse, he wasn't wearing his helmet. He had taken it off on the climb and forgotten to put it back for the descent. It was a frightening moment. Lance heard a ringing in his ears and felt the right side of his face beginning to swell up. One of his teammates called for an ambulance.

The worst of his injuries was just a slight concussion, but Lance was advised to take a couple of weeks off. To an athlete preparing for a major event, this can seem like an eternity. It could, however, have been worse, and Lance would never again forget to wear his helmet in practice. A month later, he was back on the Hautacam, completing the training schedule that had been interrupted by the crash. Once again, all his focus pointed to the Tour de France. In July, it was time to strut his stuff once more.

As usual, there was a highly competitive field, and a ton of reporters and media people were present. Most of them were asking the same questions: Could Lance Armstrong do it again? The course of the Tour is never the same two years in a row. In 2000, the course was mapped out to go counterclockwise around France, and it included some very difficult stages. It would open, as usual, with a time trial of just over ten miles. The riders wouldn't go into the mountains until stage ten. Lance and his teammates felt they were ready.

The Tour began with the time trial on July 1. Lance wanted to get off fast just as he had last year, and that meant winning the opening time trial. But when David Millar of Scotland sailed over the course with a blistering time of 19:03, Lance knew it wouldn't be easy. He attacked as always, and his time in the early going was better than the other competitors'. But by the halfway point, he was three seconds behind Millar. Once again, Lance picked up the pace and went as hard as he could to the finish line. When he looked at the clock, Millar had beaten him by two seconds. This time, Lance wouldn't be wearing the yellow jersey on the first day. But that didn't really matter. It was more important who would be wearing it on the *last* day.

This was a different race from last year's. For Lance, it was more tactical. He watched the riders whom he felt were the most dangerous and tried to stay ahead of them. He didn't win any of the first nine stages, and just before the Tour entered the mountains, he was in sixteenth place, almost six minutes behind the leader, Alberto Elli of Italy. At first glance, that didn't seem very good. But a closer look showed that Lance had set himself up in a very solid position. For openers, he was in front of the other top riders. He was forty-three seconds ahead of Ullrich and led Zulle by 4:05, Pantini by 5:12, and Virenque by 5:32. The tenth stage was a climb to Hautacam, where Lance had been injured the past May. It was a cold, rainy day, but Lance planned to launch an all-out attack. He knew most of the other riders didn't like the rain.

Lance felt as if it was going to be his day from the start. He had someone pulling him, as well. A Basque rider named Javier Otxoa, who was not in contention for the overall title, seemed to make this stage his personal Tour. He began attacking right from the start and opened up a huge lead. By the time Lance got ready for the final, steep climb to the Hautacam, Otxoa had a lead of 10:30, which seemed totally insurmountable. Lance was also on his own

now. His teammates were all exhausted by the combination of the bad weather and the strenuous climb. Now Lance was riding in a chase group that included Pantini, Zulle, and Ullrich, as well as a number of other riders. All of them were way behind Otxoa, but Lance decided this was his time. He would not only try to destroy the rest of the field, but would also try to catch Otxoa.

Pantini and Zulle attacked first, but Lance took the cue and also attacked, passing both of them quickly. He then surged past another seven riders. Finally, only Otxoa remained in front of him. He surged again, then again, then once more. The gap of 10:30 had closed to 4:48 with five kilometers left. His coaches kept telling him the time through the two-way radio. With three kilometers left, Lance was within 3:21 of Otxoa. Another kilometer and he had cut the gap to 2:14. Though he continued to close the gap, there just wasn't enough course left. Otxoa crossed the finish line just forty-one seconds ahead of Lance. Lance hadn't won the stage, but when he looked at the times, he realized that he had just done something special.

Starting the day some six minutes behind the leader, he had not only made up every second of that, but had emerged from the climb

with the yellow jersey once again his. He was now in the overall lead once again. In fact he already had opened a gap of 4:14 over Ullrich, considered the biggest threat to Lance's repeating his victory of a year earlier. With more mountain stages looming ahead of the riders, Lance Armstrong had once again become the favorite to win. His surge over the final miles had impressed some of the other veteran riders. Frenchman Raymond Poulidor, known as a strong climber himself, said Lance's final ascent was "unprecedented in the annals of cycling." Another French rider, Stephane Heulot, put it this way: "When I saw Armstrong I had the impression I was watching someone descending a hill I was trying to scale."

On another tortuous climb Lance found himself racing to the summit with Marco Pantini. They had broken away from the rest of the pack. Though he had the overall lead, Lance had not won a single stage. This one appeared to be well within his grasp. The two riders struggled through sharp wind and fatigue, with the finish line looming ahead. Lance, ahead of everyone but Pantini, suddenly slowed and allowed the Italian to win the stage. Once again, he was thinking about the politics of the Tour. It wasn't always the best idea to try to win too many stages, especially for the rider with the overall lead. He can be perceived as being greedy, as a slap in the face of the other riders.

It was something that Lance conceded Americans wouldn't understand. The mentality in the United States is to win, win, win. But when Pantini didn't take Lance's gesture in the spirit that it was offered, pronouncing after the race that Lance was simply not the strongest rider that day, Lance became angry. Next time, he'd be more choosy when he decided to concede a stage. Though Pantini would win another mountain stage a few days later, he had pretty much burned himself out. In stage sixteen, he weakened and fell back, finishing some thirteen minutes behind the lead group. The next day he withdrew from the Tour, citing stomach pains.

Lance was also tiring. Pantini had set a blistering pace before dropping back, and the other riders all paid the price. Lance lost 1:37 to Ullrich, but still led the German by more than five minutes. It was a scare, because at the end of that race he felt he had nothing left to give. He called it one of his worse days ever in a stage race. Fortunately, his will kept him from losing any more time.

Though there weren't as many rampant accusations of drug use against Lance in this

Tour, drugs were still one of the prime topics during the race. The talk of drugs made Lance recall reading a 1995 poll of mostly Olympic-caliber American athletes. According to the poll, more than fifty percent said they would take a drug that would enable them to become a champion, even though they knew there was a good chance that drug would kill them within five years.

"I've seen those results [of the poll], and I find them hard to believe," Lance said. "If they are true, then those people are crazy. Look, I live for cycling right now, but one day it's going to end, and then there are going to be no more yellow jerseys, no more adoration—we don't want your autograph, we don't want your picture, we don't want you to write a book. One day I'm going to be a normal guy, and that's going to be fine."

It was just another way of Lance reiterating that he wouldn't take a performance-enhancing drug that could harm his body. His secret wasn't really a secret—it was just constant, intense training. He put in the work, the hours on the bike, something that his wife could attest to easily.

"For nine months out of the year it's like we're living in a monastery," Kristen Armstrong said, describing how Lance spent up to seven hours on his bike some days. "[Then] he comes

home just like any other guy comes home. The first thing he always says is, 'Where's my boy!' He doesn't look tired. He looks so happy and peaceful. Then he has a bite, naps, has dinner, spends a few hours around the house and goes to bed. And that's that. Day in, day out, that's how we live. People see the highlights, but they don't see that it's a very, very serious commitment."

In effect, Lance was simply outworking everyone else; no frills, no secret methods, and no drugs. And now, another victory was well within his grasp. Despite his lead, however, he was concerned after stage sixteen because he had felt so exhausted. He felt that Ullrich was still a threat, especially if he showed any weakness. If the other riders perceived that he was weakening, there would be a feeding frenzy to catch him. He also wanted to win at least one stage. It just didn't seem right to win the overall Tour without winning a stage. That opportunity finally came in the nineteenth stage and final time trial. It would be 58.5 kilometers at full speed.

On this day, Lance had it. He felt good as soon as he began, and he attacked the course. He didn't stop until he crossed the finish line, winning the stage by twenty-five seconds and roaring over the course with an average speed of

53.98 kilometers per hour. It was the second fastest time trial speed ever, just behind the record set by the other American winner, Greg LeMond. Lance felt it was imperative to make the statement he had just made.

"It's important for the [rider wearing the yellow jersey] to show himself in the time trial because it's the race of truth," Lance said. "So it would have been easy to ride easy and ride conservative and not take risks, but I think it's important for the race leader to make that demonstration. I really wanted to win this stage. I had a lot of stress and a lot of anger and a lot of pressure. The Tour wouldn't be complete for me if I won the Tour without winning a stage."

When Lance held on to his solid lead during the next stage, he had once again all but won the race. Now came the ceremonial final ride to Paris and his second straight Tour de France victory, the one that should have silenced the skeptics once and for all.

10
Going for a Triple

Every Tour de France victory is special in its own right. Lance once again had all kinds of feelings as he crossed the finish line to repeat his victory of a year earlier. He proved once again that he had indeed become the best, a thought echoed by the second-place finisher, Jan Ullrich.

"Armstrong is a worthy champion," Ullrich said. "He was the strongest man, and he met our every attack. He earned his victory."

The detractors were slowly melting away, but for the moment Lance didn't care about that. He sought out his family, hugged them, then lofted his nine-month-old son, Luke, above his head. He had tears in his eyes.

"This one's even more special than last year,

partly because of this little guy," he said.

It was a victory with a contradiction of a sort. In one sense, Lance said it was more difficult than the year before since the course was more physically demanding, with four very difficult mountain stages through the Alps and Pyrenees. He said he was a more tired athlete this time. Mentally, however, he admitted it wasn't as difficult as the first time around.

"I was mentally exhausted at the end of last year's Tour," he said, "partly because of all the controversy and accusations. This year has been much more positive, a real vindication in many ways, and I can carry all that positive energy into the Olympics."

Lance's next goal was already the 2000 Summer Olympics in Sydney, Australia. He was pointing toward winning a gold medal in the time trial event.

"Winning gold is a big objective," he admitted in an interview just after the Tour ended. But he also told reporters that no matter how successful he was on his bike, he still had a purpose in life that would always override everything else.

"The fight against cancer is still my biggest ambition," he said. "It's nice to win the Tour de France, and to win it a second time, but [helping to fight cancer] is something that will be going on when I'm fifty."

Lance didn't need any special encouragement to continue his campaign to help with cancer research and encourage cancer patients. He continued to be an inspiration to many people. There weren't a whole lot of Americans on the Champs-Elysées to see Lance cross the finish line, but those who were there were not only rooting for him, but full of admiration for what he had accomplished and what he stood for. One spectator, Kevin Fink from Denton, Maryland, expressed his thoughts to an American reporter. "Everybody knows somebody who's suffering from, or died from, cancer—and everybody knows he beat a terrible case of cancer," the man said. "It's frankly just amazing to see him participating, never mind dominating the sport. He gives everyone a feeling of hope."

Lance returned home for another round of interviews and to make some appearances for his sponsors. He and Kristen went to New York, Los Angeles, then Austin. They then returned to Nice, France, so that Lance could begin training for the Olympics. Coming so soon after the Tour made it difficult. He had to regain his fitness and then peak in time for Sydney. What he didn't count on was the bane of all cyclists at one time or another—a car in the wrong place at the wrong time.

About a month before the Olympics, Lance

was training on a narrow, twisting road where he rarely saw any cars. He knew the mountain roads well, and in all the years he had trained there, said he had never seen any cars on the particular stretch where he was riding. He was moving at a very fast pace and taking a sharp turn when suddenly there was a car coming right at him. There was absolutely no time to react. It was a head-on and Lance went into the air.

Lance literally flew over the hood of the car and landed in the road, headfirst. This time, Lance was wearing a helmet and felt he had come through the accident without real injury. His bike had been mangled, but he felt no bones were broken and the helmet had protected his head. Lance called Kristen on his cell phone and asked her to come pick up his fellow rider and him. He told his wife he was all right, but when he awoke the next morning, he wasn't.

The pain in his neck and upper shoulders was severe. Lance couldn't turn his head and felt sharp, stabbing pains every time he moved. Kristen drove him to the hospital where an MRI revealed a fracture of the C-7 vertebra. In layman's terms, Lance had a broken neck. Suddenly, the best cyclist in the world was a questionable choice for the Olympics. But in Lance's mind, he was riding in Sydney, no matter what. When he got back on the bike, he found he still couldn't turn his head easily, which made it difficult for him to see things on both sides. But he could ride straight ahead, train, and improve his fitness as his neck slowly improved. When he made the trip to Sydney about a week before the start of the Olympics, he admitted he was probably about eighty percent healthy.

The two Olympic cycling events were a daylong road race and a time trial. The road race was on a flat course that favored sprinters, and Lance didn't feel his chances for a medal were that good. But he hoped he could attack quickly in the time trial and then gut it out to take the gold. That's where he was pinning his Olympic hopes. When he could do no better than thirteenth in the road race, an event won by Jan Ullrich, he focused even more on winning the time trial.

By the time it was his turn in the time trial, one of his U.S. Postal teammates, Vyacheslav Ekimov, was in first place with a very fast time of fifty-seven minutes and forty seconds. Lance started out quickly and with his usual focus and determination. But as he sprinted through the course he knew he was losing time to Ekimov, falling behind. He was going as fast as he possibly could that day, and it just wasn't good enough. When he crossed the finish line he was thirty-three seconds behind Ekimov's time and twenty-six seconds behind Ullrich, who finished second. Lance managed third for a bronze medal, but it was disappointing, nevertheless.

"I came to win the gold medal," Lance admitted, "but I did everything I could. I went as hard as I could. My heart rate was pegged the whole time. I could not have gone any harder. I'm glad the race is over and I can enjoy myself. I had hoped to make it a double celebration but I can't complain."

The other celebration was the October 2 anniversary of Lance's cancer diagnosis. It had now been four years. "Every year we have a party or have some special time with friends and family," Lance said. "They've occurred all over the world, sometimes in Austin, sometimes in France, and this year in Sydney."

No one can win them all, not even Lance Armstrong. Had he not had the neck injury a month before the Olympics, he might have fared better. But then again, maybe he just wouldn't have been good enough that day. In truth, Lance's focus had changed. He had really geared all his racing efforts toward winning one race, the Tour de France. If he won others, that was fine. He certainly had the ability on any given day to win almost any cycling race, but his talents as he had honed them were made for the most grueling stage race of them all. The mountains had been his weakness in the early days of his career, before his illness. Now, he was without a doubt the very best mountain rider and climber in the world. His competitors in the Tour knew that even if he didn't seem to be near the lead, once the race reached the mountain stages everyone else had better look over their shoulders. Lance Armstrong was coming.

It was no different in 2001. All his efforts again pointed to the Tour, where he would try to become the first American to win the race three consecutive times. He didn't waver from his intense training schedule and his goal to come into the Tour even stronger than he had been the two previous years. The U.S. Postal team added two new riders, both climbing specialists, with the objective to give Lance even more support when the big race arrived. Everyone was once again geared for Lance to again wear the yellow jersey as he rode down the Champs-Elysées.

As usual, he entered a number of early-season races for the purpose of conditioning, not necessarily to win. In April he rode in one of his favorite races, Amstel Gold, and ended up in a two-man sprint with Erik Dekker. The two rode together over the final miles of the race and, in the final burst to the finish line, Dekker was the winner. Lance simply said that his rival was the better man that day.

Then, just a couple of weeks before the Tour, Lance entered the Tour of Switzerland. He started it by winning the Prologue time trial and stayed among the leaders right up to the mountain time trial a week later. When he won that, he was in the overall lead and he held it the rest of the way. There was little doubt that he was ready to defend his title in the Tour de France.

With a number of the top cyclists recovering from injuries and a couple of others not in good form, only Jan Ullrich was considered a major threat to Lance. This time, he was the clear favorite. He served notice that he was ready when he finished second in the Tour's Prologue time trial. Then, as had become his pattern, he rode comfortably through the early stages, just setting back and seemingly waiting for the mountain stages to begin. At one point he was in twenty-fourth place, and after nine stages he was still only twenty-third. Those who didn't know him might have figured he didn't have it this year. After all, if there were twenty-some-odd riders ahead of him, a few of them might be able to hold him off. However, those familiar with the Tour and the riders, and with

Lance's ability, knew how quickly things could change once he got into the mountains. But no one was prepared for what he was about to do in the next two stages of the race.

The first mountain stage was the famed climb up to the Alpe d'Huez. The riders were on their bikes for some six hours when they came to the base of the final, twelve-mile climb, a brutally steep and daunting task for any rider. Lance was riding near the rear of the peloton, and to the other riders he appeared to be winded and out of breath. That was all part of the plan. All of a sudden he looked directly at Ullrich. Those seeing it said it was a cold stare, a challenge he knew couldn't be answered, not by Ullrich, not by anyone. With that, Lance began to climb, perhaps as he never had before.

When he began his attack, France's Laurent Roux was the stage leader, some six minutes ahead of Lance. Yet within an incredibly short amount of time he passed Roux, who later said, "I had the feeling I was being passed by a motorcycle." Lance continued to attack the steep grade and his opponents. Ullrich tried to go with him, but simply couldn't keep up. Finally, Lance crossed the finish line for his first stage win of the Tour. He had blown away the field, winning the race by two full minutes over the second-place finisher. In fact, he beat one rider by an incredible forty-two minutes. Seven riders never even finished the tortuous climb.

Lance still wasn't the overall leader, but he was getting much closer. He knew he had expended a huge amount of energy, maybe too much; he commented, "I may pay for this." He was concerned because the next stage was a mountain time trial, where the riders go individually up a mountain as fast as they possibly can. It was called "The Ride of Truth," to the top of Chamrousse, the ski resort where the legendary Jean-Claude Killy won three gold medals in the 1968 Olympics. Only this time the headlines were made by Lance Armstrong.

Once again he attacked the course, his legs pumping, his body not wavering, his form almost perfect. When he reached the top he had the best time of the day, giving him another stage win and bringing him even closer to the overall lead. The frightening part for the other riders was that his main rivals for the overall title were already behind him. Those in front of him must have known that a riding machine was getting ready to blow them away. Perhaps it was one of his teammates, Tyler Hamilton, who put it best after Lance's two straight stage wins.

"American doesn't understand," Hamilton said. "What [Lance] did here these last two days was like John Elway winning those two Super Bowls."

When Lance returned to Kristen after winning the two stages, she showed him a letter from her obstetrician. She had once again undergone in-vitro fertilization with the sperm Lance had preserved before his chemo treatments. Both of them anxiously opened the letter and couldn't believe the news. Test results confirmed that the in-vitro fertilization had worked again. Not only that, this time Kristen was carrying twin girls! The two of them were overjoyed, and Lance had further motivation to go on and win his third Tour.

When the thirteenth stage of the race had arrived, Lance was in third place overall. He was four minutes ahead of Ullrich, but still nine minutes behind François Simon, the race leader. This was another hard climb to a jagged summit called Col du Portet d'Aspet, followed by a steep, dangerous descent. It was the same route where Lance's former teammate with Motorola, Fabio Casartelli, had been killed six years earlier. As expected, Lance left everyone behind on the climb. As he sped down the descent and past the memorial that marked the spot where Fabio had been killed, he said he felt a surge of confidence.

"I knew I was going to win that day," he said later.

He not only won, but he made up so much time that he once again emerged as the overall leader. It was his third stage win over the last four stages and, for the first time in the 2001 Tour, he was wearing the yellow jersey. There probably wasn't another rider in the field who didn't think the jersey would stay where it now sat for the remainder of the Tour, on the back of Lance Armstrong.

In the fourteenth stage, yet another climb, this time to Luz-Ardiden, Ullrich made a last-ditch effort to attack. His respect for Lance had grown since during stage thirteen. He had taken a fall and, seeing that, Lance slowed his charge, waiting for Ullrich to get back up on the bike before continuing. It was a great gesture of sportsmanship. This time when Ullrich attacked, Lance pulled up even with him and the two rode together to the finish line. Neither would win the stage, but as they crossed the line together, Ullrich extended his right hand and Lance took it. Ullrich would later say his gesture was a concession, as well as one of respect. He knew now that he simply couldn't win, that no one could beat Lance Armstrong.

The rest of the race was almost a formality. Lance won the eighteenth stage and an individual time trial, then two days later once again rode down the Champs-Elysées at the head of his U.S. Postal team and crossed the line as the winner for a third straight time. He finished some six minutes and forty-four seconds ahead of Ullrich, a sizeable margin of victory. He had also completed the entire course in eighty-six hours, seventeen minutes, and twenty-eight seconds, making his the third-fastest Tour in the history of the race. There was little doubt now about his place in history. No matter what happened in the future, his name would always be synonymous with the Tour de France. He was now one of only eight riders to have won the Tour three times, and one of just five who had won three in a row.

There is an expression for a dominant Tour rider, one that is reserved for a special few. They are called the *patron,* the unquestioned boss of the peloton. The patron can be described as "a dominant personality who commands favors, respect, even fear from the other riders in the Tour. He admonishes and badgers, bestows blessings and bears grudges."

It was said that there hadn't been a true patron since the great Bernard Hinault's last Tour in 1986. Was Lance now falling into that role? He didn't seem to think so, perhaps more because of changing times. "I think the days of the true patrons are over," he said. "There are a lot of leaders, a lot of guys who command a lot of respect. Maybe I'm one of those."

Lance certainly had the respect of former champions. Eddy Merckx, who won the Tour five times and had known Lance for some time, marveled at his skills and tenacity. "Armstrong could win five, he could win six, he could win seven," Merckx said, "as long as he stays focused on the Tour de France."

Johan Bruyneel, director of the U.S. Postal Service team, felt that Lance's achievements and abilities could no longer be ignored by the other riders. "It's been a long time since cycling had a real boss," Bruyneel said. "Right now in the Tour de France, people consider Lance the boss."

Italian rider Davide Bramati echoed those thoughts when he said, "[Lance] is the big sheriff. He is the law in the peloton."

But there was still some backlash, perhaps because of the culture clash of an American dominating a traditional European event with old European values. The Tour's general director, Jean-Marie Leblanc, criticized Lance in a French newspaper, citing, among other things, his lack of "warmth, " his unwillingness to speak French, and his decision to employ a pair of bodyguards that Leblanc referred to as "gorillas."

Lance replied by saying, "I've really tried to respect the event and the French people."

While staying in Nice he often signed autographs and did interviews in French, though he admitted, "the little French I do have is brutal and ugly and sparse."

The French fans, who represent the majority of spectators watching the Tour, also seemed to harbor some resentments against Lance, though some of that can come under the category of sour grapes. A number of French riders were found to be using illegal drugs while Lance, the American who was dominating their most prized sporting event, had always tested clean and continued to do so. There were still many people who simply could not believe that he could be so dominant without using something to enhance his performance.

Most of them just didn't know of the intensity with which Lance trained, the enormous amount of work he put in every year while preparing for the Tour. Johan Bruyneel recalled a training session the previous May, when Lance rode hard up the Col de Madeleine, a mountain course, on a rainy day. At the top, Bruyneel opened his car door, ready to load the bike on top and give Lance a ride back home. He already had a hot cup of tea ready to give him.

"Anyone else would have gotten in the car, had some hot tea and gone home," Bruyneel said. "Lance just turned his bike around, rode to the bottom of the Madeleine and went up it again, just so he could get another big climb that day."

In some ways, Lance will probably always remain a "foreign" presence within the Tour. But even if some fans couldn't appreciate the full depth of his talents, the other riders could. Dutch rider Erik Dekker, a world-class rider who won three stages during the 2000 Tour, said this about the man he could never catch: "I am very passionate about cycling, but I cannot match Lance. Mentally, he is unique."

11

Can He Do It Again?

Despite participating in a sport that was still nowhere in the United States, Lance had now become a full-fledged national celebrity. His story by this time was well-known, as was his work on behalf of cancer research and the encouragement he was constantly giving to other cancer patients. People who know virtually nothing about cycling or racing know that Lance has been winning a race called the Tour de France every year.

On November 20, 2001, Lance and Kristen were blessed once again. Their twin girls, Isabelle Rose and Grace Elizabeth Armstrong, were born and were healthy. Life was getting better as Lance fully appreciated and loved the growing family he once thought he would never have. Despite all the time and hard work that went into remaining on top of the cycling world, Lance tried to include his entire family in everything he did.

"When we go on vacation," he said, "we go with the entire family. We want to have those experiences with our children. If we're on a beach, we want them there kickin' sand and if we're in Europe, we want them to be there, living the European life."

Lance was also very proud of his wife. He said that Kristen completely understood what he had to do to prepare for his races and especially for the Tour, and was always ready and willing to make sure he could do it. "Being an athlete, you need a few things," he said. "You need to eat, you need to train and you need to sleep. [Kristen] is completely understanding of that and she knows that if I've just [trained] for six or seven hours and I need a good sleep, she will not interfere with that."

Lance also said immediately after winning the 2001 Tour that he would be returning to the Tour de France in 2002, which prompted questions about how long he could go on, and if he had thought about retirement.

"I may get to the end of [next year's] Tour de France and say, 'Man, I've just had enough;

I'm outta here.' Ultimately, I want to decide when I leave [the sport]. I want to sit down with my family and decide when I leave. It's not going to be 'cause of some whacked-out journalist, or because of a contract, and it's not going to be because of a win or a loss. It's just going to be between us and we're going to say, 'You know what? It's been great. See ya later.'"

But Lance wasn't ready for that yet. When the 2002 cycling season began he was once again focused on the Tour. The early season events meant less than ever. The Tour was the thing. It was not only the race he enjoyed the most, but the one that was most conducive to the kind of cycling skills he had developed over the past five years. But as the Tour approached, there was something bothering Lance and he decided to go public.

It seems that during the 2000 Tour two years earlier, a French TV crew filmed U.S. Postal team officials disposing of what appeared to be medical waste from the team hotel. French officials immediately launched an investigation. Now, nearly two years later, that investigation was still open, though no evidence of wrongdoing had ever been found. In early June, about a month before the beginning of the Tour, Lance released a statement in which he voiced his objections to the continuing investigation.

"Once again, this so-called investigation by the French Judicial System baffles me," the statement said, in part. "It was with great disappointment that I read Saturday's *Le Monde* article regarding the 'US Postal Affair.' I am still confused as to why it has taken nearly two years to validate what I said after first learning of this investigation: The investigation will find nothing because there is nothing to find.

"I do not condone the use of banned substances and certainly understand how problematic this issue has become in sport. In my case, it's unfortunate that some people, including a few in the French Judicial System, are seemingly unable to acknowledge that intense and calculated training, not drugs, has been the key to my success on a bicycle.

"What more can I do? In Saturday's *Le Monde* article, Mr. François Franchy said the investigation has found no evidence of wrongdoing by our team and that there is no reason to put me under further examination. Yet, they will not declare this case closed. They will not clear my name. I find this ridiculous."

Lance went on to say that the U.S. Postal Service team had cooperated with the French authorities in every conceivable way. He had even written a French judge who was overseeing the investigation, offering to meet him anytime and anywhere to help with the investigation. His letter, he noted, was never answered. He also said that it was a shame that the nation of France and its many cycling fans would have to endure another Tour with a cloud hanging over it.

"As comparison," his statement continued, "it usually takes no more than two days to test competitors' samples for banned substances at the Olympic Games. The French investigators have taken nearly two years. Can anyone explain this in a way that makes sense? As in sport, when you challenge someone and then lose, you should have enough dignity and respect to admit you have lost. For some unknown reason, the French Judicial System refuses to concede."

He closed by saying he appreciated the support of his fans over the years and still considered the Tour de France the greatest athletic event in the world. As for the investigation, he said he considered it a dead issue and would concentrate his focus on the upcoming race.

It was almost as if some people still couldn't believe that a cancer survivor, a man who had a terribly advanced case of the disease, could come back and win the Tour de France three straight times without some kind of help. Yet Lance had done it with help from his support team and had never failed a drug test in his life. Even when he began the quest for a fourth straight victory, he still heard occasional cries of "*Dop-AY! Dop-AY!*" (Doped! Doped!) from heckling fans. It was just something he would have to live with.

When Lance won the Prologue time trial in 2002, many of his competitors were deflated already. But some of the Spanish riders began talking about his vulnerability, saying that he could be beaten. They pointed to the fact that while he had won two tough, multiday stage races before the Tour, the Dauphiné-Libéré and the Midi Libre, he didn't win the individual time trials. And that, they said, used to be his strength.

Then, in the ninth stage, Lance finished second in the extended time trial. He was not wearing the yellow jersey then, and the man who was, Spaniard Igor Gonzalez de Galdeano, announced brashly, "The Tour has changed."

Two days later the riders started up the mountains. Going into stage eleven, a climb from Grenoble to Chamrousse, Lance trailed Gonzalez de Galdeano by twenty-six seconds. As usual, Lance barreled up the mountain, leaving most of the other riders in his wake. In the final two hundred meters, he pulled away from the final pair of challengers to not only win the stage, but to recapture the yellow jersey, as well. The Tour had changed? What is it they say? The more things change, the more they remain the same! And when Lance donned the yellow jersey, it was simply more of the same.

He cemented his lead the next day, winning a second straight mountain stage and pretty much putting his stamp on yet another championship. A reporter asked him around this time if Lance felt he was too much of a force for the Tour's own good. He turned to the reporter and said, "I don't know. But I know that I love the race. I love everything that it stands for. It is what they pay me to do. This is my job. They say, 'Lance, we want you to win the Tour de France.' That's what the team wants, what the sponsors want, what cycling fans in America want, what cancer survivors around the world want."

Lance was also winning more respect than ever back home. During the first week of the Tour he was nominated for Best Male Athlete at the ESPY Awards in Los Angeles. The honor went to golfer Tiger Woods, but all-time hockey great Wayne Gretzky, who was at the award ceremony, was just one of the people who couldn't stop talking about Lance Armstrong.

"I follow the Tour de France about as much

as the average North American person," Gretzky said. "I only know of it because of the success that Lance Armstrong has had. Michael Jordan was the greatest athlete I ever saw. Tiger Woods is now at a point where he is going to go down in history as something special. There's not a question that Lance Armstrong belongs with those two guys. Not only because of what he has done as an athlete, but also what he has been able to come back from."

By this time everyone knew what Lance was doing was special. The other riders, even the ones who thought he might be beatable early in the Tour, were now convinced. As fellow American rider Levi Leipheimer said, "After the first two mountain stages people realized Lance was as good as ever."

As for Lance, he was still all for giving credit to his teammates. "Every year the media comes up with something to describe my race," he said. "The first year it was 'the comeback.' Then it was 'the confirmation.' I don't know what it was last year. This year, for me, it's 'the year of the team.' I can't say how I compare to the rider I was in 1999 or 2000 or 2001, but this team is much stronger than it has ever been. It has made it easier for me."

When Lance took the individual time trial in stage nineteen, his fourth stage win of the race, it was again all but over. Once again he had put away the opposition in methodical fashion. A rider might keep up with him for several stages, maybe even finish ahead of him in a couple. But sooner or later he would wear him down; he would wear them all down. No one had his overall consistency and ability to dig deep and add those extra minutes and seconds to his lead when it really counted. Even many of the French fans, some of whom kept looking for reasons to dislike or distrust him, now had to admire his dominance.

"A man's value is in his spirit, not his country, and Armstrong is a super champion," said Dominique Audusseau, a wine dealer who is a huge cycling fan. "I adore the guy. He'll be the first to win six Tours."

There were still some taking potshots at him. Some journalists pointed out that Lance would go back to his trailer immediately after a stage was over instead of hanging around and talking to people as the other American champion, Greg LeMond, used to do. Some continued to point out that he often seemed to isolate himself behind his bodyguards. Perhaps it was difficult for some people to understand how focused Lance was, that he had to stay within himself during the Tour. Some athletes like to be out there talking to fans and competitors. It fuels them. Lance had to concentrate, follow a routine, eat a certain way, get enough sleep, and prepare himself for the next stage.

Slowly, it seemed, more people began to admire him for the rider he was. Five-time winner Bernard Hinault said, "Armstrong masters his style—calm, steady—and rides like the champion he is."

Taxi driver Jean Nustadt praised Lance from another perspective. "Don't you listen to any badmouthing," he said. "[Armstrong] is tremendously loved in France. His courage is enormous. Enormous." More praise came from Christophe Gilardi, a worker in a bike shop in the city of Draguignan. "Sure, you see some jealousy, and there's always suspicion of drugs," Gilardi said. "But the truth is that he is very, very strong. His technique is almost perfect. He is amazing."

As for Lance, he had heard it all during his four years atop the Tour. His answer to critics about his style versus his substance was simple. "This is not theater, it's sport," he said. "I believe in performance and the beauty of the race."

When Lance completed the formality of crossing the finish line in first place, he had won his fourth Tour de France by more than seven minutes over his nearest rival. He had almost made the most difficult and debilitating race in the world look easy, as he continued to ride into the history books.

"It's an honor and it makes me happy to be able to win again," he said after the race. "It's what I devote my life to. If I lost this race, I would be extremely disappointed. Much more disappointed than anyone can guess. It was a long three weeks. With so many mountains, it was hard on the head as well as the legs. It's hard to know the significance of it. I just live for the moment."

The Tour de France had, in effect, become the Tour de Lance.

12

What Comes Next?

After four straight Tour wins the obvious question might be, what could Lance Armstrong do for an encore? There really was only one answer. Win more Tours. But how many? He had already become a Tour legend. Four riders had won the Tour five times, Lance had now won four. Two of the other riders had won four in a row, as he had, while Miguel Indurain of Spain held the record of five straight. If Lance could win again in 2003, he would tie two records, the most Tour wins and the most Tour wins in succession.

That, in itself, would seem to be motivation enough. Lance told the crowds and the press right after winning his fourth that he would return in 2003. He also said it was getting more difficult to leave his family, especially now that there were three children. That, it would seem, might be the thing that eventually breaks Lance's streak. Once he loses the smallest iota of his desire, or wavers from his spartan training methods, he may lose the edge, that little extra that allows him to stay ahead of the pack. However, that didn't happen after his 2002 victory. By October, he was back in training. Lance always uses the fall for structured workouts. There's never an off season for him, his theory being that if he allows his fitness level to drop, he'd have to waste valuable time reclaiming his fitness. He would have to take weeks to get back to where he started instead of being ahead. His training goal is to constantly move forward, to never take a step back.

In the fall he also moves into the weight room, working on his range of motion and flexibility while doing resistance training. As his trainer/advisor Chris Carmichael explained, "We use weight training in conjunction with on-the-bike resistance work to increase Lance's peak power. When you increase an athlete's peak power, you often see a corresponding increase in that athlete's sustainable power output. The movements we use in the gym start in broad ranges of motion and progress to ranges similar to what Lance uses on the bike."

These were the kinds of workouts that helped give Lance a leg up on the competition. It wasn't all riding, climbing, and sprinting on the bike. In fact, Chris Carmichael said that these early workouts were extremely important to his eventual ride in the Tour.

"Lance's fall and winter training is critical to his success in July," Carmichael explained. "This is the time of year when he can actually concentrate on making significant strength and power gains. So much time each year must be spent on aerobic and threshold training that it would be easy to overlook the need for resistance training and peak power development. Lance's hard work in the winter reaps great rewards in the summer."

Of course, Lance also had to deal with his growing celebrity status. There was no way to avoid it. He simply couldn't train, spend time with his family, and forget about the rest of the world. In mid-December, *Sports Illustrated* magazine named Lance their Sportsman of the Year for 2002. The story told how he received about three hundred pieces of mail each week, mostly from people with cancer looking for encouragement. Lance is happy the mail comes to him and wants to help. He described his role as "the obligation of the cured."

Then he added, "There's never been a Tour de France victory by a cancer survivor before me. That's what I'd like to be remembered for."

In the story, Lance said he was looking to ride into history in 2004 by becoming the Tour's first six-time winner. One of the five-time winners, Eddy Merckx, told *Sports Illustrated* he thought Lance could do it.

"There are no limits for [Lance], and he will be around a long time," Merckx said. "He's a great racer and a great person."

More recognition came. Less than two weeks after he was named Sportsman of the Year, the Associated Press named Lance their Male Athlete of the Year, topping baseball star Barry Bonds. Interviewed in Austin, he again talked about what it took to win the Tour and how being a cancer survivor helped him.

"Anytime you have three weeks of open road, you need some luck," he said. "One night you get some bad food, you can't do anything the next day and you lose half an hour." He also said riders can crash, get an ill-timed tire puncture, or even become sick. It all has to fit into place.

"When I came back [from cancer] I said if I ever get a chance to do this, I'm going to give it everything. I'm going to train correctly, eat right. I'm not going to mess up. That's why I say all the time that the illness is the best thing that ever happened to me. I would never have won one Tour de France if I hadn't had [cancer]. No doubt."

Lance also mentioned something that rarely came up in discussion—his age. "As you approach the mid-thirties, it's difficult to maintain a high level," he explained. "But I don't feel weaker, I don't feel less motivated, and the team is strong. I know what I'm doing in 2003 and I think I know what I'm doing in 2004. But after that, I don't think about it."

Lance had become a national celebrity and a sports superstar in a country where his sport was considered minor at best, an afterthought. Sure, he would have liked to see the popularity of cycling grow in the United States, but he could also live with things the way they were. Being well-known was the best way to continue to get his message across to cancer patients and fellow survivors, and to keep his foundation going strong.

In early January of 2003, he announced that the U.S. Postal Service team would feature the same eight support riders that supported him in 2002 for the upcoming Tour.

"I think we have started to really hit our stride in terms of teamwork, communication, and camaraderie," he said. "I'm really looking forward to 2003 with these guys."

There was little doubt that Lance was going full steam ahead in his quest for a fifth straight Tour victory. Oddly enough, a week after Lance announced that his team was set, there was a story out of Paris in which he was quoted as saying he wasn't sure about coming back to the Tour in 2004.

"Who can say what my motivation will be like in 2004, or what shape my body will be in," he told the French newspaper, *Le Figaro*. "Nobody escapes from the passage of time."

If nothing else, life has made Lance Armstrong a realist. On the one hand, he knows he has the opportunity to become arguably the greatest cyclist ever in the history of the Tour de France. He also knows that his quest, if he chooses to pursue it, can end at any time. No one knows that better than he. Right now, if things continue without one of the x-factors kicking in— a crash, illness at the wrong time, bad food—there aren't many who feel that Lance can be beaten in 2003. Beyond that, no one can know.

One thing is certain. Lance Armstrong has written a story that transcends sports. Yes, he is a great athlete, one of the greatest the sport of cycling has ever produced. But he is also a man who has conquered much more than the winding roads and steep climbs of the Tour de France. He has, in effect, conquered life. By coming all the way back from a very advanced case of cancer, he once again proved that the human spirit can be indomitable, that a cancer survivor can achieve anything he wants.

Perhaps one reason Lance has been so successful in his cycling career is that he knows that life itself is precious, that riding a bike isn't the only thing out there for him. Recently Lance and Kristen admitted to needing time to work on their family life. "We are working through these sensitive issues in the same way we have met other challenges in our life together with determination and dedication. We may experience a period of time apart from each other as we reflect on our relationship and work to preserve and protect the interests of our family and children," they announced in a statement emailed to the Austin American-Statesman. But Lance knows that if his career ended tomorrow, he would still have the really important things in his life.

"Seeing your kids tomorrow isn't guaranteed," Lance has said. "Look at this life like it's a gift. That's the way I try to view my life, my family—as a gift."

Biography

Bill Gutman has written more than two hundred books for children and adults in a writing career spanning thirty years. His most recent books are *Won for All,* the story of the New England Patriots 2001 Super Bowl season, written with former Giants' All-Pro linebacker and current Patriots inside linebackers coach, Pepper Johnson; and *Being Extreme,* a study of athletes who participate in high-risk, adventure sports such as mountain climbing, BASE jumping, and big wave surfing. His previous biography subjects for Simon & Schuster include Michael Jordan, Tiger Woods, Brett Favre, Ken Griffey Jr., Sammy Sosa, Shaquille O'Neal, Marion Jones, and Grant Hill. Mr. Gutman lives in Dover Plains, New York, with his wife, Cathy.

PENDRAGON

Bobby Pendragon is a seemingly normal fourteen-year-old boy. He has a family, a home, and a possible new girlfriend. But something happens to Bobby that changes his life forever.

HE IS CHOSEN TO DETERMINE
THE COURSE OF HUMAN EXISTENCE.

Pulled away from the comfort of his family and suburban home, Bobby is launched into the middle of an immense, inter-dimensional conflict involving racial tensions, threatened ecosystems, and more. It's a journey of danger and discovery for Bobby, and his success or failure will do nothing less than determine the fate of the world. . . .

PENDRAGON

A new series by D. J. MacHale
Book One: The Merchant of Death
Available now

Book Two: The Lost City of Faar
Book Three: The Never War
Book Four: The Reality Bug
Coming Soon

From Aladdin Paperbacks
Published by Simon & Schuster